# NEW THERAPEUTIC VISIONS

## Progress in Self Psychology
## Volume 8

# *Progress in Self Psychology*

Editor, Arnold Goldberg, M.D.

# NEW THERAPEUTIC VISIONS

## Progress in Self Psychology
## Volume 8

## Arnold Goldberg

### editor

 THE ANALYTIC PRESS

1992    Hillsdale, NJ                    London

ISBN 0-88163-150-7
ISSN 0893-5483

Printed in the United States of America
10  9  8  7  6  5  4  3  2  1

# Acknowledgment

We would like to thank Ms. Chris Susman, who provided secretarial and editorial assistance.

# Contents

## III   APPLIED

## IV   FURTHER CONTRIBUTIONS

# Contributors

Linda Atkins, C.S.W., Training Analyst, Senior Supervisor, Faculty, The Psychoanalytic Institute of the Postgraduate Center for Mental Health, New York City; private practice, New York City.

Michael Franz Basch, M.D., Professor of Psychiatry, Rush Medical College; Training and Supervising Analyst, Institute for Psychoanalysis, Chicago.

Beatrice Beebe, Ph.D., Core Faculty, Institute for the Psychoanalytic Study of Subjectivity; Clinical Associate Professor, New York University Postdoctoral Program in Psychoanalysis.

Bernard Brickman, M.D., Ph.D., Faculty, Training and Supervising Analyst, Southern California Psychoanalytic Institute; Faculty, Training and Supervising Analyst, Institute of Contemporary Psychoanalysis, Los Angeles.

Doris Brothers, Ph.D., Member, Board of Directors, and Faculty and Supervisor, Training and Research Institute for Self Psychology, New York City; author *Falling Backwards: An Exploration of Trust and Self Experience* (Norton, forthcoming).

Jill Cooper. Ph.D., author *Successful Psychotherapy: Curing Codependency and Other Compulsions*; private practice, San Francisco.

James L. Fosshage, Ph.D., Core Faculty, Institute for the Psychoanalytic Study of Subjectivity; Clinical Associate Professor (Faculty and Supervisor), New York University Postdoctoral Program in Psychoanalysis.

Judith Kaufman, C.S.W., Codirector, NIP Regional Psychoanalytic Training Program at Kansas City; Supervisor, Postgraduate Center for Mental Health, New York City.

Frank M. Lachmann, Ph.D., Core Faculty, Institute for the Psychoanalytic Study of Subjectivity; Training Analyst, Postgraduate Center for Mental Health, New York City.

Elliott Markson, M.D., Member, The Canadian Institute of Psychoanalysis; Associate Professor, Department of Psychiatry, University of Toronto.

Donna M. Orange, Ph.D., Psy.D., Institute for the Psychoanalytic Study of Subjectivity, New York City.

Harry Paul, Ph.D., Member, Board of Directors and Faculty, Training and Research Institute for Self Psychology, New York City; coauthor (with R. Ulman) *Narcissus in Wonderland: The Self Psychology of Addiction and Its Treatment* (The Analytic Press, forthcoming).

Carl T. Rotenberg, M.D., Assistant Clinical Professor of Psychiatry, Yale University School of Medicine; Faculty Member, Psychoanalytic Institute of New York Medical College.

Estelle Shane, Ph.D., Training and Supervising Analyst, Los Angeles Psychoanalytic Society/Institute; Training and Supervising Analyst, Institute of Contemporary Psychoanalysis, Los Angeles.

Robert D. Stolorow, Ph.D., Faculty, Training and Supervising Analyst, Institute of Contemporary Psychoanalysis, Los Angeles; Core Faculty, Institute for the Psychoanalytic Study of Subjectivity, New York City.

Maxwell S. Sucharov, M.D., Member, Vancouver Psychoanalytic Psychotherapy Society; Clinical Instructor, Department of Psychiatry, University of British Columbia.

Richard Barrett Ulman, Ph.D., Member, Board of Directors and Faculty, Training and Research Institute for Self Psychology, New York City; coauthor (with H. Paul) *Narcissus in Wonderland: The Self Psychology of Addiction and Its Treatment* (The Analytic Press, forthcoming).

Bonnie Wolfe, Ph.D., Faculty, Institute of Contemporary Psychoanalysis, Los Angeles.

# Introduction

## *David M. Terman*

This volume continues to chronicle the evolution of thought by those influenced by self psychology. As numerous authors have noted, the changes are in many areas and lead in many different directions. Subjects range from quantum physics to codependency, and from a discussion of subjectivism, relativism and realism to the function of transitional selfobjects in the genesis and treatment of addictive personality.

There is, of course, considerable work and thought concerning the selfobject, one of the most important concepts in the theory of self psychology. One group of authors attempts to integrate the concept with the classical model. Beebe and Lachmann offer a developmental approach to such an integration. They make a distinction between representational configurations and selfobject configurations. They define the latter as those which are concerned with the maintenance of the selfobject tie and with the cohesion, articulation, and vitality of the self. Representational configurations, on the other hand, have to do with "the qualities of self and other and themes of their interrelationships." Beebe and Lachmann go on to explore the subtle changes in development in which differentiated patterns of experience in interaction intersect with ongoing, self-perpetuating inner patterns of organization.

Sucharov attempts another solution at the philosophical level. He sees self psychology as offering a mode of description complementary to that of classical theory. Like the wave and particle theories of light, self psychology and classical theory offer complementary views of phenomena that neither alone can explain completely and for whose explanation both are necessary. Classical theory is appropriate when the observer and the observed are separate; self psychology is appropriate when they are one.

Other authors extend the concept of the selfobject. Brickman explores the vicissitudes of the selfobject bond in the articulation of affect. Ulman and Paul introduce the ideas of a transitional selfobject that is part of normal development and of an ersatz transitional selfobject that is characteristic of the addictive personality. Shane's reviews of recent works by Wolf, Bacal and Newman, and Lichtenberg reveal other attempts at extension. Wolf proposes the concepts of the adversarial selfobject function and the efficacy selfobject function. Bacal and Newman want to extend, perhaps even alter, the meaning of the selfobject to become the self's object. Shane wonders whether that alteration would, in fact, run the danger of losing the distinction between object and selfobject. Nonetheless, though the meaning may remain the same, the applications and reexamination of otherwise understood phenomena stimulate rethinking of the nature and implications of the selfobject experience.

Whatever its ultimate shape and extent, the selfobject experience in development is of central importance in determining the therapist's approach to the patient. For this aspect of the theory of self psychology has shifted the understanding of the genesis of the inner world from an exclusive preoccupation with a person's solipsistic construction to the consideration of the importance of the inner experience of interaction. Wolfe's exploration of the sets of therapeutic values is an outgrowth of the increasing attention paid to the importance of the therapist's contribution to the construction and reconstruction of the patient's inner world. She offers an insightful critique of the slightly different prescriptions for health that are implicit in the works of Kohut, Basch, and Stolorow. She exhorts us to be aware of our own therapeutic values, for they are of critical importance in shaping our work. The power to shape the self inheres in the mirroring process, but that phenomenon is not inert. That is, the way in which the mirroring experience is perceived by the patient has not only to do with the patient's psychological organization, but with what is communicated, that is, what the therapist (or parent) actually says or does. That response arises from the therapist's personality and his or her view of the nature of human experience and development.

There is also a tendency to normalize the construction process.

Atkins and Kaufman find the "truths" embodied in the patient's delusions. Ulman and Paul find nonhuman activities or things that provide psychological functions that enhance the self and can be transformed into structure. Cooper finds that codependency is both protective of injury and "yet seeks continued development of faulty self structures. . . ." Though the structures may, in this instance, be faulty, these authors nonetheless see the patterning activity to be as an attempt to increase organization. The accent is on the adaptive developmental thrust. Gitelson (1958) pointed out that the essence of the problem of the narcissistic character was not some kind of inherent weakness of psychological structure. Rather, he saw narcissism as a highly adaptive response to extraordinary conditions — extraordinarily adverse conditions. This view of development has broadened to encompass psychological activities as attempts to embrace and organize the world and oneself. Taking his cue from modern neurophysiology, Basch (1975) sees ordering as the basic function of the brain. Hence, the central organizing principle of psychological function is also ordering. The central questions do not have to do with tension discharge but with the elaboration of inner patterns as they reflect exchange with the world. How, when, and where these patterns emerge in pragmatic, nondemonic modes are the issues.

As Basch convincingly shows, such first principles fit our clinical data much better than the 19th-century principles of homeostasis used by Freud. Selfobject affect regulation is an aspect of ordering, and Brickman details numerous aspects of affect regulation that had to develop in the resolution of a psychosomatic illness.

I think there is another central organizing principle of psychological function, and that has to do with self-esteem. Self psychology has certainly highlighted its importance both in development and in the clinical situation; but as important as it is, I do not think it can be classified as a variety of ordering without doing violence to both concepts. What is the sense of self-esteem? I think it is an experience of loveableness. It is a sensed quality that engenders the expectation of positive, warm, pleasureable responses in others, and it arises mainly in transaction — out of the experience we have labeled mirroring. Although it is very important to specify certain subsets or particular systems in which this quality is experienced (as Lichtenberg (1989) has done), the architectonic nature of the quality of loveableness is not sufficiently emphasized in such an effort. The explication of such a primary organizing principle is, in my view, one of the important next steps in the development of self psychology.

The rich variety of this volume may stimulate the reader to his or her own particular vision of the next steps. It certainly helps prepare the way.

## REFERENCES

Basch, M. F. (1975), Toward a Theory of Depression. Depression and Human Existence, ed. Anthony, E. J. Benedek, T. Little Brown: Boston. pp. 485–534.
Gitleson, M. (1958), On ego distortion. *Internat. J. Psycho-Anal.*, 39:24–257.

# I

# Development

# Chapter 1

# Representational and Selfobject Transferences: A Developmental Perspective

*Frank M. Lachmann*
*Beatrice Beebe*

The clinical discoveries of Heinz Kohut, the empirical studies by a host of infant researchers, and the formulations of developmental theorists offer a challenge and expanded opportunities to the psycho-analytic clinician. Jointly, they promise to increase our understanding of the patient–analyst interaction and the patient's organization of that experience, the transference. A clinical vignette will illustrate the contributions from these various sources to our understanding. We will focus on the role of repetition and transformation in two dimensions of the transference: the selfobject dimension and transference as organized by representational configurations.

The illustrative clinical vignette is taken from the first year of the analysis of a 39-year-old divorced woman who was anxious and despondent to the point where she occasionally could not function in her work as a travel agent. After several months of treatment these symptoms had abated somewhat. Then, over the course of several sessions she described the following events: She had met a man who thought she was an emotional person and thought of himself as blocked and distant. In his relationship with her he hoped he would learn how to be emotionally freer. The patient stated that she made it clear to this man that she did not want to be his teacher. In the following session she reported a dream about her former therapist and depicted her as her daughter. The next session contained descriptions of numerous incidents with friends in which the patient had accepted their preferences about planning various activities and

3

later felt angry with herself for being so compliant. In the final session of this sequence, she reported a dream in which she and her daughter's cat were being drenched in a rain shower. Her associations led her to recall that she had to take care of the cat while her daughter was spending the night at a girlfriend's house. The patient felt resentful about being burdened with this chore. In addition, she described feeling resentful about her work. While feeling depressed and anxious, she still had to conduct her business and take care of her clients.

This is clearly a selective account of four consecutive sessions. However, implicit in this clinical material were the patient's descriptions of herself as burdened, resentful, feeling deprived of protection and nurturance, and angry for being overly accommodating and for being a caretaker or mother to "mother" figures and an authority for a man she had met. Others were described as demanding her care, with the expectation that she serve as the adult, parent, mother, teacher, companion, and provider.

These affect-laden descriptions of self and other constitute a series of representational configurations. Experiences of self and other are organized in line with expectations derived from an earlier time and with facets of the current analyst–patient interaction as well. Such configurations may be rigidly repeated and imposed on ongoing experience. Optimally, they are flexible. They transform and are transformed by ongoing experience.

What do we mean by "transformation"? Beginning in early development, transformations are a consequence of the continuous interaction between the person and the environment. With the advent of symbolic and other capacities, representations of interactions that have been generalized (Stern, 1985) evolve into the more complex scripts (Stern, 1989), internal working models (Bowlby, 1969; Ainsworth, Blehar, Waters, and Wall, 1978; Stern, 1989), unconscious organizing principles (Stolorow, Brandchaft, and Atwood, 1987), model scenes (Lichtenberg, 1989; Lachmann and Lichtenberg, 1992) selfobject functions, and representational configurations of self, other, and self-with-other (Stern, 1983, 1985; Beebe and Lachmann, 1988a; Lachmann and Beebe, 1989). Intrapsychic changes produce changes in the environment and vice versa so that neither the person nor the environment remains static from one point of time to another (Piaget, 1937; Sameroff and Chandler, 1975). The transformational model of development recognizes the contributions of each stage of development, not just the earliest. In the case presented here we illustrate the crucial transformations of the patient's resources and defenses during puberty.

A transformational model of development posits that experiences at each stage of development are continually reorganized. Descriptions of these stages differ according to different theorists. Self psychology addresses the selfobject needs required at various developmental stages and the progressively more sophisticated selfobject functions that are internalized (Kohut, 1984; Lachmann, 1986; Wolf, 1988).

There is controversy among developmental theorists and researchers as to predictability from one developmental stage to another. Sameroff and Chandler (1975) argue that prediction is possible when a transformational model is used and when the nature of the transaction within the dyad is the focus of study. Zeanah, Anders, Seifer, and Stern (1989) hold that continuity "is clearly not at the level of individual behaviors in the infant but in the relationship patterns" (p. 665). It is representations of the experiences in the dyad that undergo transformations throughout development.

In the treatment dyad, representations of experience can be delineated along two dimensions: selfobject and representational configurations. Whereas in early development these two dimensions are indistinguishable, the distinction between them is crucial in the treatment of the adult because they address different functions. One dimension addresses the maintenance of the tie between the self and the other and the requirements for cohesion, articulation, and vitality of the self. The other depicts the qualities of self and other and the themes of their interrelationships. We speculate that representational configurations provide the context for selfobject experiences and, in turn, selfobject experiences provide access to representational configurations. Although representational configurations are shaped by the transactions of important relationships, they are also shaped by the person's effort to construe experience in such a way that vital archaic selfobject functions may be derived.

Our use of the term *representational configurations* does not exclude the possibility that selfobject experiences are represented. We use the term to refer to those transferences that have been traditionally described within psychoanalysis as "object-related," the products of displacement, projection, and regression. Stolorow and Lachmann (1984/1985) reformulated transference as the organization of experience and proposed that selfobject and other transferences occupy a figure–ground relation to each other (Stolorow, Brandchaft, and Atwood, 1987; see also Lichtenberg, 1983). When these other transferences, the product of repetitive, rigid representational configurations, shape the patient's treatment experience, they become foreground requiring analytic attention.

In the treatment of adult patients these representational configurations may integrate and synopsize the subjective elaboration of
important interactions from any phase of the person's life. Under
optimal circumstances they continue to be open to reworking, that is,
past experience is transformed at various times in life and in analysis.
As past themes are reworked and relived (for example, in the case to
be illustrated the theme is that self-sacrifice maintains a necessary tie),
both newly acquired resources and defensively instituted restrictions
may be integrated. When these representational configurations are
based, for example, on a dread of repeating a traumatizing experience
(Ornstein, 1974), they remain rigid and stereotypic. In psychoanalytic
treatment these inflexible themes are often seen as the patient's
transference "distortions." When they dominate the organization of a
person's experience, they impose past dreads, needs, and expectations on current experience and thereby preclude the continuing
transformation of experience.

In the case of the patient presented here, the figure–ground
distinction between the representational configurations and the selfobject transferences emerged in the following way: After the four
sessions described, on the basis of the patient's description of herself
and her interactions with others, the analyst commented that though
she, the patient, might want to be taken care of, she so frequently
found herself in the position of the caring, self-sacrificing mother.
This interpretation described a representational configuration based
on the patient's narratives, associations, and dreams. No developmental origins were suggested, and no statement about the transference was directly made.

The patient immediately supplied confirmatory material with respect to her family, her parents, her brother, her ex-husband, and her
daughter. Apparently, she felt understood and used the interpretation to further organize past events in line with the interpretation and
in a manner that seemed to promise her a greater sense of efficacy.
However, shortly after the session she became increasingly depressed
and confused, to the point where she felt she was unable to function
in her work. She, feeling profoundly disorganized, telephoned the
analyst in the evening after the session in which the interpretation
was offered and asked what she could do. In the brief phone
conversation the analyst connected the patient's disorganized state to
the preceding psychotherapy session, a connection that had not
occurred to the patient. She was told that an attempt would be made
in future sessions to understand what had occurred that disturbed
her so.

How shall we try to understand the patient's debilitating anxiety?

For example, is her reaction to be seen as a resistance, as a negative therapeutic reaction, as a masochistic enactment in the transference, or as an empathic rupture in the selfobject tie? Should the analyst consider the disorganization as emanating from a threat to her need to maintain her self-sacrificing position, in which she displaced her "victimized" mother as an oedipal rival? Rather than viewing the patient's response as organized entirely by her own pathology, the interactive contributions from the analyst–patient dyad as well as the patient's propensity toward repetitive, stereotypic responses must be recognized.

When the analyst suggested to the patient that there might be a link between her overwhelming anxiety and the preceding session, the suggestion had a multitude of meanings for her. It meant to her that the cause for her disorganized state was not being located solely within her. That is, it provided a valuable contrast for the self-accusations that were prompted by her disorganization. She blamed herself for being too "vulnerable," for being unable to retain a sense of the analyst as a protective figure, and she accused herself of attempting to "destroy," "undermine," and "undo" the help she received from the analyst. These self-accusations had been reinforced by her previous analyst, who, she reported, took the stance of "observer" of her pathology. In discussing the impact of the telephone call, she felt particularly relieved because she feared that she would be rejected, abandoned, or blamed for her disorganization. She said that she now expected that her propensity toward disorganization and disruptive anxiety states would be open to understanding.

Although clarified only subsequently, the connection made between the patient's pervasive anxiety and the preceding therapy session led to the restoration of a ruptured selfobject tie. The maintenance of this tie and the patient's feeling that the analyst was invested in retaining it enabled her to traverse the troubled waters of the crisis. Her dread that the analyst would be hell-bent on severing this tie harked back to her feelings of abandonment by her mother.

From the analyst's perspective, the interpretation that though the patient might want to be taken care of, she so frequently found herself in the position of the caring, self-sacrificing mother was an attempt to address her masochistic character structure. She was understood as longing for nurturance and feeling threatened by her desires to be taken care of, which were defended against through her excessive caretaking of others. Thus, through the analysis of the function served by her masochism (Stolorow and Lachmann, 1980), it was anticipated that the patient's sense of competence would increase, her dependent longings would become tolerable, and her sense of efficacy would solidify.

The patient, however, did not share the analyst's perspective. The analysis of the rupture revealed that she felt that her sense of cohesion was derived from feeling vitally needed, though self-sacrificing and overburdened. She perceived herself as a caregiver and depicted those under her care—her cat, her daughter, and her analysts—as essentially helpless in the face of an inundating, "rain-drenching," hostile world. She felt effective in helping them. The interpretation undermined this source of efficacy.

From the perspective of the selfobject dimension of the transference, the patient's complaints in relation to her friends and daughter were *not* expressions of a desire to change those interpersonal relationships. The complaints conveyed that she had succeeded in establishing the necessary prerequisites to sustain and consolidate her self-organization as an overburdened caretaker.

In her early years the patient lived in dread of being abandoned by her mother. Her mother's attention was devoted to community affairs and to maintaining her tie with her own parents and sisters. Her father's political activities had required frequent moves: the family was uprooted several times during the patient's first eight years. She described constraining herself, since she felt that any demand on her mother would unduly burden her. She expected to be able to ensure her mother's attention by being undemanding and expecting little from her. Her ability to nurture her mother provided her with a feeling of stability. That is, in enabling her mother to derive selfobject functions from her, she avoided the experience of her mother's absence. Furthermore, she ensured her own cohesion and survival by fulfilling vital selfobject functions for her mother (Stolorow et al., 1987). Though initially derived from her relationship with her mother, her self-organization underwent a crucial transformation during her puberty years with respect to her need to retain her father in an idealized position.

Although the original interpretation—that she might want to be taken care of but found herself in the position of the self-sacrificing mother—did not address the transference per se, it nevertheless had a powerful effect on the patient's immediate experience of the analyst. She felt as if he had said to her, "You are a victim like your mother, and I do not need you to sacrifice yourself." She felt implicitly rejected, which contributed to her profound experience of disruption. In exploring the nature of this rupture, the hitherto silent selfobject dimension of the transference became clearer. Exploration of the tie led to the understanding of its organization during her puberty years in relation to her father. At that time it was coupled with an array of newly developing resources and provided the patient with the sense of efficacy and competence that she drew upon in much of her later and adult functioning. Thus, in the treatment situation, with the ruptured selfobject tie restored, the patient felt she could address those aspects of the representational configurations that had been activated and had turned out to be so disruptive.

The representational configuration, the "figure" from the analyst's perspective (as opposed to the ground), contained a vital selfobject tie. In making the interpretation, this tie was ruptured and no longer remained silently in the background. Through the rupture, the selfobject tie became "figure" and required attention and repair.

In retrospect it became clear that prior to the interpretation the patient had established an idealized selfobject tie with the analyst. This tie was an outgrowth of a bond with her father, organized during puberty and based on the conviction that *he* needed *her*. In contrast to the feeling of self-abnegation that was part of her provision of a supportive milieu for her mother, through the bond with her father she felt needed, valuable, and capable. Subsequently, this tie to the father was repeatedly ruptured through disappointments. A combination of unfortunate external circumstances and "bad choices" diminished her father's stature in the family and in his community. The patient explained, "My father was politically very active in those years, and I thought of him as a rather daring man. As he began to decline, I wanted my competence to be of benefit to him. It would make him feel strong and effective. He could brag about me to his cronies and the family. He could feel proud and that made me feel really good." A salient feature of the patient's organization of the treatment was her proclivity to experience ruptures in the selfobject tie. The later tie to the father had been characterized by continual disappointments and ruptures, for which the patient held herself responsible. This representational configuration containing the self-object tie organized the transference. The representational configuration depicted her father as having been restored by her to his idealized position, as active and daring. Inherent in this representational configuration is the selfobject tie in which the daughter benefits her father. She makes him strong, an idealized source of vitality, and thereby derives her sense of coherence and competence. The vulnerability inherent in the selfobject dimension of the transference organized the disruptions.

The patient's representational configuration of self-sacrifice, established initially to provide stability for her mother and cohesion for herself, was later activated and transformed to restore her father's idealized position and sustain herself. She was thereby able to protect herself against being disappointed by him. She imagined herself as part of her father's world, which provided her with a sense of vitality and promoted her intellectual curiosity. Her academic work flourished; her world of skills and interests expanded. Thus, a general masochistic pattern, first organized to retain a connection with her mother and to derive some nurturance through self-abnegation, was later refined and its function transformed. In being activated in relation to her father, the pattern enabled the patient to acquire a sense of pride and competence, as well as the feeling that she could be thought of as needed and interesting. Thus, her representational configurations expanded and became more varied. However, the selfobject tie on which they were built retained points of urgency. Unless the patient could experience herself as all-giving and self-sacrificing and thereby bolster her potentially faltering father, who she felt needed her to restore him to an idealizable position, she feared that her precariously built world would collapse. After a similar idealizing selfobject tie with her analyst was established, the interpretation aimed at the representational configuration had the capacity to rupture this tie. It repeated her feeling of disappointment in that the idealized analyst also made a "wrong choice," that is, in offering the interpretation. It indicated to the patient that she had failed to maintain the analyst in an idealized state. Her depression, her sense of emptiness and worthlessness, and her panic-like anxiety states were the results.

How do we understand the origins of the patient's sense of emptiness and worthlessness, her panic-like anxiety, her wish to be cared for, and her disorganized reaction? Must these states be rooted in an early pathogenic tie to the mother based on mismatches and disruptions that were merely repeated and exacerbated in her later relationships? Are the disappointments in her father merely screens for the early deprivations she experienced in relation to her mother? Does an explanation that emphasizes later transformations and disruptions fit this patient better?

We are arguing for a model that recognizes both the continuous construction and potential reorganization of experience at various stages as well as the repetition of ways of organizing experience shaped by early interactive patterns. Such a model recognizes the constant shifts and transformations that provide a complex texture to ongoing experience and avoids reductionism (see also Mitchell, 1988). It also acknowledges that each transformation generates the possibility that new resources may be acquired as well as provides new ways of organizing past experience (Loewald, 1980).

In the patient's continuous construction of her experience, the transformations at puberty provided vital resources for her ongoing development. At that time the patient had turned to her father in part as a reaction against her mother's chronic sense of victimization and in part for self-restoration. Thus, there was a decisive time period when the patient resourcefully attempted to restructure her experience in the context of a more responsive mutual regulatory system. Feeling supported by her father, she felt protected and valued. When the father's stature began to falter, she then needed to shore him up to retain her sense of adequacy, efficacy, and pride in accomplishments and her expectations of some responsiveness and mutuality. She imagined that he needed her support and could be strong again. She attempted to be neither a victim nor demanding like her mother but a caretaker and, thereby, an ally to her father in a mutually beneficial relationship. That is, she attempted to restore her father to his preeminent idealized position. Although she maintained her intactness and efficacy, she was more rigidly restricted in that she had to organize her experience to emphasize her caretaking to the point of self-sacrifice. The initial tie of self-abnegation to her victimized mother was thus transformed at this stage through her attempt to restore her father. Silently, this precarious balance had been reestablished in the treatment and then ruptured.

This case illustrates a distinction that became apparent when a masochistic representational configuration, the necessity to repeat the experience of burdened caretaking, simultaneously performed archaic selfobject functions. As a burdened caretaker the patient could maintain a needed tie. We suggest that representational configurations provide the necessary context in which disruptions of the selfobject tie can be understood. Thus, the analyses of selfobject transferences and representational configurations must go hand in hand, since they address different functions.

If the analyst is bound to a model that explains the current manifestations of pathology in terms of the earliest prototypes, then the masochistic stance of this patient only as it evolved in relation to her mother would be addressed; this relationship would be seen as the deeper and more influential layer. But the later feelings of worth and competence, dearly acquired and constructed in relation to her father, would then be bypassed. Though fragile and derived through a self organization that required self-sacrifice, they nevertheless provided the patient with intellectual and interpersonal resources. They rescued her from the isolated, victimized life that she felt her mother led and pointed her toward a more socially engaged, intellectually challenging one associated with her father. If the analyst were to ignore these resources, he would be continually reflecting back to the patient a sense of her that overemphasized her limitations, her sense of victimization, and the masochistic self-abnegation that were organized in relation to her mother.

Should the interpretation not have been made? Ruptures in the selfobject tie are inevitable and lead to increased understanding. As Kohut has so crucially described, their repair is one source for the transformation and formation of new themes and expectations in treatment. The intervention jarred the patient because the analyst seemed to reject her as his needed, self-sacrificing caretaker. Indeed, he appeared to her to be distinguishing himself as her rescuer, saving her from her repetitive self-sacrificing behaviors. The patient even wondered aloud if the analyst were unduly anxious about her ability to survive in her hostile environment. Did the timing of the interpretation, the breach of empathy that it conveyed to her, reflect the analyst's anxiety? Was the analyst as worried about her as she had been about her father when she felt that he was being overwhelmed and could not survive in his hostile environment? This perception of the analyst's anxiety had contributed to the patient's increased anxiety and had escalated her disorganization. In appearing as a rescuer to the patient the analyst became unavailable to her as a necessary participant in the organization of her crucial theme. The analyst was needed as the helpless and benign ally who had to be rescued by the patient through her sacrifices. His enlivened presence would serve as a source for her self-consolidation. These various themes became clarified subsequent to the rupture of the idealized selfobject dimension of the transference.

The interpretation was based on the assumption that when the patient's sense of self was strengthened or, put differently, when the necessity to protect her vulnerable self was diminished, she would feel freer to experience her competence with a sense of pride. The interpretation also touched on the patient's shame-filled wish to be more dependent. Integration of her dependent wishes would then contribute to the transformation of other rigidly retained configurations, for example, her overaccommodation. The interpretation of the representational configuration furthered the transformational processes of the analysis by illuminating and engaging these dominant organizing themes of the patient's experience.

In the process of interpreting the representational configuration, the idealized selfobject dimension of the transference was disrupted. When this rupture was addressed, it provided an opportunity to transform a rigid representational configuration. Analysis of the rupture established for the patient the expectation of being understood, of retaining a valued tie through interactive efforts with the analyst and without self-sacrifice. Addressing the rupture established the expectation that ruptures can be repaired and disappointments understood.

Thus, it is necessary for the analyst to address both dimensions of the transference. Analysis of the patient's representational configuration affected, ruptured, restored, and thereby transformed the selfobject dimension. Restoring the ruptures in the selfobject dimension permitted the representational configurations to assume the foreground. The analysis and transformation of the recurring representational themes of the burdened, self-sacrificing caretaker of the weak, needy, but idealizable father could thereby continue.

We have elaborated on Kohut's description of the rupture and repair of the selfobject tie. Kohut (1984) emphasized that through disruption and repair, psychic functions that had not been acquired could be transmuted and internalized, thereby building psychic structure. In the repair process the functions that the patient provides for himself (e.g., soothing, self-regulating) are emphasized. In this repair the analyst's role is to recognize, acknowledge, and be empathically attuned to the rupture. We have added an emphasis on the acquisition of expectations of mutuality during the repair phase of the rupture. In addition to the role that Kohut gives to the analyst, we see the repair process as involving dyadic regulation. Both patient and analyst influence each other to develop a new interaction pattern. The analyst and patient together examine not only the impact of the selfobject failure but also the efforts at restoration. Through this very process of analyzing disruptions of the selfobject tie, a representation of the expectation of mutuality accrues for the patient. This is our two-dimensional view of the transference. The specific way in which the tie is ruptured and interactively repaired transforms rigid, repetitive expectations and establishes new expectations and representational configurations. The patient's reaction to the analyst's efforts to restore the tie are viewed both within the perspective of selfobject needs and within the perspective of recurring representational configurations. Rather than view the repair solely as the source of a new inner function, we emphasize that a new interactive pattern evolves. This pattern will contain a selfobject tie and at the same time will be represented, thereby diminishing the power of repetitive configurations that had been engaged in the transference.

In the course of this patient's analysis, the most frequent ruptures of the selfobject tie were instances in which the patient's need to feel the analyst's investment in retaining the tie was jarred. Later in the analysis, when a disjunction along this line again occurred, the patient was able to say, "Look, you make sure that our tie is retained, and I'll take care of my own autonomy." By this time the patient's self-expectations, as well as her expectations of the analyst, had been transformed. The analyst was no longer required to be the needy, weak ally whom she had to support. He was now expected to carry his own weight. A step had been taken toward being able to derive selfobject functions from an occasionally playfully adversarial relationship with the analyst (Lachmann, 1986). Through the analysis of the rupture and its repair the patient could integrate the resources she had acquired in puberty, which she had been able to use only sparingly, with self-sacrifice and disruptive anxiety. She became more gutsy, assertive, intellectually active, fun-loving, and popular with her peers.

In conclusion, although the concept of developmental transformations has long been accepted in developmental psychology, it has not been consistently applied to psychoanalytic treatment. Reorganizations occur as both child and environment (or patient and analyst) influence each other in a mutual regulatory system at each phase of development (or analysis).

We have illustrated the distinction between the selfobject and the representational dimensions of the transference and the necessity to continuously address both during analysis. These dimensions serve different functions, and each may illuminate aspects of the other. If we confine ourselves to selfobject transferences, as crucial as these are, we may neglect a level of dynamics, namely, the themes that organize the patient's representation of past experiences. If we confine ourselves to the interpretation of representational configurations, we may lose our attunement to the vulnerabilities in the patient's sense of cohesion.

In the clinical illustration, the analyst interpreted a specific representational configuration to the patient and thereby ruptured her experience of the analyst as a sustaining selfobject. Exploration of the rupture of this selfobject tie revealed its specific function, its developmental history, its transformation, and its place in the analyst–patient relationship. In addition, the ongoing transformation of the patient's experience in the treatment was promoted through the establishment of new, interactively organized expectations of mutual participation. Rather than emphasize the early mother–infant dyad, uncovering and reconstructing this phase of development as the sole focus of therapeutic action, we placed equal emphasis on the contributions from later phases of development. Analyst and patient were then alerted to the resources and defenses derived from various developmental transformations as well as from currently activated themes.

# REFERENCES

Ainsworth, M., Blehar, M. Waters, E. & Wall, S. (1978), *Patterns of Attachment*. Hillsdale, NJ: Lawrence Erlbaum.

Beebe, B. & Lachmann, F. M. (1988a), Mother–infant mutual influence and the precursors of psychic structure. In: *Frontiers in Self Psychology: Progress in Self Psychology, Vol. 3*, ed. A. Goldberg. Hillsdale, NJ: The Analytic Press, pp. 3–25.

_____ & _____ (1988b), The contribution of mother–infant mutual influence to the origins of self and object representations. *Psychoanal. Psychol.*, 5:305–337.

Bowlby, J. (1969), *Attachment*. New York: Basic Books, 1982.

Kohut, H. (1984), *How Does Analysis Cure?* ed. A. Goldberg & P. Stepansky. Chicago: University of Chicago Press.

Lachmann, F. M. (1986), Interpretation of psychic conflict and adversarial relationships: A self-psychological perspective. *Psychoanal. Psychol.*, 3:341–356.

_____ & Beebe, B. (1989), Oneness fantasies revisited. *Psychoanal. Psychol.*, 6:137–149.

_____ & Lichtenberg, J. D. (1992). Model scenes: Implications for psychoanalytic treatment. *J. Amer. Psychoanal. Assn.*, 40:117–137.

Lichtenberg, J. D. (1983), An application of the self psychological viewpoint to psychoanalytic technique. In: *Reflections on Self Psychology*, ed. J. Lichtenberg & S. Kaplan. Hillsdale, NJ: The Analytic Press, pp. 163–185.

_____ (1989), *Psychoanalysis and Motivation*. Hillsdale, NJ: The Analytic Press.

Loewald, H. (1980), *Papers of Psychoanalysis*. New Haven, CT: Yale University Press.

Mitchell, S. A. (1988), *Relational Concepts in Psychoanalysis*. Cambridge, MA: Harvard University Press.

Ornstein, A. (1974), The dread to repeat and the new beginning: A contribution to the psychoanalysis of the narcissistic personality disorders. *The Annual of Psychoanalyis*, 2:231–248. New York: International Universities Press.

Piaget, J. (1937), *The Construction of Reality in the Child* (trans. M. Cook). New York: Basic Books, 1954.

Sameroff, A. & Chandler, M. (1975), Reproductive risk and the continuum of caretaking casualty. *A Review of Child Development Research, Vol. 4*, ed. F. D. Horowitz. Chicago: University of Chicago Press.

Stern, D. (1983), The early development of schemas of self, other, and "self with other." In: *Reflections on Self Psychology*, ed. J. Lichtenberg & S. Kaplan. Hillsdale, NJ: The Analytic Press, pp. 49–84.

_____ (1985), *The Interpersonal World of the Infant*. New York: Basic Books.

_____ (1989), The representation of relational patterns. In: *Relationships and Relationship Disorders*, ed. A. Samaroff & R. Emde. New York: Basic Books, pp. 52–69.

Stolorow, R. D., Brandchaft, B. & Atwood, G. (1987), *Psychoanalytic Treatment*. Hillsdale, NJ: The Analytic Press.

_____ Lachmann, F. (1980), *Psychoanalysis of Developmental Arrests*. New York: International Universities Press.

_____ & _____ (1984/1985), Transference: The future of an illusion. *The Annual of Psychoanalysis*, 12/13. New York: International Universities Press, 19–38.

Wolf, E. S. (1988), *Treating the Self*. New York: Guilford Press.

Zeanah, C., Anders, T., Seifer, R. & Stern, D. (1989), Implications of research on infant development for psychodynamic theory and practice. *J. Amer. Acad. Child Adolesc. Psychiat.*, 28:657–668.

# Chapter 2

# Commentaries

## SELF PSYCHOLOGY AND THE TRANSFERENCE
### Michael Franz Basch

Drs. Lachmann and Beebe have presented us with a very interesting clinical case illustrating a point that is well taken. Lachmann has often emphasized in these forums that, to use his words, "the jump from the cradle to the couch" is an unwarranted one. We cannot assume that whatever the patient is struggling with in the analysis simply repeats a significant trauma of the patient's early mother–infant relationship.

The first impact, and perhaps one of the most important, that Kohut's (1971) clinical discoveries had on our practice was to undo the certainty that ultimately it was the analysis and interpretation of the oedipal conflict that was both definitive and curative for whatever the patient complained of or was suffering from. Lachmann and Beebe call attention to the fact that if we now were to simply assume and interpret a linear connection between what the patient tells us and the selfobject failures in his early development, we would only be repeating the same fallacy of constructing a theory that is much too narrow to accommodate all that happens in our consulting room.

Lachmann's case illustrates that the crucial developmental issues around which the patient's defenses against the transference were organized were those of the patient's puberty. I would say this emphasis on the continuity of development is very much in keeping with what modern-day infant research has taught us. As Daniel Stern (1985), in his classic book *The Interpersonal World of the Infant* makes very clear, the development of the sense of self is an ongoing proposition that continues until, as Kohut also pointed out, the life of the person has ended.

I have no quarrel with the manner in which the case was handled. I would, however, disagree that Lachmann's patient had formed an idealizing transference that was ruptured by his interpretation of her need. In my opinion, the patient's masochistic attitude, in and outside the analysis, was a defense, a defense against incurring a repetition of the disappointment she experienced when her need for an ideal was frustrated by her father's failures. In other words, the patient was defending against transferring her need for an idealized selfobject experience to the analyst—I believe it is this adaptive defense that Lachmann calls the representational situation or configuration. Lachmann explicitly acknowledged to the patient that it may well have been the session and, by implication, his interpretation that had created a problem for her. This calmed the patient, restored the bond between her and the analyst, diminished the need for defense, and let her begin meeting her need for an idealizing selfobject experience.

Having agreed with Lachmann's proposition that we should focus our therapeutic efforts on the developmental issues truly crucial for the patient, without assuming that we are thereby necessarily gaining an understanding of that patient's infancy or, for that matter, early childhood, I would now like to qualify that. What Lachmann's patient seems to have done is attempt to use her relationship with her father to build what Kohut (1977) called compensatory structure. That is, having been significantly disappointed or traumatized in her selfobject needs by her mother, she turned to her father, with whom, unfortunately, she was only temporarily more successful.

As Kohut said, compensatory structures should not be confused with makeshift or defensive compromises. Compensatory structure is strong, viable, and flexible, it truly compensates for earlier damage, and it is only when the compensatory structure is endangered that symptoms develop. So it is not totally out of order to speculate about what happened in this patient's early childhood, given the way she conducts herself in the therapy, the history that she is able to recount, and the historical issues indirectly uncovered in the therapy. However, Lachmann's experience is very much in line with Kohut's clinical judgment that a patient will usually not permit us to deal with the basic or primary infantile trauma. To reopen that situation would be too damaging for the patient's self system, and the risk of fragmentation involved in reactivating it precludes analytic examination. Instead, the patient will work with us at the level of the damaged compensatory structure, and when successful, we help the patient to restore, expand, or otherwise improve that manner of coping both with the world and her subjective needs. In other words, I believe that Dr. Lachmann's initial interpretation to his patient of her wish to be cared for and her need to defend herself against that wish by caring for others was, though not focal for her analysis at that point, not necessarily incorrect.

I am not so sure that I agree with what I understand to be the authors' conclusion, namely, that the way in which we help a patient to build new structure is somehow different from what Kohut tried to teach us. Kohut (1971), as Lachmann and Beebe mentioned, emphasized that through disruption of empathy and its repair the patient acquires new psychic functions, that is, learns and makes his own the manner in which the therapist deals with empathic breaks that inevitably arise between them—this process he called "transmuting internalization."

I do not think that Kohut excluded analysis of the empathic break in those patients able to participate in the process. I agree with Kohut (1971) that in cases like that of Miss F one cannot interpret initially; for a long time all one can do is to mirror the patient through echoing her words. This is a merger form of the mirror transference and, in my opinion, indicates that Miss F was a borderline patient. In the patient who, like Lachmann's, is much better put together (i.e., who has a higher-level character disorder), acknowledgment of the empathic break and an interpretation of its significance for the patient go together. Lachmann and Beebe say that it is the specific way in which the tie is ruptured and interactively repaired that establishes new themes and transforms psychic structure. I do not see this as contradicting what Kohut said. Perhaps I do not understand the authors, but it seems to me that Kohut too was talking about the fact that we have our clinical theories about what happened to the patient, hazard an intervention, find that the intervention hurts rather than helps, acknowledge that to the patient, and enlist the patient's cooperation in getting on the right track. Is it not in this very process that Dr. Lachmann's patient learned that the analyst, the current focus of her defense against the idealizing transference, was not as fragile as either mother or father had been and that the analyst could deal with difficulties in a relationship in a very different way from what the patient had heretofore experienced? I am of course not suggesting that this was a conscious kind of learning but, rather, that this was learned unconsciously and that the *effects* on the patient's psychic structure would be expected to appear in the patient's future relationship with the analyst and with others. That is, I would expect the patient, as a result of working through repeated miscommunications and misunderstandings in the analysis, eventually to deal differently with disruptive situations. For example, instead of decompensating she might at some future date call attention to the fact that the therapist is, in her opinion, mistaken in his assumption, whatever that assumption may be. In this way, the patient would be demonstrating that she had indeed acquired new psychic structure—a relatively stable and more optimal way of functioning with stress in her relationships.

Kohut expanded the range and efficacy of psychoanalysis. He did not simplify it, nor in his emphasis on introspection and empathy did he provide us with a shortcut to what remains, at best, a challenging and difficult task: the formation and resolution of the analytic transference. Lachmann and Beebe's elucidation of the phase of empathic immersion during the defense transference is an excellent illustration of how one may work toward that goal.

## REFERENCES

Kohut, H. (1971), *The Analysis of the Self.* New York: International Universities Press.
_____ (1977), *The Restoration of the Self.* New York: International Universities Press.
_____ (1984), *How Does Analysis Cure?* ed. A. Goldberg & P. Stepansky. New York: International Universities Press.
Stern, D. (1985), *The Interpersonal World of the Infant.* New York: Basic Books.

## TRANSFERENCE AND STRUCTURE FORMATION
### Elliott Markson

Lachmann and Beebe examine the relationship between transference and the process of structuralization. Like many others, they see the disruption and subsequent mending of selfobject transferences as a major route for structuralization in treatment. Transference is seen as operating within an interactive system, or intersubjective context, and not simply as a replication of the past. There is a basic theoretical assumption here of a representational world, that is created through the internalization of experience and that can be altered by treatment.

This is a particularly useful metatheory because it is experience—near, unlike much of metapsychology.

While Kohut emphasized transmuting internalization in the formation of psychic structure, he did not examine the nature and function of these representational configurations. Nor did he give a great deal of attention to other forms of internalization that were not the result of disrupted selfobject transference. Apart from his concept of disruption within a selfobject transference, Kohut's view of internalization is rather similar to classical theory, which also sees frustration and disappointment as the impetus for development. In fact, it is the mending of these disruptions that appears to be the mutative agency. It seems likely, however, that most structuralization occurs without the disruption–restoration sequence and without unpleasure.

Lachmann and Beebe are advocating a transformational perspective, which, in contrast to a linear perspective, stresses the continuous construction and reorganization of experience. This model emphasizes the exploration of selfobject transference ruptures whereas the uncovering of the past is the focus of the linear model. The authors caution us against the hazards of reductionism inherent in the linear model. They also want us to see, I think, just how complex are the manifold transference meanings of a single clinical event. This complexity not only is the result of the patient's accumulated experience but also reflects the therapist's contribution to the disruption and its repair. Linear genetic interpretations do not do justice to this complexity.

However, I think there are "dominant organizing themes" (to use the authors' own term), which run through the treatment, that may have a linear connection to early experience. Early traumatic experience may, in fact, remain ongoing and cumulative through childhood but be subject, of course, to transformation at different levels of development. So I think there is still room for a linear perspective provided the therapist does not lose sight of the intersubjective aspect of treatment and of subsequent contributions to development. I think Lachmann and Beebe's reminder that later transformations of structure have significant potential for preserving the patient's self-esteem and sense of competence is important. The authors describe how their patient's self-esteem and capacity for hopefulness were sustained through her experience of being a competent, self-sacrificing caretaker. They show how this vital structure was endangered by the intervention of the therapist, because the selfobject dimension was overlooked. There has been a growing interest in the issue of competence or efficacy in recent years because of its developmental and clinical relevance.

I think Lachmann and Beebe make an interesting statement on how transmuting internalization operates. Whereas Kohut viewed it as a process in which the patient takes over or identifies with the therapist's selfobject functioning, Lachmann and Beebe emphasize "the acquisition of expectations of mutuality" resulting from the interactive repair of disruptions. For them it is the mending of disruptions through the efforts of both patient and therapist that is crucial to structural change.

I would like to add a few comments on the sense of competence or efficacy, which is involved in transmuting internalization and in structure formation generally. It is an integral aspect of the mending or restoration process, which ought to follow disruptions in the selfobject transference. Transmuting internalization, as Kohut described it, had a passive tilt to it: the patient is narcissistically injured within a good-enough selfobject transference relationship, and the injury is dealt with intrapsychically. That is, the patient has internalized selfobject functions provided earlier by the therapist. There is an identification with the provider in the service of self-maintenance or self-righting. But there is no struggle here, no attempt to alter a disappointing object. There is no work of conquest, no attempt to use the object in order to elicit a more satisfactory response. There is no manifestation of protest or of attachment behavior; the patient makes no active attempt at mending. We would not want to see disjunctions in the selfobject transference consistently dealt with in this way by our patients. What we want to see some of the time when there is an intersubjective strain are active efforts at restoration by the patient and not just by the therapist. There is, for the patient, a great pleasure premium attached to successful efforts of this kind, that is, a pleasure in functioning, in mastery, and in being an agent of change. Of course, there is also a need for what Lachmann and Beebe term an "interactive effort," where patient and therapist work together toward repair, but this is a different kind of experience, with different results.

There are developmental parallels to these clinical issues. The child's capacity to effect optimal responsiveness (Bacal, 1985) results in the structuralization of such basic capacities as self-esteem, initiative, hopefulness, and a sense of competence and of entitlement. In Lachmann and Beebe's case illustration, as in other cases of masochistic-depressive disorder, these structures are impaired or deficient. There is a predisposition to this syndrome when an early sense of competence has been compromised.

Clearly, not all transformation of structure is the result of optimal failure and subsequent mending. Many of us would agree with the observation of Stolorow and Lachmann (1985) concerning "the ubiquitous curative role played by the silent . . . selfobject dimension of the transference [and] that every mutative therapeutic moment includes a significant element of selfobject transference cure" (p. 34). The worry here, of course, is that self psychology might be seen as advocating a cure through love or manipulation. Perhaps Ornstein (1990) shares this concern; she does believe, I think, that supportive and reassuring comments may be counterproductive and that they may interfere with the mobilization of the selfobject transference and eventually create a malignant form of dependency. She advocates instead what she terms "validation," and only within the context of an interpretation. I think, however, there are times when something more than interpretive validation is required, when educative measures and overt expressions of support, hopefulness, and encouragement are justified. They may or may not be accompanied by interpretation and need not place the treatment at risk. For example, if the therapist is enjoying the patient and experiencing a sense of admiration of the patient's achievements, surely this is not to be concealed. This may, in fact, be a necessary experience for the masochistic-depressive patient, such as the one described by Lachmann and Beebe. These patients may also need the therapist's hopefulness, since they have little of their own.

Eventually, we will learn more about the limits of interpretation and the limits of both silent and overtly supportive measures. We need a clearer idea of the relationship between interpretation and support, and of the different structures created by them. I think we can say that both implicit and explicit supportive measures may enhance the mutative power of explanations and that in themselves they are probably capable of structure formation or modification.

My impression is that in areas of conflict, interpretation is central, and when deficit is the issue various forms of support are the essential element. Optimal responsiveness in the treatment situation would involve one or the other or both at different times. As you know, Kohut struggled brilliantly with these issues in *How Does Analysis Cure?* But much remains to be understood.

The supportive elements of treatment that can be subsequently internalized are sometimes provided in an attenuated form and sometimes in more explicit ways. They fall into three broad categories: (1) tension and affect regulation; (2) recognition and support of the evolving self and its aims, capacities, and vitality; and (3) the provision of meaning to experience. These supportive functions address the selfobject needs that may be mobilized in the transference. The available selfobject function, however, may or may not be used or internalized by the patient. There is an assumption here of a corrective experience capable of transforming structure. In fact, classical theory assumed there was therapeutic value in the patient's ability to recognize the discrepancy between transference distortions and the true qualities of the analyst. This provided a perceptual correction, if not an experiential one.

But there are obstacles to the internalization of new experience and the use of the analyst. How do we modify the "rigidly retained configurations" of which Lachmann and Beebe speak? As Ornstein (1990) asks, how do we overcome "the patient's difficulty in perceiving the analyst's empathy and using her selfobject functions"? Is transference always the obstacle? Is Kohut's valuable concept of the fear of retraumatization always a sufficient explanation? Is defense in general always implicated? Is the therapist somehow falling short? Is there an impediment in the area of fantasy and illusion that compromises the creative area of the transference (Bacal, 1985)? Are there other deficits that interfere with structure formation? What is it that so often prevents masochistic-depressive patients from recognizing and internalizing our pleasure and admiration of them or from believing in our authenticity when they do recognize these responses? Can they, in fact, benefit fully from treatment without the experience of being enjoyed by the therapist? I think this is a central issue in these patients, one that has an intimate connection with the selfobject transferences.

Masochistic–depressive patients are burdened, guilty, and unhappy people with very poor and precariously maintained self-esteem. They display little sense of being truly entitled to a better life, as Ornstein (1990) mentions. Instead, they are driven to self-sacrifice, often to an appalling degree. Suffering in servitude has become idealized. This is clearly seen in Lachmann and Beebe's patient, who strove to maintain her self-esteem and relatedness through masochistic behavior. A similar character structure is usually seen in one or both parents. The mother has usually been experienced as a burdened and self-sacrificing person who has been drained of vitality through service to her family. The child experiences himself or herself as a source of pain and disappointment to the parent rather than as a source of pride and pleasure. Usually, the child's reparative efforts are thwarted by the parent's own masochistic need to repudiate pleasure. Mending is not possible. The developmental consequences are manifold, particularly in the evolution of self-esteem, of a sense of effectance, and of an ordinary sense of entitlement. These deficits constitute a predisposition to depression and reflect a failure in mirroring.

In my own experience with these patients it has been difficult to mobilize an overt mirror transference with a full and clear expression of the related selfobject needs. Within this transference patients seek evidence of the therapist's pleasure and admiration, and confirmation of their value as persons. The mobilization of a mirror transference may be essential to structural change here. Ornstein (1990), while not speaking directly of the mirror transference, observes that in these cases "infantile narcissism has not been transformed into pride and pleasure in the self and its activities" and that "this condition is extremely resistant to change." I am certainly in agreement with her views here.

While selfobject needs for mirroring are usually provided silently via optimal responsiveness, I think we ought to consider whether there may be times when these patients need something more concrete, some spontaneous expression of our admiration and pleasure. This does not preclude the necessary interpretive work, but interpretation and the silent selfobject dimension may be insufficient because the obstacles to the internalization of new experience may be so daunting. Enactments judiciously, but not reluctantly expressed may be essential to these patients' eventual sense of pride in themselves.

I wonder if Lachmann and Beebe's patient was able to openly and unambiguously express her need for the therapist's admiration and enjoyment. Certainly, as they say, the therapist wanted to help the patient experience "a sense of pride and efficacy," and they clearly recognized the patient's need to feel that her reparative strivings were valued. While the relationship with the father was highlighted in this case, I wonder whether the mother might have been experienced as a burdened and self-sacrificing person and whether the patient felt unenjoyed and responsible for her mother's pain, which she was unable to mend. There seems to be some evidence for this. At the risk of sounding like a mother blamer and like someone hopelessly fixated on a linear perspective, I suggest that this patient may have turned to her father in the hope of remedying earlier and ongoing problems with her mother. I don't think that this is falling back on the earliest possible cause, as Lachmann and Beebe mention. I think of this more as an ongoing, cumulative narcissistic disturbance in the relationship with the mother and certainly as one that can undergo structural transformation during the course of development.

While a linear perspective can blind us to the adaptive and defensive achievements of later development, I do not see it as necessarily in opposition to a transformational view. In fact, the emphasis on transformation may tend to obscure the significance of early experience. Nor does a therapeutic focus on later development necessarily remedy the effects of early conflict and deficit. We have to be careful not to swing too far in either direction.

## REFERENCES

Bacal, H. (1985), Optimal responsiveness and the therapeutic process. In: *Progress in Self Psychology, Vol. 1,* ed A. Goldberg. NY: Guilford Press, pp. 202–227.

Ornstein, A. (1990), *Transference and structural change.* Presented at the Annual Conference on the Psychology of the Self, New York City.

Stolorow, R. & Lachmann, F. (1985), Transference: The future of an illusion. *The Annual of Psychoanalysis,* 12/13:19–38. New York: International Universities Press.

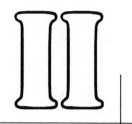

# Clinical

# Chapter 3

# Problems for a Rational Therapeutics in Self Psychology

## Bonnie Wolfe

Self psychology lacks an adequate theory of treatment. In his posthumously published book *How Does Analysis Cure?* Heinz Kohut (1984) described the action of psychotherapy, but he did not give a sufficiently comprehensive description. He characterized psychotherapy in broad terms as a reinstatement of development and as a process of structure building via transmuting internalization. These ideas reflect a distinctive set of beliefs increasingly articulated over the course of Kohut's writing, which form a coherent view of psychological health and help and of the essential qualities of human nature.

But Kohut never fully resolved the tension between his new ideas and his wish for their acceptance by the psychoanalytic community. There is a fundamental ambiguity in his description of the therapist's role in facilitating development. This has led to confusion about the basic stance of the therapist and the nature of therapeutic influence. In addition, Kohut's idea that the domain of psychoanalysis is defined by and limited to the information available through empathy and introspection has obscured our understanding of the forces at work in the treatment process.

This chapter describes three different theories of treatment proposed by psychologists interested in the self—Kohut himself, Robert Stolorow and his colleagues, and Michael Basch. I show that each of these theories is predicated on a different concept of self and point out certain problems inherent in each. Finally, I describe an additional dimension—the arena of values—that needs to be considered in formulating a rational basis for therapeutics in self psychology.

## KOHUT'S CONCEPT OF CURE

By the late 1960s Kohut had developed two new ideas that were to become hallmarks of self psychology. One was that certain needs implicit in the manner in which patients related to him revealed the cause of their distress. Kohut believed that the communication of these needs via the selfobject transferences indicated an absence or insufficiency of requisite responsiveness in early development at the same time that they revealed an essential vulnerability in the present day. A second important discovery was that the systematic employment of empathy played a pivotal role in the recognition, reception, and resolution of such needs in the psychoanalytic situation, and particularly in the transference relationship.[1]

These ideas were criticized as attempts to "cure through love" and to provide a "corrective emotional experience." Kohut took pains to defend his views. He insisted that the aim of analysis was to understand, not to fulfill such longings. The indulgence of a transference wish—for example, by giving a patient the necessary "emotional echo or approval" not previously received—might be a "temporary tactical requirement," Kohut (1968) said, but the true analytic aim was "mastery based on insight, achieved in a setting of (tolerable) analytic abstinence" (p. 111). Furthermore, he warned that the active attempt to provide needed responses could lead to the establishment of a "tenacious transference bondage" and hamper the "gradual alteration of the existing narcissistic structures" (p. 102). Instead, he believed, an in-depth reactivation of these "archaic attitudes" would provide an opportunity for them to be "tamed and neutralized" through the traditional analytic methods of interpretation and working through of the transference. A corrective emotional experience might be a corollary of successful psychoanalysis, but Kohut did not uphold it as a principle guiding the conduct of treatment.

By 1977 Kohut had developed a more comprehensive theory of the self, largely dispensing with classical drive–defense terminology. His earlier descriptions of cure, involving the integration of split-off narcissistic structures, the neutralization of narcissistic energies, and the establishment of ego dominance in the narcissistic sector of the personality, were replaced with the idea that cure involved "filling in

---

[1]For a detailed discussion of the development of Kohut's concepts of the self, selfobjects, and the action of psychotherapy, see Wolfe (1989b). Clinical illustrations of these concepts are presented in Wolfe (1985, 1989a, 1991).

the defects in the structure of the self via selfobject transference and transmuting internalization" (p. 134). Increasingly, Kohut emphasized the role of the selfobject transference itself in the functional rehabilitation of the self.

By 1980 he described the essential therapeutic task as "reentering into the course of the line of development of self–selfobject relationships at the point where it had been traumatically interrupted in early life" (p. 453). To "fill in defects" in the self and to "reenter into" a course of development are, however, ambiguous projects. Neither the nature of the filling-in process nor the manner in which the relationship between therapist and patient promotes the resumption of a course of development was made clear. Empathy was said to play a role in the process, but Kohut's use of the term was equivocal and his description of the role of empathy in the therapeutic relationship was incomplete.

Kohut's well-known description of empathy as "vicarious introspection"—a form of observation used in the clinical situation as a data-gathering tool—refers to the therapist's capacity to recognize complex mental states that may be inarticulately or incompletely expressed by patients. Kohut made it clear that empathy is not equivalent to a comprehensive understanding of the larger patterns of a patient's experience or of their etiology and interrelationships. It can, however, provide a basis for understanding such patterns, and it can therefore alter the way in which the therapist thinks about a patient and influence decisions about the conduct of treatment. Empathically informed understanding is not, by itself, therapeutic, but when it is conveyed to the patient and contributes to the patient's experience of feeling understood, it becomes a mode of therapeutic action. Empathy may also profoundly alter the therapist's deeper feelings and attitudes toward the patient and thereby color many of the therapist's reactions to the patient—a powerful additional source of influence.

As Kohut gained a greater empathic understanding of the painful states of mind he described in *The Analysis of the Self*, he became more tolerant of them and more interested in their origin and meaning. He developed a new conceptual framework in which he defined the self as an irreducible experiential construct, regarded such states of mind as evidence of weakness or threat to the self, and developed the notion of the selfobject as the needed and painfully missing component of self. At the same time, he increasingly came to regard an emotionally expressive and actively encouraging attitude on the part of the analyst as appropriate in working with the "disorders of the self." He encouraged therapists to "quietly welcome" the expression of selfobject needs (Kohut, 1968, p. 100). He criticized the usual analytic ambience of "muted responsiveness and presumed neutrality" as being "grossly depriving" of ordinary human needs (Kohut, 1977, pp. 249–266) and especially deleterious for patients with narcissistic personality disorders who might feel that their "germinally displayed exhibitionism" or "cautiously offered" idealization had been rejected, thus causing a delicate aspect of the transference to break down.

Kohut (1977) suggested that the analyst adopt an attitude in harmony with the needs of such patients, one that is derived from a "deep comprehension of the genetic core of the analysand's disturbed personality" (p. 258). He never made plain the less muted responsiveness he had in mind, but he clearly regarded the analyst's kindly acceptance of and emotional resonance with the patient's feelings as indispensable to the establishment and maintenance of the selfobject transferences and, *pari passu*, of the therapeutic relationship. Kohut (1984) further believed that an analyst's "comfortable warmth" toward a patient and "life-affirming enjoyment" of the patient's activity might inadvertently respond to the patient's deepest need and have a beneficial effect (pp. 91–94, 145). Still, he thought such attitudes and responses were not sufficient to produce a cure. He described the basic principle of growth as a process of transmuting internalization, whereby functions necessary to the establishment and maintenance of a self are gradually developed as internal capacities rather than supplied by others.

Kohut variously invoked the concepts of insight and frustration to explain the process of transmuting internalization in psychotherapy. His views about the importance of insight were inconsistent. He asserted that an increase in the scope of consciousness does not always occur and is not essential but that the aim of cure is the establishment of a bond of "empathic in-tuneness" between self and selfobject on mature adult levels (pp. 64, 66). At other times, however, Kohut (1980) described a shift from "the enactment of a selfobject transference" to the "introspectively accessible experience of the need for such a selfobject" (p. 534), and he claimed that insight-promoting dynamic-genetic interpretations of the patient's psychological reactions, especially his transference experiences, are necessary in order to transform an ephemeral experience into a lasting one (Kohut, 1984, pp. 105–106), to permit a lessening of the "archaic merger bond" with the analyst, and to promote its replacement with an "empathic bond on a more mature level" (pp. 184–185). In any event, he regarded insight as being important insofar as it promotes the development and maintenance of the "mature empathic bond" to which he alluded.

Kohut's (1984) views on frustration were more consistent and more controversial.[2] He maintained that frustration is a necessary prerequisite of the move from archaic to more mature forms of self–selfobject relatedness, both in early life and in psychotherapy, and that it stimulates the internal development of psychic functions formerly provided by others. The occurrences that build up a healthy self during childhood are, he claimed, a basic "in-tuneness between the self and its selfobjects" and selfobject failures of a nontraumatic degree (p. 70), which serve as an impetus to development. Using this developmental model, he described an understanding phase of psychotherapy—which would include many sequences of need-activation, nonfulfillment of need, and substitution of direct need fulfillment with "a bond of empathy" between self and selfobject—and a succeeding explanatory phase, which would broaden and deepen the patient's empathic-accepting grasp of himself and strengthen his trust in the empathic bond with the analyst (pp. 103–104). Thus, he regarded frustration, like insight, as furthering the development of a "mature empathic bond," which sustains a sense of trust in being able to be understood empathically by another, and a capacity to understand and accept oneself.

Again and again in Kohut's writings a "bond of empathy with the analyst" is invoked as a curative agent, but it is not adequately elucidated. A bond of empathy, while not sufficient to produce a cure, is regarded as indispensable to the process. It is described as the necessary prerequisite for the resumption of development, the substrate of new psychic structure, the context within which frustration can be nontraumatic and disappointment can be assimilated, the successor to archaic experiences of direct enactment and need fulfillment, and, in mature form, as the intrapsychic essence of emotional well-being. A bond is not equivalent to a mode of observation by the therapist, an inquiring stance, or a type of responsiveness, although all of these may promote and reflect such a bond, nor is it equivalent to an experience of being understood in depth by a therapist, however reliably and repeatedly this occurs. Since empathic understanding can be used for destructive as well as beneficial purposes, its presence is not a sufficient guarantor of therapeutic agency. An adequate explication of the concept would need to include a description of the therapist's aims and attitudes.

When Kohut (1977) described the events that contribute to the

---

[2]Kohut (1984) himself wondered whether abiding psychic functions could be acquired without a preceding frustration and whether the presence of the so-called selfobject might activate innate functions (pp. 100–101). He also anticipated a number of other criticisms of his paradigm of development, including the idea that there may be a difference between the way structure is acquired in adult life and in childhood.

development of psychic structure in childhood, he emphasized the caregiver's ability to empathically perceive the child's disrupted feeling states and "to include the child within its own psychological organization" (pp. 85–87). The caregiver, he said, creates conditions that enable the child to experience the caregiver's more mature feeling states *as if they were his own* (italics added). The child can then learn to experience affect as a signal instead of feeling overwhelmed by affect spread (p. 87). Numerous such sequences, during which the child recovers from experiences of disintegration through empathic merger with the caregiver, establish "one of the pillars of mental health throughout life" (p. 87). But when Kohut described the therapeutic interaction, he did not give a comparable degree of attention to similar elements in that process.

An empathic bond with the therapist might involve the patient's vicarious participation in the therapist's states of mind. A bond of empathy might refer to an extended experience of in-depth understanding of the patient by the therapist, one who is more mature than the patient and who feels accepting, compassionate, kind, and warm—simple words for an "enormous country where all is silent."[3] A systematic description of a mature empathic bond would then need to include a better understanding of the ways in which the therapist conveys kindly acceptance, comfortable warmth, and life-affirming enjoyment to the patient and enables the patient to participate in them. To understand and be understood in this way is a singular achievement.

In addition, we would need to understand what the therapist's more mature psychological organization consists of and how the values and aims of the therapist are embedded in the therapeutic project. Kohut's writing is shot through with his ideals. When he encouraged analysts to welcome reactivated mirroring and idealizing needs and merger transferences (Kohut, 1968, pp. 100; 1980, p. 534), when he cautioned against moralizing about a patient's narcissism or disparaging a patient's idealizations, and when he admonished against subtle rejections that might be concealed in prematurely given interpretations (Kohut, 1968, pp. 100–106), he set forth an outstanding example of tolerance and acceptance of human vulnerability. When he wrote about the individual's continuing search to complete his development and fulfill his innermost aims (cf. Ornstein, 1980, pp. 138–142), he expressed his own compelling interest in the inner experience of freedom and his abiding optimism about the

---

[3]Guillaume Apollinaire, "La Jolie Rousse," *Poemes* (Paris: Editions Gallimard, Livre de Poche, 1956), 161.

human potential for growth. The totality of his work stands as an exhortation and inspiration to the community of therapists.

These and other beliefs, which are neither self-evident nor universally accepted, permeate the work of many of Kohut's followers, invariably find expression in their attitude toward patients, and are a powerful source of influence in the therapeutic relationship. And although they inextricably inform the concepts and practice of self psychology, Kohut's theory of cure does not adequately take account of their impact.

## INTERSUBJECTIVITY

Stolorow and his collaborators have clarified a number of concepts used by Kohut, and they have formulated a different theory of treatment. Two separately developed lines of thought come together in their idea of psychoanalytic treatment as a science of intersubjective fields. The first involves a systematic application of the idea of self as a structure of experience. The second is an attempt to extend and systematically apply Kohut's definition of the domain of psychoanalysis in order to address the issue of the analyst's subjectivity.

A principle of the so-called projective techniques for assessing personality is that projection is not simply a defense against and attempt to eliminate unwanted mental contents but is an instance of the tendency to screen, select, order, and interpret stimulation from the outside in accordance with already existing patterns of affect, habitual response and perceptual tendencies, persistent aims and action propensities, and recurrent wishes and fantasies (cf. e.g., Henry, 1956, pp. 8–9, 31–32). The order and meaning attributed by a subject to external objects (such as clouds in the sky or Rorschach cards in the consulting room) reflect, to some extent, existing tendencies in the subject. This understanding of mental processes derives from an intellectual tradition dating back to Immanuel Kant.

Following a similar reasoning, Stolorow and Atwood (1979) argued that personality theories themselves are examples of the reification of subjective experience. Differently organized patterns of subjective experience color both the empirical observations and the general propositions about human nature made by various theorists, and these patterns, in turn, can be inferred by examining their intellectual productions. In an expanded application of this idea, Atwood and Stolorow (1984) pointed out that reification of subjective experience is an everyday phenomenon, that people are often unaware of their role in partially constituting the reality of the world in which they live, and that they tend to see the uniquely personal patterns and themes into which they organize events "as if they were properties of those events rather than products of [their] own subjective interpretations and constructions" (p. 36).

Unlike many theorists, including Kant and Kohut, these authors do not claim that there are any universal primary patterns of mental life, other than the tendency to organize experience and the need to maintain the organization of experience (p. 85). Stolorow (1986) therefore believes Kohut's idea of a bipolar self, with grandiose and idealizing poles, unnecessarily narrows our thinking about "the vast array of selfobject experiences that can shape and color the evolution of a person's self organization" (pp. 392–393). Nor do Atwood and Stolorow (1984) postulate the general presence of any particular motives informing human behavior, such as libidinal and aggressive aims or mirroring and idealizing needs. Rather, they believe that, for various reasons, people may strive to actualize the central patterns of their inner experience in recurrent patterns of conduct, thereby making concrete the configurations of their mental life (pp. 34, 35). From this vantage point—without normative assumptions or nomothetic declarations, without embracing or offering a theory of personality—the authors provide broadly encompassing definitions of psychological health and illness, interpretation, transference, and psychotherapy.

Atwood and Stolorow recognized in Kohut's thinking a focus on the nature of subjectivity, and with this concept squarely in mind they clarified certain terms that he had used inconsistently. A self, understood as a structure of inner experience, is different from a person, understood as an observable entity, they pointed out (pp. 34–35). Similarly, the concept of selfobject refers neither to other persons nor to their behaviors but to a dimension of the subjective experience of the behavior of others, namely, the experience of others as serving functions needed for consolidating and maintaining the organization of self experience (Stolorow, Brandchaft, and Atwood, 1987, pp. 16–17). Atwood and Stolorow (1984) found Kohut's ideas about the development of self especially relevant to their efforts to describe the structuralization of subjective experience (p. 39). Because there are broad areas of similarity between their views and those of Kohut, significant differences in their basic assumptions may tend to be obscured.

Kohut's ideas about the role of mirroring and idealizing experiences in the consolidation of self derive from an ontological premise. He believed that two basic kinds of experience are a function of the condition of being a human infant in a caregiving relationship: the experience of being perfectly wonderful and the experience of being less than perfect relative to caregiving others. The incompatibility between these two experiences gives rise to an "abiding, action-promoting tension," he said (1977, p. 183). He believed that an individual's inner experience of enduring sameness might ultimately be derived not from any particular content of the nuclear self, not from the lifelong sameness of basic ambitions and ideals, but from the "unchanging specificity of the self-expressive creative tensions that point toward the future" (p. 182). He further believed, as his last paper makes clear (1982, pp. 404ff.), that it is in the nature of human beings to establish such caregiving conditions for their infants.

Atwood and Stolorow (1984) make no such assumptions about human nature or infantile life. Rather, they formulate a model of psychological health based on the concept of optimal structuralization. This they define as "an optimal balance between the maintenance of . . . psychological organization on the one hand and . . . openness to new forms of experience on the other" (p. 39). Such a balance would allow a person to assimilate new experiences into existing psychological structures so that inner integrity and stability could be retained; at the same time, it would allow a person to accommodate to new experiences so that psychological organization could expand in complexity and scope.

This is a value-neutral definition of health, deriving from the concept of growth and resembling the notion of virtue in Aristotelian ethics, a kind of golden mean. It stipulates that flexible stability is the measure of psychological health, although the parameters for appropriate and undue amounts of each quality are left unspecified, as are the criteria for determining their sufficiency. This can be contrasted with Kohut's belief that the inner feeling of fulfillment and the sense of the wholeness and meaningfulness of one's life are the yardsticks of therapeutic success and of mental health (Kohut, 1980, pp. 455, 509). Kohut's (1977) experiential self—an experience of being "a unit, cohesive in space and enduring in time, which is a center of initiative and a recipient of impressions" (p. 99)—is different from a self as structure.

A structure is frangible for two reasons: it can be too rigid or too weak. Stolorow et al. (1987) describe the therapeutic enterprise in terms that derive directly from the notion of self-as-structure and the associated definition of health as flexible stability. Treatment, and the transference relationship, are described as having two poles—the conflictual/resistive/repetitive pole and the selfobject or developmental pole—each with an associated mode of therapeutic action (pp. 25–26, 101–102). When overly ossified, or "pathological," structures are salient, interpretation, conjoined with the "newness" of the analyst, can promote reorganization—the synthesis of alternate modes of experiencing the self and the object world. When structuralization is insufficiently cohesive, the selfobject bond with the analyst can promote structure formation.

Rather than being mutually exclusive, these two "poles" of the treatment represent two different dimensions of the transference, which "oscillate between the experiential foreground and background of the treatment" (Stolorow et al., p. 102). Indeed, Stolorow and his colleagues criticize the idea that there is a dichotomy between interpretation and affective bonding. They believe that interpretations are an inseparable part of the relationship with the therapist. "Good" interpretations strengthen and expand the selfobject transference bond while incorrect interpretations can threaten the bond. We can understand this from a different perspective by realizing that every time we evaluate a structure as being too rigid, by virtue of interpreting it, we are attempting to create a new and expanded structure, one that includes our assessment of and reactions to the patient's established modes of experience and will include, if all goes well, the patient's positively toned experience of being understood and responded to in a new way.

But what are the criteria for deciding when a structure is ossified and in need of interpretation? In principle, the therapist might "interpret" any invariant pattern of mental activity, any of the patient's established and unquestioned interests, values, and judgments. And any interaction with the analyst that contributes to the structuring of experience in the course of treatment might be considered an element of the selfobject bond and therefore therapeutic, regardless of the content of the structures that are formed. It is not possible to be more specific about the nature of help when the definition of health is so abstract. In practice, however, the authors usually focus their attention on the affective dimension of experience. The ossified structures they propose to interpret are primarily recurrent affect states, particularly the patient's fears of traumatic experiences with the analyst, and the various means of attempting to cope with such fears. And the selfobject bond with the analyst is described as an "affective bonding" (Stolorow et al., 1987, pp. 66–87). According to Socarides and Stolorow (1984), selfobject functions "pertain fundamentally . . . to the need for phase-appropriate responsiveness to affect states in all stages of the life cycle" (p. 105).

But the apparent gain in specificity provided by the focus on affect states is lost when it comes to articulating the principles guiding interpretation and the criteria for determining what kind of responsiveness is phase-appropriate. According to the authors, interpretation should elucidate the "developmental origins and functional significance" of the patterns of self-and-object relating embodied in the patient's fears, especially those that characterize the transference relationship (Atwood and Stolorow, 1984, pp. 31-33, 46). Such functions might include wish fulfillment, self-guidance, self-punishment, adaptation, restitution, reparation, and defense. These may be conscious or unconscious, can undergo various developmental vicissitudes, generally co-occur clinically, are combined and amalgamated with each other in highly complex ways, and typically change over the course of treatment and even within a single session, with regressive and progressive shifts in the organization of the patient's experience (cf. Stolorow et al., 1987, pp. 37-38).

How can the analyst determine which functions are at work and which to interpret? Terms like *wish fulfillment, adaptation, reparation, defense,* and *regression* sound like the language of classical psychoanalytic metapsychology. But the authors do not intend to invoke these theories because they do not espouse any particular model of normal or pathological self-structure. They suggest that interpretation be guided by "an assessment of the relative motivational priority or urgency of the meanings or purposes of the configuration currently under study" (Atwood and Stolorow, 1984, p. 46), but they provide no theoretical framework for assessing developmental status, motivational priority, or functional urgency. Such evaluations are occasionally illustrated by clinical vignettes but are basically left to the discretion of the individual analyst.[4]

Matters are not more specific with regard to the selfobject bond. When Kohut described transmuting internalization during childhood, he said that the child is enabled to experience the caregiver's more mature feeling states as if they were his own. Socarides and Stolorow (1984), by contrast, focus on the caregiver's responsiveness to the child's affect states. Rather than referring to vague and unknowable processes, such as an infant's inner sense of merging with a caregiver and acquiring functional capacities by a kind of mental metabolism, they list the specific types of response by the caregiver that promote the acquisition of specific structures by the child. These include affirming, accepting, differentiating, synthesizing, and containing replies to the child's affect states throughout the

---

[4]Brandchaft (1985) describes self-development as involving two intertwined and overlapping processes—the consolidation of a nuclear self and the differentiation of self from other—and says that psychic conflict occurs when differentiating strivings are felt to be inimical to the maintenance of a vitally needed selfobject tie. Rather than being a fully articulated theory of development, however, this is a statement about the intersubjective origin of psychic conflict.

course of development.[5] But the manner of applying these ideas to the treatment of adults is far from obvious. Stolorow, Brandchaft, and Atwood (1987) describe the selfobject dimension of the transference as a "holding environment," an archaic intersubjective context in which developmental processes are reinstated (p. 44). They say that the understanding of ruptures in the selfobject bond is particularly valuable because such understanding provides an opportunity to "mend and expand" the affective tie between patient and analyst.[6] This tells us about the importance of interpreting problems when they become apparent but not about the essential nature of the selfobject bond or how it becomes established in the first place.

Sometimes the authors seem to suggest that the analyst's responses should be matched to the level of reactivated needs and developmental strivings of the patient. They describe the traditional analytic attitude of abstinence as inimical to the reinstatement of aborted developmental strivings, "[e]specially in the treatment of severe developmental arrests" (Atwood and Stolorow, 1984, p. 45). And they propose that the analyst's interventions be guided by an assessment of "what is likely to facilitate . . . the unfolding, illumination, and transformation of the patient's subjective world" (Stolorow et al., 1987, p. 10). Such assessments would need to be based on an understanding of the meanings of the analyst's actions or nonactions to each patient.

An advantage of nonspecific guidelines such as these is that they can be understood in a variety of individual ways. A disadvantage is that imprecision courts misunderstanding. The principle of responding in a manner likely to facilitate the unfolding, illumination,

---

[5]These authors regard the mirroring and idealizing processes Kohut described as pertaining only to certain affect states, albeit very important ones—reactive states of anxiety, vulnerability, and distress, on one hand, and affect states that accompany developmental progress, such as pride, expansiveness, efficacy, and pleasurable excitement, on the other. In their view, responsiveness to the entire range of the child's affect states throughout development contributes to the articulation of affect, establishes the rudiments of self-definition and self-boundary formation, makes contradictory affect states intelligible as issuing from a unitary self, and makes possible the containment of strong affects so that they can function as self-signals rather than threaten to rupture the continuity of self-experience (see Stolorow et al., 1987, pp. 92ff.).

[6]In contrast to Kohut, they contend that the therapeutic value of frustration does not reside in the opportunity to master disappointment but in the experience of having narcissistic injuries "confirmed and validated by empathic understanding" (Brandchaft, 1983, p. 350). The "benefit of analyzing ruptures in selfobject bonds" is said to lie in the "integration of the disruptive affect states that such ruptures produce and in the concomitant mending and expanding of the broken selfobject tie" (Stolorow et al., 1987, p. 104).

and transformation of the patient's subjective world has been misunderstood as implying that the analyst should acquiesce with the patient's wishes. Some clinicians have felt in danger of being "imprisoned" by their patients' needs or of relinquishing their own values to a psychological relativism. But the authors do not intend that the analyst's responses be dictated by the patient's needs. Indeed, they note that while "relentless abstinence" may obstruct the developmental, or selfobject, dimension of the transference, so may an attempt "literally" or "actually to fulfill the patient's archaic needs" impede the development of "more advanced modes of organization in the transference" (Stolorow et al., 1987, p. 42).

Brandchaft (1988) points out that if the analyst's responses are designed to avert experiences that appear too painful to the patient, the opportunity for empathic understanding of "poorly resolved issues" and "sequestered affect" may be cut short.[7] He describes a difference between a posture "necessary to establish a safe milieu, in which analysis and revived developmental processes can evolve" and responsiveness that "goes beyond the bounds of maximal affective engagement." And he warns that "enactments" that "collude in the patient's assessment" and spring from the analyst's need to be loved and not identified with frustrating others will eventually be experienced by the patient as a seduction. He holds up an "investigatory stance" toward "whatever needs or feelings may arise in the patient or analyst in the course of treatment" as the quintessential selfobject response.

Stolorow and his colleagues clearly intend that analysts use their own judgment in assessing the patient's current and potential level of affective maturity and in deciding when responsiveness that is organized around the patient's affective needs may promote further analysis and development and when it may obstruct these aims. Although a patient's perceptions and subjective experience are described as being just as real as those of the analyst, the authors believe that his "personal universe" may be "archaically organized," compared with the "relatively structured world of the analyst" (Stolorow et al., 1987, p. 2). More problems are raised than resolved by these cautionary comments, however. If selfobject responses are defined as

---

[7]For example, the therapist who reassures a patient against his fears of being rejected may obstruct his reexperiencing and integrating painful affect and may prevent him from revealing deeper fears, such as the fear that his affective longings are themselves repugnant (see Atwood, Stolorow, and Trop, 1989; Brandchaft, 1991). And the therapist who reassures a patient about the validity of his perceptions may inadvertently reinforce an archaic organizing principle—the belief that another person's judgment is more objective than his own.

those that are experienced as structure-building at any point in development, then there is no means of distinguishing conceptually between actions that "actually" or "literally" fulfill selfobject needs and those that do so in some "more advanced" way. Nor is it possible to distinguish an empathically informed response from an enactment, except by knowing more about the therapist's motives. On a practical level, it is not possible to know, in advance, which responses are necessary in order to establish a safe milieu that permits the optimal unfolding and transformation of the patient's affectivity and which will divert that process along lines dictated by the therapist's needs. When is the patient's assessment of his affective needs the best guide for deciding how to respond, and when is the therapist's judgment more reliable?

The more general problem is that the authors provide no model of development by which the analyst can assess the level of maturation that has been reached by the patient and devise a phase-appropriate complementary response. These decisions, like decisions regarding interpretation and appraisals of pathology, would depend on classifications and evaluations the analyst has derived from other sources, which are not explicated. It is precisely these issues the authors would address in defining psychoanalytic treatment as a "science of the intersubjective." They deplore the "tendency of classical analysis to view pathology in terms of processes and mechanisms located solely within the patient" because it "blinds the clinician to the profound ways in which he is himself implicated in the clinical phenomena he observes and seeks to treat" (Stolorow et al., 1987, pp. 3–4). Each analyst, they say, interprets the *purposes* of the patient's organizing activity in the light of his own subjective experience (Atwood and Stolorow, 1984, p. 47). His ability to understand the *meanings* of the patient's experience depends on his own organizing activity and patterns of creating meaning. Even the patient's *subjective reality*, as it is articulated during treatment, is shaped by the analyst's subjectivity "because . . . the analyst's psychological structures . . . delimit and circumscribe his capacity for specific empathic resonance" (p. 8).

If the analyst's subjectivity is an inseparable element of the patterns and meanings evoked and observed in the patient, how can the treatment proceed? Stolorow and his colleagues hope that analysts will recognize that psychoanalysis is an "indissoluble system" of mutual and reciprocal interaction and that they will continually strive to become aware of and "decenter from" the structures of their own experience, without necessarily abandoning them, in order to investigate their impact on the patient and on the analytic process. By this means, the authors believe, the theory as well as the practice of psychoanalysis will become "exquisitely self-reflexive and potentially self-corrective" (pp. 1–14, 17).

In accordance with this idea, the authors have defined psychoanalysis as an attempt to illuminate the phenomena that emerge from the interplay between two differently organized subjective worlds (Atwood and Stolorow, 1984, p. 41; Stolorow et al., 1987, pp. 1–15). What the analyst knows in the psychoanalytic situation is not seen as being more real than what the patient knows. "All that can be known psychoanalytically," they say, "is subjective reality – the patient's, the analyst's, and the evolving, ever-shifting intersubjective field created by the interplay between them" (Stolorow et al., 1987, p. 8). Thereby, they seek "to push to its limits Kohut's . . . proposition that the empirical and theoretical domains of psychoanalysis are defined and demarcated by its investigatory stance of empathy and introspection" (p. 5). But in so doing, they compound the problems they are attempting to address, namely, the presence of the powerful influence of the analyst's idiosyncracies and the absence of a substantive view of health to guide the treatment process.[8] The analyst is expected to be more mature than the patient, but no clear definition of maturity is articulated.

Kohut said that the empathic-introspective method of observation defined his domain of study, the domain of complex mental states (Kohut, 1959, pp. 479–482; 1977, p. 306; 1980, p. 488). In fact, however, it was because he had marked out a particular domain of interest that a particular observational method became relevant. He was deeply interested in certain inner states – particularly experiences of "choice, decision, and free will" – and he argued that they were legitimate subjects for study *because* they were observable by the accepted psychoanalytic methods of introspection and empathy (Kohut, 1977, pp. 243–245).[9] What is more, he thought there was a hidden morality associated with the "extrospective" method of observation – a "facing-the-truth" morality based on the concepts of drive, psychic determinism, and social adaptation – that was interfering with the "analyst's ability to allow his analysands to develop in

---

[8]The authors describe several criteria for evaluating theoretical concepts and interpretations (Stolorow et al., 1987, p. 8), but these criteria are not framed with reference to health or structuralization.

[9]In another paper (Wolfe, 1989b, p. 549), I have described the importance of Kohut's interest in the experience of volition, and the role this played in his concepts of a bipolar self and a two-stage sequence of self development.

accordance with their own nuclear programme" (Kohut, 1982, p. 399; see also 1983, p. 397).

Kohut (1982) outlined the borders of psychoanalysis, and he defined its essence by the operations of introspection and empathy in order to prevent it from becoming a form of moral education (p. 399). He noted that empathy is "a value-neutral mode of observation" (p. 396), but he was far from neutral in his own moral priorities. He believed that people have a lifelong need to live in a matrix of sustaining self–selfobject relationships (1980, pp. 478–479), but he also believed that it is better to feel creative than to be immediately accepted by one's social environment (see Kohut, 1977, pp. 53–54; 1980, pp. 478, 509). Kohut (1980) thought the capacity "to go it alone" and to act according to one's own convictions, while attempting to impress others with one's own truths, was a sign of inner strength (p. 498)–a fair description of his own professional life.

Kohut (1980) believed that psychological theories are an attempt to explain in experience-distant terms our naive perceptions regarding health and cure (p. 493). His concept of the ideal life–the intrafamilial and intergenerational relations he described as embodying the "nuclear essence of humanness" (Kohut, 1982, p. 405)–derives from his belief that the mirroring and idealizing processes that emerge in the family are the cradle of the inner experience of freedom, volition, and self-determination. The inner experience of freely striving to unfold one's innermost self was, to him, the essence of psychological health and maturity.

Stolorow and his colleagues propose "distinctively *hermeneutic* criteria" for evaluating psychoanalytic concepts and explanatory constructs (Atwood and Stolorow, 1984, pp. 5–6; Stolorow et al., 1987, pp. 8–9). Their "avowedly subjectivist and relativist position" regarding psychoanalytic knowing and reality places the analyst's values in the field to be investigated by each analyst. The personal values that inform their work with their patients, which play a powerful role in their assessments of the kind of organization that is "more advanced" and the kind of transformation that should be facilitated, can sometimes be inferred from their clinical reports but are not held up for debate or emulation. By their reckoning, a progressively deepening, empathically and introspectively derived understanding of the course of a therapeutic relationship can, in principle, be beneficial. But a "science of the intersubjective" is more like a theory of literary criticism than a theory of aesthetics. It is a tool for analyzing the play and course of any relationship. A more specific understanding of the nature of the therapeutic disappears from view.

## THE SELF SYSTEM

If some writers have difficulty addressing the fact that therapists attempt to influence their patients in accordance with their own view of health and maturity, Michael Basch is not one of them. "[T]he art of psychotherapy," he says, "lies in promoting and then using one's influence skillfully" (1980, p. 6). His prescriptions for doing psychotherapy (1980, 1988)—an unabashed effort to "change the patient's mind" (1985a, p. 34)—derive from a fully articulated theory of personality that includes a statement of the core characteristics of human nature and the primary aim of human behavior, a description of the sequence of normal development through which universal tendencies lead to individually differing styles of behavior, and an explanation of the way in which pathologies of different kinds result from an inappropriate interface with the environment at various stages of development. Each of these principles is carefully defined and elaborated.

Basch's theorizing, unlike Freud's, does not begin with the study of disease. And, unlike Kohut, Basch (1985b) does not look to the clinical situation, and specifically to the transference relationship, as a source of information about the universal features of personality functioning. In his view, narrow foci such as these reveal only limited ranges of types of difficulty and yield a flawed and restricted explanation of human behavior (pp. 4–5, 7–9). Basch (1981) has created a comprehensive model of normal psychological functioning by integrating concepts from the fields of neurobiology, communications and systems theory, cybernetics, cognitive psychology, and developmental research (pp. 165ff). From this model he derives a framework for explaining a broad range of psychopathologies, a schema for differential diagnosis, and a guide to the differential treatment of malfunctioning self-systems.

A self-system, as defined by Basch, is fundamentally different from the self conceptualized by Kohut and from the idea of self articulated by Stolorow and his colleagues. Basch (1988) defines the self-system as the superordinate structure whose functioning is synonymous with psychological life (p. 103). But psychological life means something different to Basch than the "pure psychology" envisaged by Kohut (1982) and the intersubjectivists (p. 402). By *psychological* Basch (1988) means "whatever takes place at the interface of the environment and an affectively responsive brain" (p. 103, n. 1).

For Basch the brain, and not the mind, is the basic element of explanation—the explicans. Like other empiricists, Basch (1976a) prefers explanatory terms that refer to operations that can, in principle, be observed in public and validated by consensus. He regards the use of terms like *mind* and *thoughts* as being equivalent to the invocation of ghosts (pp. 391–392; 1978, p. 260). Mind, Basch (1976a) says, is not a governing agent within the brain but a "particular kind of order between elements of a complex relationship that happens to . . . occur in brain tissue" (p. 399). And the things Basch, like other behaviorists, is interested in explaining are publicly observable events—behaviors—not recondite entities like affects and meanings. There is, he says, "no such thing as affect apart from action or disposition to action." Affect is "a measure of symbolic significance, or meaning," and meaning is measured by its dispositional power, that is, "the intent or behavior to which it gives rise" (pp. 417–418; 1981, p. 166; 1988, pp. 8–11).

This does not mean there is no place in Basch's psychology for the uniquely personal subjective experiences that can be observed only by introspection and empathy. On the contrary, it is precisely such phenomena—affective constellations, meaning and significance, purpose and conflict—that are the focus of psychoanalytic study and treatment (Basch, 1976a, pp. 399–400; 1981, p. 165; 1985a, p. 34). These are the formations that occur at the interface. Events in the brain and the environment are the underlying causes, behavior the result. "The psychological is not to be found in" or equated with patterns of neuronal activity, he says, but in "the dispositional effect of those patterns on behavior" (Basch, 1981, p. 158). Basch is an anomaly among behaviorists because the domain he investigates and manipulates is immaterial, while his explanatory constructs seem to have the impersonal authority of scientific objectivity.

The concept that bridges the gap between these apparently different realms is the idea of competence. "The search for competence," Basch (1988) says, "is the basic motivation for behavior," and competence can be manifested in various ways:

> In the behavioral sphere, it takes the form of exercising control over external events. In respect to brain functioning and the neurophysiological substrate of behavior, competence is achieved as a result of the brain's capacity to establish order among the disparate stimuli that continuously bombard the senses. . . . On the level of introspection and reflection, competence is experienced as self-esteem. In the sociological universe of discourse, competence consists of healthy adaptation; and in the world of art and esthetics, competence is akin to harmony [p. 25].

These statements suggest that successful pattern-matching activity in the brain, effective problem-solving behaviors, healthy adaptation to the social environment, and heightened self-esteem are a unified phenomenon, differing only by virtue of the mode and vantage point of observation, or that they occur in constant conjunction. The idea of competence has never been so elastic.

One need not be a philosophical dualist to question whether these phenomena have an identical basis or to wonder how closely they may be correlated. To believe in such equivalence or correlation has important theoretical implications, however. It allows therapists to address what they perceive as incompetence along one dimension with the confidence that benefit will accrue in the others. Thus, for example, therapists may intervene in a "self-defeating developmental spiral" at the level of decision making, if they judge that to be most effective, and may expect that the patient's self-esteem and future adaptation will improve as well (Basch, 1988, pp. 30, 64). Furthermore, knowledge of developments in the brain's organizing capacities is used to help therapists make intelligent judgments about patients' difficulties, based on information other than the therapists' own immediate reactions, and design their input signals accordingly.

Elaborating on Freud's idea that defense is always against affect, Basch (1985a) describes defense against affect as a source of psychopathology (p. 14). Affect, Basch (1988) says, is initially a reflex response to the intensity and shape of stimulus waves (pp. 73–74), a response that serves as the gateway to appropriate action and healthy adaptation (pp. 65–99). Our affective responses to the environment are, he says, "the most important signals . . . the human brain has to organize" (p. 64). On the physiological level, affect is described as an inborn readiness to have particular autonomic reactions to stimuli and stimulus gradients. These visceral and vasomotor reactions, generated in the limbic system of the brain, intensify and prolong the approach and avoidance behaviors geared to adaptation and survival (Basch, 1976b, pp. 763–764; 1981, p. 157). The human infant, extensively dependent on others to carry out self-preservative behavior, communicates affect through facial expression, sounds, and bodily attitudes and in this way engages the more coordinated capacities of caretakers (Basch, 1976b, pp. 761, 764; 1988, p. 79).

Defense against affect is also described as an aspect of normal endowment—but one that can go wrong. "The brain is constantly generating more information than is needed for adaptation", Basch (1988, p. 122) says, and sorting and filtering mechanisms are therefore necessary to survival. On the behavioral level, the gatekeeping maneuvers that are presumed to be the manifestation—not the analogue—of filtering mechanisms of the brain are called defenses. Defenses normally operate to protect the self-system against unnecessary stress. But their failure, or overly prolonged usage, interferes with development and leads to symptomatic behavior and characterological problems (Basch, 1985a, pp. 34–41; 1988, pp. 108ff, 121–128). These manifest signs of psychopathology are not seen as being the basic problem but the primary source of information about the level of affective maturation at which trauma occurred. It is the level of affective maturity that indicates both the nature of the disease and the appropriate mode of treatment, in Basch's view.

Basch (1976b) says that affective development normally evolves from an unconscious, automatic, unmodulated form—an adaptive program present at birth, under the control of the old brain, and activated by particular environmental circumstances—to a consciously accessible, verbally communicable, cognitively mediated modality. In mature form, affect is a highly sophisticated activity, under the control of the neocortex, that involves abstract conceptualization, symbolic thought, logical reasoning, reflection, verbal articulation, and subjective awareness related to a concept of self (pp. 765–771). Basch (1978) describes the potential for affective maturation as being the feature that distinguishes humans from other animals, whose behavioral repertoire and range of adaptability are limited to fixed, inherited programs (pp. 261–262; 1988, pp. 103–107).

The mature human brain has the capacity to generate symbols, or "patterns created by the imaginative manipulation of previously registered perceptions" (Basch, 1988, p. 107). This allows for a greatly expanded range of alternative adaptive behaviors. The "preliminary symbolic weighing" of these various possibilities for action is subjectively experienced as the exercise of choice and free will (Basch, 1978, p. 262; 1988, p. 107). The condition of having unaltered and immutable patterns of affective expectation and response is the neurological definition of psychopathology. Disease is reflected in the failure to develop mature affective and cognitive signal-processing abilities, and it is manifested on a gross behavioral level by symptoms and dysfunctional defenses. In cybernetic terms, the pathological self is described as a system that is closed to new information, specifically, to error-correcting feedback.

Diagnostic assessment therefore begins with an identification of the patient's primary defense and the associated symptomatic phenomena. Each of the four primary defenses Basch (1988) describes— withdrawal, primal repression, disavowal, and secondary repression—is linked to a particular stage of maturation, which is seen as an indicator of the period at which the arrest occurred and the nature of the underlying problem in the nervous system. The faulty nature of the interaction with caretakers, whose responses play a pivotal role in affective maturation, is inferred from the nature of the problem. Since "traumatically induced" patterns of affective expectation and expression "sooner or later," according to Basch, "find their way into the relationship to the therapist," interventions designed to compensate for these failures by taking into account "the cognitive and affective level of development . . . of the patient" can then be introduced (pp. 129, 130, 152).

By identifying the patient's primary or characteristic defense as manifested in everyday behavior, by declaring the existence of a link between the defense and an underlying distortion of the normal sequence of neurophysiological maturation, by adducing a relationship between that distortion and faulty caretaking behavior, and by designing strategies believed to compensate for or ameliorate such failures, Basch intends to provide a "scientific basis for psychotherapy" (p. 153). Basch is not the first analyst, of course, to describe and classify defenses or to suggest that therapists should devise interventions that take into account their patients' affect states and affective capacities. But Basch has brought together information derived from a variety of disciplines that use extrospective methods of observation and offered a schema for integrating these findings with the observations psychoanalysts have made about subjective states (see, e.g., Basch, 1981, pp. 163–164; 1988, pp. 144–145).

There are two basic problems with such an approach. The first is that scientific knowledge about the correlations between behavioral difficulties, underlying neurological processes, the factors that induce these processes, and the actions that can reverse them is far from being as advanced as Basch suggests. His use of scientific language gives an air of increased authority to commonplace psychological explanations. The second problem is that systematic correlations are claimed rather than shown to exist between the cognitive processes that are "coassembled" with mature affect states and brain activities that an external observer can know about. The language of the natural sciences, which refers to operations that can be publicly observed, replicated, and consensually validated, is elided and converted into the language of psychoanalysis and self psychology, which refers to mental states that can be observed only by private operations and to complex mental acts, such as abstract conceptualization, deliberation and evaluation, and creative thinking.[10]

---

[10]For some illuminating discussions of the mind–body problem and related issues by contemporary philosophers, see Feigl (1959), Toulmin (1970), and Searle (1984). For a discussion of the use and misuse of models for scientific explanation, see Braithwaite (1955).

To illustrate: overcontrol and withdrawal from affect, secondary depression, hypochondriasis, somatization, and alexithymia are said to be among the symptoms associated with the defense called primal repression, which denotes the failure to talk about feelings and the presumed inability to do so. Basch believes that primal repression reflects a neurophysiologically based developmental failure to transform sensorimotor affective reactions into ideas, that is, symbolic concepts that can be talked about and reflected on, but this has not been demonstrated experimentally. Indeed, it is difficult to imagine how a neurological transformation of this sort could be observed. The behaviors to which affects and ideas give rise could be counted and measured, but this would be a circular description, however useful, not an explanation.

Basch further believes that primal repression results from the failure of caretakers to recognize and respond appropriately to the child's affective reactions during the period leading up to this stage of development, or from their active discouragement of affect expression. This conclusion, and some of his ideas about the nature of appropriate responsiveness, may be derived from the systematic observation of interactions between infants and caretakers, longitudinal studies of the development of those infants, and consensual assessments regarding their health or normalcy. Other notions about appropriate responsiveness are not anchored by such data or collective opinion, however, but are based on informal observations and personal beliefs about the normal relationship between the individual and society.

In cases of primal repression, Basch (1988) recommends that therapists use not only their empathic resonance with the patient but also their own more mature affective organization to "supply the words" for states the patient may be feeling but is unable to articulate (p. 222). He also illustrates a therapist's use of accepting, reassuring, and didactic statements to help such a patient overcome what he calls "pathological shame" associated with feelings of weakness and longings for love (pp. 227, 230–231). What is more, the therapist makes recommendations about the patient's behavior, based on an idea about the function of "normal shame." The therapist explains that behaving in an alienating way toward others understandably leads to shame, urges that such shame not be "swallowed" because it is "a signal that a connection has been broken and needs to be reinstated," and advises the patient to take "steps to rectify the situation" (p. 233).

These measures are wholly consistent with Basch's belief that healthy social adaptation is a manifestation of competence and that normal shame serves to terminate behaviors that are not successful in evoking affective resonance and modifies behavior "in the interest of social maturation" (Basch, 1976b, p. 765; 1988, pp. 136–138).[11] But we live in a pluralistic and rapidly evolving society, and behaviors that are scorned by some segments of society are actively prized by others. The theory cannot distinguish between circumstances in which the patient should take steps to rectify his behavior and cases in which he should find a more suitable social milieu.

The strategies designed to deal with disavowal even more clearly illustrate the extent to which the therapist is encouraged to assess normalcy and maturation in terms of social adaptation. The defense of disavowal, which denotes the failure to attach affective significance to potentially traumatic events, is said to occur later in development, to be superimposed on earlier defensive reactions, and to be less easily corrected (Basch, 1988, pp. 236–239). The neurological process underlying the defense is described as a blocking of the link between perception and affective reactions (p. 125). In developmental terms, this is believed to be reflected in a series of difficulties, including precocious self-reliance and adaptation to the needs of others, followed by fantasies of omnipotence and omniscience to compensate for the misunderstanding of affective needs and communications, followed by the disavowal of the affective importance of reality as a means of maintaining an exaggerated sense of self and denying the existence of limitations (p. 237).

Basch believes that disavowal is the most often misunderstood and therefore most neglected of the defenses and that the mishandling of disavowal accounts for a large percentage of therapeutic failures (pp. 124–126). Therapeutic interventions in these cases must take into account earlier defenses as well as the defense against the transference.[12] It is an error to wait for the patient's associations or for the transference of underlying affect, Basch says. These patients have unconsciously deceived themselves about the true emotional significance of events, and they need their therapist's help in finding and

---

[11]"The utility of the shame reaction . . . is perverted," Basch (1988) says, "when the child's need for the parents' validating affective response or mirroring is consistently ignored, misunderstood or punished." Children may then become ashamed of their affective lives generally, "rather than of specific behavior," and retreat defensively from the mobilization of affect (p. 138).

[12]By this, Basch (1988) means that such patients protect their self systems by not bringing "thwarted affective needs into the therapeutic relationship" (pp. 135–136), because of the "chronic shame-producing tension" described in n. 11, above. Of course, these patients transfer to the therapeutic situation their existing patterns of affective expectation in the form of defenses.

expressing the affect that "needs to be attached" to memories and in learning how to respond to events in an affectively appropriate way (pp. 126–127). In these cases therapists must do more than rely on their affective resonance with the patient's states of mind. They must guess what the patient might be feeling, or ought to be feeling, based on their own experience and that of other people. In addition to active questioning and exploration of inconsistencies, therapists may need to point out logical errors and confront the patient with what they believe to be the affective significance of the patient's nonverbal behavior. The therapist may thus be in the position of challenging the patient about his thinking and feeling, and this will unavoidably mobilize a sense of shame, which must then be dealt with therapeutically (Basch, 1985a, pp. 39–40).

Clearly, the therapist using this model of treatment is called upon to make definitive assessments of "the affective significance . . . a particular event would and should have" (p. 39). Since affect and significance are behavioral dispositions, the therapist is also called upon to recognize the most appropriate and effective ways of behaving in the segment of society to which the patient must or should adapt. Basch's (1985b) broad characterizations of psychoanalysis as a "method of investigating purposefulness in human behavior" (p. 7), of "establishing new affective and cognitive constellations," and of "enhancing the ability to see new meanings" (Basch, 1976a, p. 418) do not sufficiently describe the kind of influence the therapist would thereby exert.

Basch (1988) describes patients' efforts to seek validation and approval from their therapists as a manifestation of the basic "need to be united with someone one looks up to, . . . [with someone] who can lend one the inspiration, the strength, and whatever else it takes to maintain the stability of the self system when one is endangered, frustrated, or in search of meaning" (pp. 141, 223). In this, Basch goes far beyond his original formulation of "the search for competence" as the basic motivation for human behavior.[13] But any effort by patients to obtain validation and approval represents an attribution of authority and an opportunity to be influenced. Basch says that the analyst helps raise early affective experiences to a "verbal, reflective level" (p. 99), and at the final stage of maturation helps "raise the level of cognitive functioning from the concrete to the formal" so that

---

[13]A number of such needs, which Basch may consider to be variants of a "basic search for competence," appear throughout his writings. These include longings for love, the need for validation and approval, and the need for attunement to and acceptance of one's affect states by others.

the patient can describe his behavior objectively (Basch, 1977, p. 261). These abstract formulations do not tell us enough about the kinds of words that are used, and they obscure the fact that the therapist's subjective assessments do not constitute an "objective" or scientifically grounded reality.

When Basch (1985b) says that "we act the part of the corpus callosum, so to speak," by using words to help "join affect and cognition appropriately" (p. 11), he is using an illustrative metaphor, not giving a neurophysiological explanation of therapeutic influence. But when he says that our "better knowledge of how the brain works enables us to correlate what we observe in the psychoanalytic situation with what transpires in the underlying structures" (p. 11), he is reproducing a fallacy he has already exposed—that of "adducing unprovable brain hypotheses to account for . . . behavior" (p. 4). "All the neurones of the brain," Basch (1976a) notes, "are in constant activity" and each of the ten billion or more cells in the human brain "may have functional connection with up to 60,000 of its neighboring cells" (p. 396). Given the associational potential of the human brain and the model of motivation cited by Basch—which stresses the "affinity for order and avoidance of the dysrhythmia of unintegrated novelty" (p. 397)—it is sounds as though it might be possible to construct an explanation of human behavior that would encompass its enormous variety and complexity. But technological possibilities are often grossly exaggerated. We do not, in fact, know anything about the correlation between particular patterns of brain activity and particular sets of beliefs—a mind-boggling project.

We may imagine that each bit of information conveyed by a therapist contributes to the budding of a dendritic spine in the brain. But whether this is for better or worse depends on the nature of the new values and ideals thus created. From the perspective of brain activity, values can be described as highly developed cognitively and affectively organized neuronal hierarchies of symbolic patterns for ideal behavior, and ideals can be described in cybernetic terms as perceptual sets that serve as a reference pattern for error-correcting feedback programs that are used as a guide for actions (see Basch, 1978, p. 262). But the apparent equivalence between brain activity and "minding" is misleading because it suggests that the therapist can have certainty about right behavior, and this ignores the ten thousand forms the good might take.

## CONCLUSION

Values can be understood as a set of beliefs about what is intrinsically good. Closely held and deeply cherished, they often have the quality of being self-evident truths. Values include what Kohut (1980) called "our naive perceptions" regarding health. Although he believed that "psychological health cannot be described in terms that have universal validity," to him psychological health meant the inner experience of an "unbroken, functioning continuum" in at least one sector of the personality (p. 496), the sense of "an uninterrupted flow of . . . narcissistic strivings . . . proceed[ing] toward creative expression" (p. 509; 1977, p. 54). Flexibility and openness to further development, however defined, were not, to Kohut (1983) necessary markers of health or maturity so long as an individual's innermost goals could be realistically achieved (pp. 396–397). Nor did he care how insignificant one's creative activity might appear to others or how limited one's social impact on, acceptance by, or adaptation to one's social environment might be so long as one could feel that the basic design of one's nuclear self was being fulfilled (Kohut, 1977, p. 54). Thus, the man who conceived of the very existence and survival of self as being inextricably dependent on the social surround was a radical individualist at heart.

Values can also be understood as a set of principles for acting one way rather than another (see Hare, 1952, pp. 56–78, 111–136). Kohut, alone among the theorists I have discussed, used evaluative language in a systematic way to commend and condemn certain attitudes and actions to the community of therapists. He thereby made plain certain underlying beliefs that were undoubtedly expressed in his work with patients, even though he did not include an adequate account of their influence in his theory of treatment.

Values are the province of the individual. It is fitting that therapists should strive to become aware of their own moral principles, to recognize the complexity of moral judgments in our pluralistic society, and to appreciate that attitudes regarding such issues can be a powerful undercurrent in the therapeutic relationship. But values are also the province of the community. The acceptance of a set of shared values is one way by which a community is defined. It is often assumed that self psychologists share Kohut's (1980) conviction— inspiring to many of us—that the inner feeling of freedom and fulfillment, and the sense of the meaningfulness of one's own life are the primary indicators of mental health (pp. 455, 509). But there are other criteria by which clinicians may assess a patient's health or maturity. If we are to develop a rational basis for an applied therapeutics in self psychology, we need to consider carefully whether we share Kohut's outlook and to recognize how our views are embedded in our work with patients and help determine the outcome of the process.

# REFERENCES

Atwood, G. & Stolorow, R. (1984), *Structures of Subjectivity*. Hillsdale, NJ: The Analytic Press.

_____ & Trop, J. (1989), Impasses in psychoanalytic therapy: A royal road. *Contemp. Psychoanal.*, 25:554–573.

Basch, M. (1976a), Psychoanalysis and communication science. *The Annual of Psychoanalysis*, 4:385–421. New York: International Universities Press.

_____ (1976b), The concept of affect: A reexamination. *J. Amer. Psychoanal. Assn.*, 24:759–777.

_____ (1977), Developmental psychology and explanatory theory in psychoanalysis. *The Annual of Psychoanalysis*, 5:229–263. New York: International Universities Press.

_____ (1978), Psychic determinism and freedom of will. *Internat. Rev. Psycho-Anal.*, 5:257–264.

_____ (1980), *Doing Psychotherapy*. New York: Basic Books.

_____ (1981), Psychoanalytic interpretation and cognitive transformation. *Internat. J. Psycho-Anal.*, 62:151–175.

_____ (1985a), Interpretation: Toward a developmental model. *Progress in Self Psychology*, Vol. 1, ed. A. Goldberg. New York: Guilford Press, pp. 33–42.

_____ (1985b), New directions in psychoanalysis. *Psychoanal. Psychol.*, 2:1–13.

_____ (1988), *Understanding Psychotherapy*. New York: Basic Books.

Braithwaite, R. (1955), *Scientific Explanation*. Cambridge: Cambridge University Press.

Brandchaft, B. (1983), The negativism of the negative therapeutic reaction and the psychology of the self. In: *The Future of Psychoanalysis*, ed. A. Goldberg. New York: International Universities Press, pp. 327–359.

_____ (1985), Self and object differentiation. In: *The Development of Self and Object Constancy*, ed. R. Lax, S. Bach, & J. Burland. New York: Guilford Press, pp. 153–177.

_____ (1988), The developmental line of empathy. Panel presentation at the 11th Annual Conference on the Psychology of the Self, Washington, D.C.

_____ (1991), To free the spirit from its cell. Presented at the 14th Annual Conference on the Psychology of the Self, Chicago.

Feigl, H. (1959), Philosophical embarrassments of psychology. *Amer. Psychol.*, 14:115–128.

Hare, R. (1952), *The Language of Morals*. Oxford: Clarendon Press.

Henry, W. (1956), *The Analysis of Fantasy*. Huntington, NY: Robert E. Krieger.

Kohut, H. (1959), Introspection, empathy, and psychoanalysis: An examination of the relation between mode of observation and theory. *J. Amer. Psychoanal. Assn.*, 7:459–483.

_____ (1968), The psychoanalytic treatment of narcissistic personality disorders: Outline of a systematic approach. *The Psychoanalytic Study of the Child*, 23:86–113. New York: International Universities Press.

_____ (1971), *The Analysis of the Self*. New York: International Universities Press.

_____ (1977), *The Restoration of the Self*. New York: International Universities Press.

_____ (1980), Reflections. In: *Advances in Self Psychology*, ed. A. Goldberg. New York: International Universities Press, pp. 473–554.

_____ (1982), Introspection, empathy, and the semi-circle of mental health. *Internat. J. Psycho-Anal.*, 63:395–407.

_____ (1983), Selected problems of self psychological theory. In: *Reflections on Self Psychology*, ed. J. Lichtenberg. Hillsdale, NJ: The Analytic Press, pp. 387–416.

_____ (1984), *How Does Analysis Cure?* ed. A. Goldberg & P. Stepansky. Chicago: University of Chicago Press.

Ornstein, P. (1980), Self psychology and the concept of health. In: *Advances in Self Psychology,* ed. A. Goldberg. New York: International Universities Press, pp. 137–159.

Searle, J. (1984), *Minds, Brains and Science.* Cambridge: Oxford University Press.

Socarides, D. & Stolorow, R. (1984), Affects and selfobjects. *The Annual of Psychoanalysis,* 12/13:105–119. New York: International Universities Press.

Stolorow, R. (1986), Critical reflections on the theory of self psychology: An inside view. *Psychoanal. Inq.,* 6:387–402.

_____ & Atwood, G. (1979), *Faces in a Cloud.* New York: Aronson.

_____ Brandchaft, B. & Atwood, G. (1987), *Psychoanalytic Treatment.* Hillsdale, NJ: The Analytic Press.

Toulmin, S. (1970), Reasons and causes. In: *Explanation in the Behavioural Sciences,* ed. R. Borger & F. Cioffi. Cambridge: Cambridge University Press, pp. 1–26.

Wolfe, B. (1985), The costs of compliance: A patient's response to the conditions of psychotherapy. In: *Progress in Self Psychology, Vol. 1,* ed. A. Goldberg. New York: Guilford Press, pp. 147–163.

_____ (1989a), Diagnosis and distancing reactions in psychotherapy. *Psychoanal. Psychol.,* 6:187–198.

_____ (1989b), Heinz Kohut's self psychology: A conceptual analysis. *Psychotherapy,* 26:545–554.

_____ (1991), The birth of a baby during psychotherapy: A perspective from self psychology. *Psychoanal. Rev.,* 78:483–504.

# Chapter 4

# So Little Truth Was Told: The Meaning of the Delusions and Hallucinations of an Adolescent Girl

*Linda Atkins*
*Judith Kaufman*

The separate psychoanalytic treatments of two patients, a mother and her daughter, offer a unique opportunity to learn about the origin and meaning of the daughter's psychotic breakdown in adolescence. The psychotic illness of the daughter—specifically, her hallucinations and delusions—can be understood within the context of her ongoing relationship with her mother.

The therapy of the mother provided a new dimension with which to understand the experience of her daughter. This was an unusual opportunity to obtain data generally not accessible about a patient's parents.

Most important, we learned that within the therapeutic relationship the mother's analyst experienced emotions that were a microcosm of the daughter's. We propose that the content of the girl's delusions and hallucinations were concretizations (Stolorow, Brandchaft, & Atwood, 1987) of the painful truths and dilemmas that existed in her relationship with her mother. These same issues came alive in the therapist's relationship with the mother as well. We regard the girl's symptoms of mental illness as the only means available to her to give a "voice" to critical subjective experiences that otherwise could not be acknowledged.

According to classical psychoanalysis, the essential deficit in psy-

The authors wish to thank Dr. Frank Lachmann for his valuable help with the manuscript.

chosis is the loss of the reality-testing function, a loss caused by a regression to very early developmental stages characterized by denial, projection, and introjection (Freud, 1894). These processes occur intrapsychically. Later psychoanalysts focused on the interpersonal aspects of the etiology of psychosis. Sullivan (1944), Fromm-Reichman (1959), Laing (1967), Arieti (1974), and Searles (1979) viewed psychosis as the result of early traumatic interactions within the family. Systems theorists such as Bateson, Jackson, Haley, and Weakland (1956) identified double binds as the primary etiological factor in schizophrenia.

Kohut (1971, 1977), with his insights into the critical role that empathic understanding plays in the development and maintenance of the sense of self, reasoned that psychotic patients suffered from protracted or permanent fragmentations of the self caused by prolonged loss of contact with archaic selfobjects. He considered delusions attempts to repair or stave off the threatened fragmentation and permanent loss of selfobject experience. The propensity for protracted fragmentation, Kohut suggested, lies in the combination of inherited factors and in the environmental provision of selfobject supplies. In psychotics, these factors combine to prevent the formation of a "nuclear cohesive self," leaving later structures brittle and fragile. In an interview on March 12, 1981, Kohut spoke about the treatment of psychosis: "Insofar as [the analyst] can truly build a bridge of empathy to a person, to that extent he is not psychotic. Once you are with him and have built that bridge, he has ceased to be psychotic" (1985, pp. 250–251).

The intersubjective approach (Stolorow, Brandchaft, and Atwood, 1987)[1] closely parallels Kohut's views but emphasizes the self-affirming and communicative meaning of psychotic symptoms. Of particular importance, this approach encourages us to look more broadly into the meaning of psychotic symptomatology by exploring not only the subjectivity of the patient but, especially, the intersubjective matrix created by the patient and important others. We were fortunate to gain access to this intersubjectivity through the analyses of both the psychotic patient and her mother.

The concept by Stolorow and associates of the intersubjective field and their focus on the necessity for the developing child to validate subjective "realities" of self and others provide a means of understanding the crystallization of the patient's psychosis in this mother-daughter dyad. Stolorow and associates propose that persons predisposed to psychotic states have experienced insufficient validation

---

[1]See also Magid (1984) and Josephs and Josephs (1986).

of subjective experiences early in life. That is, their sense of what is going on within themselves and within the family, of what is true what is not true, is shaky at best. Psychosis is then triggered by an intense emotional reaction, that is, by not being validated by the person's object world. The delusional system is an effort to concretize, substantiate, and preserve a subjective reality that has begun to disintegrate. The essential task of psychoanalytic treatment is to enter the patient's subjective reality, to understand and then help these patients understand their own message. Thus, the analyst creates a bond in which the patient's belief in his own reality can become reestablished.

We learned that the mother of our psychotic patient interacted with her daughter in such a way as to tragically obstruct her daughter's development. More specifically, the mother's need to turn away from life, as well as her need to camouflage and deny important personal and family realities, led to her daughter's very vulnerable sense of self, her propensity to fragmentation, and ultimately to her psychosis.

Contemporary self psychology formulations that expand the concept of countertransference will provide a framework for our utilization of the experiences of the mother's analyst to comprehend the ideas encoded in the delusional system of the daughter.

Freud (1910) defined countertransference as the activation of the analyst's conflicts in response to the patient's transferences. Although the ubiquity and inevitability of the phenomenon was recognized early (Ferenczi, 1909; Deutsch, 1926; Glover, 1927), it was conceptualized primarily as an interference with the ideal objective analytic stance.

Later analysts took the more positive, less shame-inducing position that countertransference facilitates the analyst's commitment and capabilities (Winnicott, 1974), that it promotes the analyst's efforts to understand the patient (Tower, 1956), and that it contributes to the affective intensity between the analytic pair, which constitutes the basic leverage of the therapeutic process (Gitelson, 1952).

Contemporary theorists, including McLaughlin (1981), Hoffman (1983), Hoffman and Gill (1988), Lichtenberg (1990), and Fosshage (1990), reject the concept of countertransference as reactive and have reconceptualized both transference and countertransference to encompass the complex nature of the analyst's participation in the analytic dyad. Kohut (1984) identified the "personal presence" of the analyst as a facilitating or encumbering factor in the establishment of the selfobject transference.

The intersubjective approach (Stolorow et al., 1987; Beebe and

Lachmann, 1988) emphasizes that analysis is a two-person situation, a mutual influencing system created by the personalities, personal histories, and representational worlds of patient and analyst. In order to deeply understand our patients, we must attend to the shifting intersubjective field and the complex feeling and motivational states of both participants.

We will demonstrate how the organizing principles of the subjectivity of Ann's analyst, subjectivity derived from earlier experiences with her own mother, caused her to establish an intersubjective field with her patient that recreated in significant details the intersubjective field between Ann and her psychotic daughter, Margaret. Subsequently, the analyst's experience of Ann as a failed selfobject helped us gain insight into Margaret's parallel experience of her mother. This isomorphism gave us unexpected access to the meaning of Margaret's delusional system.

## MARGARET

I (LA) first learned of Margaret when her school counselor phoned: Margaret heard voices, she could not silence the voices in her head, they intruded into all her thoughts, she could not stop them in the day, she could not sleep at night. Margaret wanted to see someone. An appointment was made but not kept.

Eight months later Margaret phoned. In a whisper she asked if she could come to see me. Now she was even more afraid of the voices; they had grown louder, more insistent, and punitive. When she called, Margaret was 12 and in the eighth grade. Her older brother and only sibling had left for a job in another state in September. Her parents had divorced, and Margaret was living with her mother, a busy professional woman who now had a serious illness.

When Margaret arrived on a snowy February afternoon, my immediate response was alarm at her condition. She was skinny, ragged, cold, and shivering. She was inadequately dressed against the harsh winter, looked frail in appearance and gait, and had garish red lips and two-toned black and pink hair. She walked into the room with a certain determination. Head held high, she sat in the chair and described with great lucidity what was happening to her and the tremendous fear and pressure she was under. I had just made myself a cup of tea. Without hesitation, I offered her one too. She accepted, drinking it slowly, her hands warming on the cup. In the midst of the session she looked at me and said, "This tea is good; it's the kind I like."

At the end of our first session, I told Margaret that I usually had tea at this time and that if she liked we would continue to have tea together and together we would try to understand what was happening to her. She agreed and we set up a ritual for three sessions per week that would last for four and a half years. From the first meeting this tea ritual, which was spontaneously set up by me and willingly accepted by Margaret, was, in retrospect, the reflection of an intuitive bond on both our parts. It enacted the missing affirmation of Margaret's selfobject needs and thus established the empathic bond between us.

Each day when Margaret arrived after school, she walked to her chair and took a tea bag from a canister set out next to a thermos of hot water and a mug. She would look over the tea bags, commenting if I had put in a new brand or a new flavor, choose her tea, pour the hot water into the mug, and begin to talk. The only variation in this ritual occurred when a transference/countertransference manifestation was enacted—when I failed to respond empathically or when an action or interpretation of mine caused Margaret to feel misunderstood or invalidated. The analysis of these crucial ruptures to our relationship, which flowed from and around this ongoing tea ritual, afforded Margaret the opportunity to further understand and integrate previously warded-off fears and anxieties as they appeared and were explored by us.

In the early weeks of treatment, Margaret elaborated on the voices that plagued her existence. They scolded, told her to leave them alone, threatened her to get out of their lives, to stop thinking about them. All the voices delivered the same message: "Get out of our lives! Leave us alone! Vanish!" I established with Margaret that these voices were part of her, that they represented her real, though encoded, experience. I conveyed the idea that the voices were an attempt to concretize symbolically experience she could not verify as real to herself in her daily life and that in our work together we would seek to establish her subjective reality (see Stolorow et al., 1987).

Specifically, I told Margaret that the voices she heard were actually a form of her own worries, that the voices were telling her about things in her life that bothered her deeply but that she, for reasons we did not yet know, was afraid to think about. I said that first we would want to know everything the voices said, whether or not they made sense to her, so that we could understand what was bothering her. This concept created a bond between us in listening to the voices together and taking them seriously. Though for some weeks Margaret continued to feel them to be persecutory foreign bodies, the reflection of a telepathy emanating from her and out of her control, my consistent belief in trying to understand the voices as reflective of her inner world created a bond in listening together that helped Margaret gain control of her fear of breaking down. By sharing a concern about the voices I could begin to help her learn what it may have been that already had been experienced and was terrifying (cf. Winnicott, 1974).

Margaret approached the task of analysis with energy. She did not talk directly about her mother's illness but described her life at home as a struggle with the voices by day and with frightening dreams at night. Margaret was trying desperately to substantiate a reality that was difficult for her to grasp. Gradually, I got glimpses of how she felt in her home. She was alone most of the time. Her mother worked late into the night and rarely returned for dinner. When she did, she was too exhausted to eat. "My mother has buried herself in her work," Margaret said one day, "and it is killing her, but she doesn't care. She will never listen to me. She doesn't have real interest in anything or anyone."

In the therapeutic relationship, Margaret was beginning to experience in me the longed-for idealized maternal figure missing throughout her formative years. As I accepted her admissions of her loneliness, her expressions of deadness, her fears for her own and her mother's well-being, Margaret could begin to validate, affirm, and integrate these fears about her life to herself. One day Margaret said, "I like this kind of tea you have here; it's natural and healthy."

Margaret's voices and the fantasies around them reflected a vitality in the sessions that was disavowed elsewhere. Margaret was deadened in ordinary life. All of her attention was directed to her inner world and her attempts to save herself. By day she struggled with the voices: "Stop bothering me," they said. At night Margaret was tormented by her dreams. Policemen appeared as bulldogs that tried to make her say obnoxious things. Blackboards appeared on which "Shut up, keep peace" was written. She depicted herself as having a shut-off valve in her head, which either she or someone else was trying to gain control of. Margaret said, "When I think of others, they know it and hate me. My thoughts only make people enraged."

Margaret, her mother's favorite child, recalled that she had been described as a "twin" for her mother. Margaret was intelligent, brooding, withdrawn, and shy. She recalled lying in bed hearing her mother accuse her father of preferring her brother, Dennis. Margaret said she began at that time to wonder if this was really true, if her father really did prefer Dennis.

During the early months of treatment I saw Margaret's mother. Ann appeared to be a tense, beleaguered woman; she spoke in a curiously unconcerned manner about Margaret and the severity of her problems. During this session I learned of Ann's medical history. It was unclear just how ill she was or whether she was ill at all. I felt confused by her ambiguity; it was impossible to know. During the subsequent four years, she phoned only once to ask for a referral for herself. Completely and without question, she gave Margaret over to my care and never questioned Margaret about her treatment.

Gradually, Margaret told me of her years as a "health detective." As soon as she could read, Margaret searched the drawers and closets for medical information. She eavesdropped outside doors and looked for clues on envelopes and message pads. She knew that her mother had become gravely ill early in her adolescence, at the same age that Margaret was now, but had made medical history. Nevertheless, Margaret was worried. Since her father had left, her mother had gone twice to the original treatment hospital; although Ann said she was fine, Margaret did not believe it. According to Margaret, her mother seemed "more listless than usual." A few weeks after these sessions, Ann began medical treatment that severely weakened her and caused her to be unable to leave her bed. Just as Ann had discussed Margaret's severe state as "ordinary," so too did Margaret treat her mother's state as ordinary.

A transference enactment followed whereby I became the detective. Margaret's voices warned against discovering this information: "Go away, stop bothering me, leave me in peace." I told Margaret that her voices concretized her attitude toward me, that when I brought up her mother's illness, she was telling me to go away. Ann's outward presentation of herself as well, lively, giving, and competent, while inwardly she was exhausted, depleted, helpless, and dying, presented Margaret with a double bind, an impossible dilemma in acknowledging what she felt to be happening to her and her mother.

Margaret began to dream of dying. War threatened her dreams. Everything was contaminated with infection, and everyone was threatened with deadly sickness. In one dream Margaret's father was carrying her mother home from a treatment through a shadowy land. "Don't put her down," Margaret woke up sobbing, "the infection will rot her soles." Margaret discussed with me her fear that without her father to take care of her mother, both she and her mother would die.

Margaret's understanding of the voices evolved. During the recurrence of her mother's grave illness, she described the voices as "intensified doubts." She was beginning to understand that the voices enabled her to remain in doubt, to avoid devastating truths about her mother and her relationship with her. Specifically, Margaret was approaching one of her core themes: to keep her mother alive by never calling attention to her lifelessness, by never calling attention to her own liveliness and her own conflicted wish to live and grow. To do so would reveal her mother's lifelessness, a revelation for which she would suffer crushing guilt and vicious retribution and ultimate annihilation.

Margaret began to understand her fear that she too was dying. She realized that for many years she had feared that her "always dying" mother could not offer her strength to live. The encoded meaning of the voices ("Go away; stop bothering me") represented Margaret's attempts to keep knowledge and fear of "always dying" from both of them. Death appeared in Margaret's dreams. In one, death met Margaret and her mother at the top of the stairs. In another, Margaret dreamed she was in bed with a "mummy." She dreamed she and her mother were in a grocery store when Ann collapsed; Margaret could not revive her and collapsed at her mother's side.

Gradually, Margaret's fear that she had to keep me alive arose in the transference. For many months Margaret failed to call attention to disruptions she may have experienced in our relationship. She needed me to remain for her an idealized figure and would react to my failure in empathy by withdrawal and by an increase or reappearance of delusional material. When we were able to capture and analyze these disruptions as they occurred, they were of enormous help and relief and led ultimately to an abatement of symptomatology and a resumption of growth.

One day I forgot to take the tea can from the shelf and place it on the desk next to Margaret's chair. It remained on the shelf visible to Margaret but not to me. Margaret did not ask for the can; rather, she became at first agitated, then mute. When I commented that she was not drinking tea, she retorted angrily, "How can I when you forgot to put it out?"

My acknowledgment that I had failed to put the tea out and my inquiry into Margaret's experience of my failure led to several sessions in which aspects of her self-expression that were bound in fear and encoded in her delusional system were explored. Margaret feared I would hate her if she pointed out my weakness, if she asked for what I might not want to give her, if she made me pay attention to her needs, and if she called attention to the fact that I was getting old and forgetful while she was young and strong. Thus, within the context of our relationship the patient's subjective observations and affects could be acknowledged and affirmed. This process, repeated over time, diminished Margaret's need to encode her powerful feelings within a delusional system.

Shortly after the experience of the failed tea, Margaret reported the following dream, in which she conversed with a Pilgrim who was pouring tea for her.

> **Pilgrim:** You have been going through spiritual insight and healing.
> **Margaret:** Yes, but I went mad.
> **Pilgrim:** You have to do it to understand madness-projections and distortions.
> **Margaret:** I do understand projections and distortions. They are in my control; I can just hold them.

"Who do you suppose the Pilgrim might be?" I asked. "You, me, and my mother," Margaret answered candidly. "We are all in this room; underneath all the sickness and fear there are good wishes for me." Margaret commented that her mother never asked about analysis. "Even though my mother can't do certain things for me, she wishes me well and wishes someone could help me. That's why she pays for my analysis and leaves it alone."

Ann had indeed turned Margaret's quest for living, for resumption of her development, over to me. Ann could not bear this quest, so tragically disrupted in her own life. My initial response to Margaret, my offer of the tea, was, I believe, a complicated gesture. It was an instinctual wish to protect and take care of her, as well as to encourage her to live. My belief in the validity of the encoded messages of Margaret's voices arose out of an understanding of my own difficult experience of affirming my subjective reality during adolescence, when my separate sexual development, as well as other aspects of myself, had threatened my own mother. Like Margaret, I too had to find a way to preserve my own truths. Margaret became delusional whereas I had become rebellious.

My awareness of the fear and desperation lurking behind Margaret's odd behavior helped me to "decenter" in order to avoid becoming involved in the outer chaos and many entanglements of Margaret's life and to remain focused on her fragmented and terrifying inner world. The tea ritual receded into the background and became an essential part of our relationship and of the facilitating environment, only coming to the fore when Margaret experienced an aspect of the ritual in ways important for her to explore and affirm with me.

Margaret established a bond with me that enabled her to begin to reexperience her vitality, her energy for living. She was able to face the message of her voices. Her mother, Ann, had created the illusion that she was a loving mother within a solid family and that she had achieved an intimate relationship with her daughter and was attuned to her needs. Margaret's voices ("Go away! Stop bothering me!") represented her desperate attempt by means of concrete symbolization to preserve her own personal reality. The voices depicted Margaret's experience that her mother did not want to be bothered with her, that her mother wanted her to go away. Margaret perceived that Ann was dying, just as she had always believed that Ann was dying. Margaret's subjective truth was affirmed in the therapeutic relationship. The voices ceased speaking. She had acknowledged her mother's lifelessness and was released from its grip.

## ANN

After Margaret had been in treatment for two years, her mother requested a referral from Margaret's therapist. Ann said that she had an incurable illness and more than likely did not have long to live. She said she came to therapy not for herself but for her daughter Margaret. She was hoping she could become less depressed so she could be a better role model for Margaret.

Ann had a certain British style in both manner and dress: no nonsense, reserved but engaging, with a sense of humor that tentatively peeked out. She had a milky white complexion and seemed delicate and shy beneath her "professional" exterior. I (JK) found her to be a likable and articulate woman. Ann described the recent calamities of her life with unusual composure. A year and a half earlier she learned that she had an incurable illness; she then went through an agonizing course of medical treatment, during which time she divorced her husband of more than 20 years and Margaret had a "nervous breakdown."

Ann conveyed a pervasive sense of weariness; although she was superficially engaging, she did not feel "reachable" to me. She indicated that she wanted to be less depressed in order to help her daughter, rather than help her acknowledge and begin to cope with the fact that her mother was going to die. This was a foreshadowing of the denials and deceptions that I later learned had structured Ann's life.

Ann was the oldest of eight children of a working-class British family. She became the main caretaker of the family very early. She recalled that by the age of five, she no longer cried in front of her mother or sought her help with any problem. She described her mother as depressed and helpless while her father, a relentlessly and verbally abusive alcoholic, intimidated the entire family. As Ann grew up, she enjoyed the experience of her own competence. She was an outstanding student and a responsible caretaker of the younger children and was popular with peers. However, in early adolescence she began to experience a chronic state of exhaustion. She thought this was due to her excessive responsibilities as well as to staying out late nearly every night in order to avoid her father.

At age 17 Ann was diagnosed as having an incurable illness. She had been ill for a year but was sent to a doctor only at the insistence of a teacher. Thus began several years of treatment at a British hospital. While a patient there, Ann gained considerable attention from doctors and hospital staff. Indeed, she regards the years of treatment as the best years of her life.

Toward the end of her college years, Ann was told she had miraculously recovered and that while the disease could recur, it was not known when or if that would happen. The illness recurred 25 years later. Nevertheless, Ann had remained convinced that she was dying. This was her secret, and she told no one about it. Although in love with another man, she married her husband because she thought he could provide security. She went on to move to this country with him to establish and develop a career and raise two children, all the while thinking she was in her "final years."

Her experience of married life was fundamentally the same as her experience in childhood. Secretly, she felt herself to be an overburdened, unrewarded caretaker. Her flamboyant husband went to parties nearly every night, had affairs, and was frequently drunk and derogatory toward her. He called her a boring drudge. She submitted to sex with him but never enjoyed it and never had an orgasm.

Ann believed she was successfully maintaining the fiction that she was a happy woman. She presented herself as a loving wife and mother who despite a demanding career made the time to cook a well-balanced meal every night. She maintained she was "always there" for her children—to meet their physical needs, to help with homework, to talk about things that mattered to them. She wanted to be a good mother and provide her children with a sense of security and stability. Ann thought that no one knew that she felt she was dying.

"Always dying" was a central organizing theme for Ann. It served multiple functions. Dying made her special, worthy of the nurturance denied her in childhood and provided to her by her doctors. With its accompanying profound feelings of weariness, the sense of dying was a concretization of her feeling that she was not getting enough life-sustaining emotional nurturance. Dying also served to justify her emotional withdrawal, thereby enabling her to avoid the retraumatization that a conscious longing for dependency, intimacy, and sexuality might have brought her.

During the early months of psychotherapy a selfobject transference was established through which Ann sought the affirmation she so desperately needed. In particular, she sought a witness to her experiences of illness and dying. She tearfully described the salient traumatic events of her illness. Soon after she began a difficult medical treatment and shortly before her divorce, her husband took Margaret and Dennis to a ski resort for a weekend, leaving Ann at home alone and ill. She became so sick that she literally could not get out of bed. She felt panicky and thought she might die. But she was so ashamed that she had been left alone by her husband that she decided she would rather die than call her doctors. That weekend Ann thought she would die because no one was there. This dramatically describes the theme of her life.

Ann longed for the security for which she had married but, instead, felt unappreciated and uncared for, feelings that replicated her experience of her childhood. She also felt deeply wounded by the lack of appreciation from her children, to whom she felt she had given so much.

In the transference I was experienced as one who echoed and confirmed her and helped her articulate her emotional responses. This also came to include her many professional achievements, which she felt had either been ignored or mocked by her family. As treatment went on, I began to notice that Ann easily felt criticized when I tried to explore with her such issues as her relationship with her children or her need to limit her therapy to one session per week. When I asked her questions that departed from a previously planned private agenda, she would quickly lose interest or change the subject. It became apparent that it did not matter if the subject was emotionally charged or not; Ann simply would not address anything that was not immediately meaningful to her.

I was aware that I responded to her with annoyance and then felt guilty about feeling annoyed. Ann was dying. I believed it was morally necessary for me to enable her to use her time with me in the ways that she would find most meaningful.

Because of my difficulties and uneasiness with Ann, I arranged several consultations with Margaret's analyst, which took place during the termination phase of Margaret's treatment. These consultations brought into focus similarities between Margaret's experience of Ann and my own; through them I learned that for each of us in our own ways, Ann was a failed selfobject.

When I learned the actual content of Margaret's hallucinations and delusions I was struck with a peculiar feeling of resonance. Margaret's hallucinations brought into focus my own experience of her mother, Ann. Margaret thought people could read her mind and that people hated her because her wishes for them bothered them. She felt people were furious with her, that they wanted her to go away and leave them alone. She heard voices yelling at her, "Stop bothering me! Stop bothering me!" I realized I had similar feelings in response to Ann. I felt Ann did not want me to bother her. I felt I had angered her when I asked questions or tried to explore issues that she didn't want to talk about.

Ann's personality aroused within me a specific transference. My own mother was overburdened; she had encouraged me to look to others to be substitute caregivers. Intuitively, I knew I should not complain about her inattentiveness to me. I perceived that being warmly sympathetic about her difficult life would enable me to win her affection as well as to defeat my more demanding older sister and thus become our mother's favorite child. This particular theme of my life dovetailed with my work with Ann. My history had left me vulnerable to certain selfobject failures, which I later experienced with Ann (cf. McLaughlin, 1981).

I did not tell Ann my observations about her because I, like Margaret, imagined it would be too disruptive for those ways in which she needed to perceive herself. Margaret's treatment identified her need to keep her mother alive by not calling attention to her lifelessness. I too thought that calling attention to Ann's lifelessness would be destructive to her and to our relationship. Ann needed to sustain her belief that she had successfully concealed her sense of imminent death and that she had therefore been a good mother. The blackboards in Margaret's dreams, on which "Shut up; keep peace!" was written, concretized what I myself felt—that Ann was fragile and could be devastated by exposure of her "secrets."

Both Margaret and I knew that the truth could not be spoken. But this understanding created dilemmas about how to relate to Ann. At times I was distracted during Ann's sessions and would turn to fantasy. Margaret too turned to fantasy in the presence of Ann. I experienced being with Ann as being in the presence of dying and death. She was summing up her life; her talk was focused on her achievements, her efforts, and her disappointments. She did not look to a future. My fantasies during sessions served as a resistance to being drawn into her mood and, by extension, my own mother's lack of vitality. Fantasizing was my attempt to maintain the integrity of my own life and my future. It served a similar function for Margaret.

My subjective experience of Ann did not correspond to the person she presented herself as being. For instance, she appeared to be a responsible and reliable person, one who was always prompt and

who canceled sessions, on the rare occasions when this was necessary, well in advance. However, during the few minutes prior to
every session, I imagined that she was not going to show up, that she
was tired and had decided not to come, or that she had died and no
one had told me. Her arrival on time would momentarily throw me
off balance, and I wondered what was wrong with me. I knew that
Ann's medical condition was not acute and, furthermore, that she
was responsible. This discrepancy between my fantasies and reality
was a fleeting experience of fragmentation brought about by my
immersion in Ann's subjective reality, my capacity to decenter and
introspect upon this experience being momentarily impaired by the
activation of comparable themes from my past. It was only a moment
in which I felt disoriented and a little "crazy." But for Margaret this
sense of confusion and difficulty in preserving her subjective reality
became an ongoing terrifying existence.

To Margaret, Ann was not what she appeared to be. Her words
and actions of "being there" for her daughter belied her conviction
that she was slipping away. Long before Ann's fatal illness was
diagnosed, Margaret desperately went through Ann's drawers,
looking for concrete confirmation in the form of doctor's reports,
laboratory findings, and so on of her subjective experience that her
mother was dying. The fact that Margaret's medical detective work
preceded the diagnosis suggests that Ann had for a long time felt
herself to be dying.

Margaret and I both had the same fantasy, arrived at independently, that we would watch Ann starve to death. Significantly, Ann
was actually gaining weight as a result of her medical treatments. This
idea that we would watch Ann starve to death was a concretization of
our subjective feeling that Ann was starving emotionally and that we
could not "feed" her enough to make her live.

Both Margaret and I shared the impression that Ann did not want
to make herself live. Each of us was afraid to admit this. Margaret
needed her mother. I needed to make my patient "better," to make
Ann feel more nurtured, more cared about, more at peace with
herself before she died. By extension, I was preserving the fantasy
that I could make my mother "better" and therefore more responsive
to me. One day Ann looked at me and said, "I wish it were over
already. I've lived my life, and I want to be dead." I replied, "I know."
At last, the truth was told.

Although a full explication of the process of Ann's treatment is
beyond the scope of this paper, this session marked a turning point
in our work together. Through consultations with my coauthor I had
become aware of my countertransference, my need to be enlivening

and "gleam-inducing," and of my mini-fragmentations when Ann failed to respond. I was then able to "decenter" and allow Ann to gradually reveal in detail what she truly felt herself to be—a dying woman who felt connected and enlivened by no one but her doctors.

## DISCUSSION

As a result of our work with this mother and daughter, we suggest that the single most important factor that ultimately led to the daughter's psychotic breakdown was the impossibility of acknowledging and confirming a central "truth" about her family and herself. Her delusional system represented an encoded description of herself and her world.

To appreciate Margaret's psychosis, we must understand her mother Ann's subjective organization, particularly her need to maintain an outward image as a competent and caring mother while privately feeling she was a dying woman, a feeling that caused her to become profoundly withdrawn from all others, including her children.

As Margaret approached adolescence, her experience of herself as a developing woman, as well as her experience of the family, was essentially unarticulated and unconfirmed. Her psychosis was triggered by her intense emotional reaction to the recurrence of her mother's illness, which was also unvalidated. Her hallucinations and delusions became the vehicle by means of which her self experience could be revealed and concealed.

Ann's therapist experienced an emotional tug of war with Ann. She felt as though Ann was pulling her into death and she was trying to pull Ann into life. Ann's therapist and Margaret fantasized while they were with Ann in order to affirm the vitality of their lives. But for Margaret the pull toward death was at times irresistible. Appearing to others as "half-dead" and having dreams of dying and of being in a tomb with a "mummy" attest to Margaret's merger with her mother.

Further, Ann's therapist experienced her as confusing. Ann's need to obfuscate, camouflage, and deny important personal truths made it difficult to know what to expect from her, what was "real" about her, and what was "real" about her relationships. The way her therapist experienced her was often at odds with the ways in which Ann needed to present herself. Ann's consistent failure to substantiate the therapist's sense of reality often caused the therapist to experience during Ann's sessions feelings of confusion, disorientation, and derealization. The therapist experienced in microcosm what Margaret had experienced throughout her life. Ann's consistent failures in validating Margaret's subjectivity led first to a vulnerable sense of self and ultimately to Margaret's psychotic breakdown.

The concept of the intersubjective field, with its thesis that "the psychotic person elaborates delusional ideas that symbolically concretize the experience whose subjective reality has begun to crumble" (Stolorow, Brandchaft, and Atwood, 1987), provided a firm underpinning for the work that gradually enabled Margaret to gain a sense of the validity of her own experience.

Margaret's despair called forth in her analyst an empathy based on her own tumultuous adolescent struggles. Her empathic inquiry led to the establishment of a therapeutic bond in which Margaret could experience her own intense struggles—even in delusional form—as valid, understandable, and, above all, real. The ongoing uncovering that existed in the therapeutic relationship enabled Margaret to successfully articulate the themes and dilemmas of her life. Her delusional thoughts were viewed by her as aspects of herself and her world that she had not been able to know about.

Gradually, the analytic work helped Margaret to understand and acknowledge and then to mourn her mother's unyielding psychic death. With her therapist, Margaret was able to establish a clearer sense of her own boundaries and develop and a better sense of herself. Margaret no longer needed to so desperately try to make her mother live so that she could live herself. This separation enabled Margaret to acknowledge her desire for her father's attention. Gradually, she became able to see her father as a more complicated person, one who was capable of being kind and loving as well as insensitive and impulsive.

Ann's involvement in treatment gave her the caregiver she sought. Giving Margaret over to her analyst enabled Ann to free herself of a burden that she did not want. Ann no longer had to feel guilty or to pretend to want to live. She no longer felt guilty about not wanting to take care of Margaret. As of this writing, Ann continues to be in treatment. Her medical condition is stable. We are working on identifying the circumstances of her childhood that caused her to turn away from life.

Margaret has begun college and is now fully involved in college life.

## SUMMARY

From the separate psychoanalytic treatments of a mother and her psychotic daughter, we are proposing that the daughter's psychosis resulted from consistent failures to have her subjective experiences validated. We view her hallucinations and delusions as concretizations of intense emotional experiences and dilemmas that existed in her relationships with her mother and other family members.

We argue that in order to understand and treat the psychotic process, the analyst must address the intersubjective experiences that the patient is urgently trying to communicate and validate. The patient's delusional ideas need to be taken seriously and the interpersonal experiences they encode must be acknowledged. When the psychotic person can understand his own message and can believe in its validity, he will lose the need for a delusional system.

> *He who does not lose his mind over*
> *certain things has no mind to lose.*
>
> Gotthold Ephraim Lessing,
> in his play *Emilia Galotti* (1772)

## REFERENCES

Arieti, S. (1974), *Interpretation of Schizophrenia.* New York: Basic Books.

Bateson, G., Jackson, D., Haley, J. & Weakland, J. (1956), Toward a theory of schizophrenia. *Behav. Sci.*, 1:251–264.

Beebe, B. & Lachmann, F. (1988), Mother–infant mutual influence and precursor of psychic structure. In: *Frontiers in Self Psychology: Progress in Self Psychology, Vol. 3,* ed. A. Goldberg. Hillsdale, NJ: The Analytic Press, pp. 3–25.

Deutsch, H. (1926), Okkulte Vorgange Wahrend der Psychoanalyse. *Imago,* 12:418–433.

Ferenczi, S. (1909), Introjection and transference. In: *Sex in Psychoanalysis.* New York: Basic Books, 1950, pp. 109–121.

Fosshage, J. (1990), Toward a reconceptualization of transference. Presented to Division 39 of the American Psychological Association, New York City.

Freud, S. (1894), The neuro-psychoses of defence. *Standard Edition,* 3:45–61. London: Hogarth Press, 1962.

————— (1910), The future prospects of psychoanalytic therapy. *Standard Edition,* 11:139–151. London: Hogarth Press, 1957.

Fromm-Reichmann, F. (1959), *Psychoanalysis and Psychotherapy: Selected Papers of Frieda Fromm-Reichmann.* Chicago: University of Chicago.

Gitelson, M. (1952), The emotional position of the analyst in the psycho-analytic situation. *Internat. J. Psycho-Anal.* 33:1–10.

Glover, E. (1927), Lectures on technique in psychoanalysis: 1. Introduction: The analytic situation; 2. The opening phase. *Internat. J. Psycho-Anal.,* 8:311–338.

Hoffman, I. Z. (1983), The patient as interpreter of the analyst's experience. *Contemp. Psychoanal.,* 19:389–422.

————— & Gill, M. (1988), Critical reflections on a coding scheme. *Internat. J. Psycho-Anal.,* 9:55–64.

Josephs, L. & Josephs, L. (1986), Pursuing the kernel of truth in the psychotherapy of schizophrenia. *Psychoanal. Psychol.,* 3:105–119.

Kohut, H. (1971), *The Analysis of the Self.* New York: International Universities Press.

————— (1977), *The Restoration of the Self.* New York: International Universities Press.

_____ (1984), *How Does Analysis Cure?* ed. A. Goldberg, & P. Stepansky. Chicago: University of Chicago Press.

_____ (1985), *Self Psychology and the Humanities,* ed. C. Strozier. New York: Norton.

Laing, R. D. (1967), *The Politics of Experience.* New York: Ballantine Books.

Lichtenberg, J. D. (1990), Rethinking the scope of the patient's transference and the therapist's counterresponsiveness. In: *Realities of Transference: Progress in Self Psychology, Vol. 6.* Hillsdale, NJ: The Analytic Press, pp. 23–33.

Magid, B. (1984), Some contributions of self-psychology to the treatment of borderline and schizophrenic patients. *Dynamic Psychother.,* 2:101–111.

McLaughlin, J. (1981), Transference, psychic reality, and countertransference. *Psychoanal. Quart.,* 639–664.

Searles, H. F. (1979), *Countertransference and Related Subjects.* New York: International Universities Press.

Stolorow, R., Brandchaft, B. & Atwood, G. (1987), *Psychoanalytic Treatment: An Intersubjective Approach.* Hillsdale, NJ: The Analytic Press.

Sullivan, H. S. (1944), The language of schizophrenia. In: *Language and Thought in Schizophrenia,* ed. J. J. Kasanin. New York: Norton, pp. 4–16.

Tower, L. (1956), Countertransference. *J. Amer. Psychoanal. Assn.,* 4:224–465.

Winnicott, D. W. (1974), Fear of breakdown. *Internat. Rev. Psycho-Anal.,* 1:103–107.

# Chapter 5

# Trust Disturbance and the Sexual Revictimization of Incest Survivors: A Self-Psychological Perspective

## *Doris Brothers*

Evidence is mounting that incest leaves its survivors at great risk for further abuse. Of the 152 incest survivors in Russell's (1986) interview study, 82% revealed that in addition to having been incestuously abused they had also been raped or subjected to other forms of serious sexual victimization by nonrelatives. A number of other researchers, including Herman (1981), Frieze (1983), and Browne and Finkelhor (1986), report significant correlations between sexual abuse in childhood and sexual abuse in later life.

Since, as this research suggests, incest powerfully affects potential offenders as well as survivors, no single factor accounts for the high incidence of revictimization. For example, Russell (1986) points out that the mere knowledge that a child or woman has already been sexually abused may rouse some potential abusers to acts of sexual violence. Another factor in sexual revictimization is to be found in the powerful role that incestuous experiences play in shaping a child victim's sexual development. Many incestuously abused children compulsively masturbate or engage in sexual play, behaviors that, all too frequently, are mistaken for seductive invitations to sexual relations.

My purpose in this chapter is to explore only one of the myriad factors involved in the sexual revictimization of incest survivors: disturbed trust. That trust disturbances figure importantly in the symptomatology and treatment of incest trauma is hardly news to most experienced clinicians. As far back as 1932, Sandor Ferenczi asserted that trust betrayal was of primary significance in the sexual abuse of children. Openly challenging Freud's repudiation of the "seduction theory," i.e., the hypothesis that neuroses were caused by actual experiences of sexual abuse, Ferenczi (1933, p. 161) asserted: "sexual trauma, as the pathogenic factor cannot be valued highly enough," that it occurred "more often than one had dared to suppose," and that "people thought to be trustworthy such as relatives (uncles, aunts, grandparents), governesses or servants . . . misuse the ignorance and innocence of the child."

According to Ferenczi (1933), incest occurs because an adult with a "pathological disposition" is grossly unempathic to a child's wish for "tenderness." Confusing the child's playful emulation of its parents with the seductive behavior of a sexually mature person, the adult initiates sex with the child "without consideration of the consequences." The extremely harmful consequences, according to Ferenczi, include profound disturbances in the child's trust. Urgently needing to maintain a trusting relationship with the adult, the child, by various psychological stratagems including "identification with the aggressor," succeeds in maintaining an illusion that his or her trust has not been betrayed. However, this illusion takes a great toll on the child's trust in self: "When the child recovers from such an attack, he feels enormously confused, in fact split—innocent and culpable at the same time—and his confidence in the testimony of his own senses is broken" (p. 162).

As we shall see, Ferenczi's insights are highly compatible with a self-psychological understanding of incest trauma. More recent investigators have also attributed the psychological devastation of incest to its profound impact on the child's trust. For example, Poston and Lison (1989) state: "the most significant and deep-seated violation the incest survivor faces is the betrayal of trust in her childhood. It invades all the other areas of survival. It colors and shapes her entire approach to life" (p. 89).

The relationship between trauma and disturbed trust is brought into sharp focus with the application of self-psychological theory. Once Kohut's thesis is accepted that, from birth to death, we are utterly dependent on one another for the provision of psychological functions essential to the experience of cohesive selfhood, the need to trust others and to be trusted by them assumes a prominent position in mental life. Disturbances in trust, from this perspective, invariably and profoundly affect self-experience.

As I hope to demonstrate, a self-psychological perspective not only clarifies the relationship between trauma and trust disturbance, it also helps to shed light on the problem of revictimization among incest survivors. In what follows I first describe the realm of trust involved in trauma. Next, refining the "shattered fantasy" theory of trauma (Ulman and Brothers, 1988), I attempt to show that trust disturbance lies at the heart of trauma. I then examine a specific type of trust organization often found among incest survivors which appears to contribute to sexual revictimization. Finally, I present a portion of an illustrative self-psychological treatment case.

## SELF-TRUST: THE GLUE OF SELF-EXPERIENCE

According to Corazzini (1977), who performed sophisticated factor analyses on a number of scales designed to measure trust, including Rotter's (1967) *Interpersonal Trust Scale*, trust is a complex, multidimensional construct. "Self-trust" is the name I have given to the domain of trust that pertains to selfobject relationships. A preliminary definition of self-trust is the hope or wishful expectation of obtaining from others and providing for others (Brothers, 1990a, b) the selfobject functions necessary for the development, maintenance and restoration of self-experience. While other kinds of trust, such as environmental trust and interpersonal trust, are necessary for a sense of safety, comfort, and familiarity in the outer world, self-trust is necessary for a sense of safety, comfort, and familiarity in one's inner or subjective world.

Self-trust is implicit in Kohut's understanding of self-experience. A fundamental tenet of self psychology (Kohut, 1971, 1977, 1984) holds that the self cannot survive in a vacuum. That is to say, the experience of self always involves selfobjects. If we, on an unconscious level, could not trust others to serve as selfobjects, or, if we could not trust ourselves to serve as selfobjects for others, our emotional lives would be crippled. We would live in perpetual dread of self-disintegration and self-depletion. This is, I believe, another way of understanding "disintegration anxiety," which Kohut (1984, p. 18) characterized as "the deepest anxiety man can experience."

The idea that selfobject relationships form the irreducible units of self-experience is also fundamental to the Ulman-Brothers (1988) theory of trauma presented in *The Shattered Self*. We conceptualize self-experience in terms of central organizing fantasies, or, as we now call them, selfobject fantasies, which consist of affect-laden images of self and others. In some selfobject fantasies we are the recipients of the selfobject functioning of others and in some selfobject fantasies we are the providers of selfobject functions for others (Brothers, 1990).

Selfobject fantasies involve three main types of selfobject functions: (1) mirroring, (2) idealizing, and (3) twinship. These fantasies correspond to the "three separate lines of selfobject development" Kohut (1984, p. 198) described that are activated in the three main types of selfobject transferences: the mirroring, idealizing, and twinship transferences. Normally, over the course of development, selfobject fantasies undergo transformation from highly archaic to more mature forms.

Trauma is experienced as a betrayal of self-trust. This conceptualization refines the "shattered fantasy" theory which defines trauma as "a real occurrence, the unconscious meaning of which so shatters central organizing [selfobject] fantasies that self-restitution is impossible" (Ulman and Brothers, 1988, p. 3). Both the shattering of selfobject fantasies and faulty efforts at their restoration find expression in the dissociative reexperiencing and numbing symptoms of posttraumatic stress disorder (PTSD).

Insofar as self-trust serves as a bond between self and the principal figures in one's selfobject relationships, it may be thought of as the glue that holds selfobject fantasies together. A traumatic betrayal loosens this glue, severely damaging psychological life. With the disintegration of the bonds of trust connecting trauma survivors to those with whom they are involved in selfobject relationships, selfobject fantasies shatter and self-experience disorganizes. Survivors are plunged into a nightmare world in which sanity, indeed, the very continuity of existence can no longer be taken for granted.

The loss of selfobject functions per se does not cause disintegration anxiety—many people have endured long periods of actual separation from others experienced as selfobjects without undergoing mental breakdown—it is the loss of trust in the selfobject functioning of self and others that is unbearable. This helps to explain why the same event, for example, a specific battle in a war, may be traumatic for one soldier and not another. Only the soldier who experiences the battle as a betrayal of his trust in vitally needed selfobject relationships is traumatized.

Because every traumatic betrayal holds the specter of disintegration anxiety, strenuous efforts must be undertaken to heal damaged self-trust and, concomitantly, to restore selfobject fantasies. Ulman and Brothers (1988) found empirical support for this postulate among trauma survivors. Their efforts to restore shattered selfobject fantasies were found to be inevitable because of the primacy of the need to preserve a sense of self (Tolpin, 1985).

By way of illustration, let us consider a traumatic rape. Maggie, a 21-year-old black woman (the case is reported in detail in Ulman and Brothers, 1988) was raped on her first date with a handsome young doctor after he persuaded her to accompany him to his apartment. Prominent in Maggie's self-experience were perceptions of herself as possessing extraordinary powers to size up other people and to predict the outcome of events and situations. Maggie's expectation of receiving mirroring selfobject responses from others largely depended on her possession of these extraordinary powers. (As I explain below, her criteria for self-trust were very immature.)

As a consequence of having been deceived by the rapist, Maggie could no longer experience herself as omniscient and prescient. Without her grandiose illusions, Maggie's wishful expectation of receiving admiration and praise from those who functioned as mirroring selfobjects was destroyed. It was the "ungluing" of this connection between self and selfobjects that shattered one of Maggie's central selfobject fantasies. Maggie's trust in her capacity to elicit the selfobject functions she urgently needed for the preservation of her sense of self was dealt a severe blow. She suffered feelings of intolerable humiliation, narcissistic rage, and terrifying experiences of fragmentation and depletion.

Maggie's efforts at self-restoration included "turning the tables" on men by becoming the one who betrayed their trust. For example, after promiscuously seducing men and persuading them to provide her with money and drugs, she would suddenly drop them. In so doing she experienced herself, at least temporarily, as once again worthy of her mirroring selfobjects: her fantasy of mirrored grandiosity was briefly restored.

## THE FOUR DIMENSIONS OF SELF-TRUST

Because Maggie had grown up with a violent, alcoholic father and a remote, preoccupied mother, neither of whom reliably and predictably met her selfobject needs, her trust in other people had never been very great. Because, as a young child, Maggie had developed precocious abilities to take care of her own needs, she came to place inordinate trust in herself. Her belief that she could never be exploited reflected her extremely inflated confidence in her mental processes. Consequently, Maggie experienced the rape less as a betrayal of her trust in others than as a self-betrayal.

As Maggie's experience suggests, self-trust is not a unitary construct. I have identified four dimensions of self-trust that are commonly disturbed by traumatic betrayals (Brothers, 1989). Disturbance in one dimension of self-trust does not necessarily result in the same degree and kind of disturbance in other dimensions. Yet, the various dimensions of self-trust are complexly interrelated.

The four dimensions of self-trust are: (1) trust-in-others, (2) trust-in-self, (3) self-as-trustworthy, and (4) others-as-self-trusting. Trust-in-others involves the hope that others will serve as one's selfobjects; trust-in-self involves faith in one's capacity to elicit the selfobject functioning of others; self-as-trustworthy involves the expectation of serving as selfobject for others; and others-as-self-trusting involves confidence in the ability of others to get their own selfobject needs met.

As an example of the interrelatedness of the self-trust dimensions, consider the effect on trust-in-self when trust-in-others is confirmed by experience. We tend to trust people to meet our selfobject needs to the extent that we find them predictable, reliable, consistent, and dependable (Rempel and Holmes, 1986). These qualities give us the illusion of being in control of their responses. As Kohut (1977) points out, on an archaic level, we experience selfobjects as extensions of ourselves, more like limbs on our bodies than separate people. When others behave predictably, reliably, consistently and dependably, they tend to reinforce the illusion of our total control over them. The more others in whom we place trust serve our selfobject needs in a trustworthy fashion, the more our trust in them is confirmed and strengthened, and, concomitantly, the more our trust in our own capacity to elicit the selfobject functioning of others is also confirmed and strengthened. In other words trust-in-others promotes trust-in-self. Conversely, when others behave unpredictably, unreliably, and inconsistently, trust-in-self is likely to suffer.

As I argue elsewhere (Brothers, 1989, 1990a, b) the four dimensions of self-trust exist, at least in nascent form, in early life. Recent studies of infant-caregiver relations indicate that infants are capable of forming expectations of having their physiological and psychological needs met. Stern (1985) calls these expectations "representations of interactions that have been generalized (RIGs)." Certain RIGs involve the infant's experiences of being with others. Stern calls these experiences "evoked companions." He writes: "The infant is, in subjective fact, not alone but accompanied by evoked companions, drawn from several RIGs, who operate at various levels of activations and awareness. *The infant is therefore trustful*" (Stern, 1985, p. 118, italics added).

## DEVELOPMENTAL CHANGES IN SELF-TRUST CRITERIA

Clearly, the self-trust of infants, young children, older children and adults all differ qualitatively one from the other. One of the ways in

which self-trust is transformed over the course of normal development is that the criteria upon which self-trust is based change.
Research in trust development, (Selman, Jaquette, and Lavin, 1977;
Brothers, 1982) indicates that the criteria for trust used by young
children and developmentally arrested adults often involves magical,
highly unrealistic notions about the self and others. External, super-
ficial qualities such as physical size and attractiveness, rather than
enduring psychological qualities or the adherence to abstract principles, may determine the extent to which trust is experienced. Early in
development, trust criteria tend to be black or white (e.g., the belief
that someone is "totally reliable" or "always a liar") rather than
reflections of the multifaceted nature of human personality. Furthermore, qualities of self may be confused with qualities of others. With
increasing maturity, the criteria for self-trust become more realistic,
abstract, complex, and differentiated.

For example, one criterion for trust-in-self of a little boy might be
that he, like the Superheroes he watches on TV, is invulnerable to
harm. That is to say, his experience of himself as capable of eliciting
the selfobject functioning of others depends, in part, on enactments
of his imperviousness to injury. In his play he might imagine himself
surviving unscathed the villainous attacks of hordes of "bad guys."
He unconsciously experiences his fantasized relationships to mirroring selfobject as dependent on this grandiose illusion. If another
child insists that this boy has been "shot dead," he might object
strenuously; his trust in his ability to receive the mirroring responsiveness of others has been placed in jeopardy.

By the time the boy reaches adolescence, his trust-in-self would no
longer be based on such an unrealistic criterion. Instead, if his
development proceeded normally, he might place trust in himself to
the extent that he earned good grades, achieved popularity with
friends, and behaved like a responsible son. As an adult, his criteria
for trust-in-self might also include his ability to sustain love relationships, the extent to which he realized his professional goals, and such
abstract concepts as his allegiance to his country and his adherence to
a religious or moral creed. A similar process of maturation would be
expected to occur in the criteria used for self-trust in the other three
dimensions as well.

Trauma profoundly affects the criteria upons which self-trust is
based. As a consequence of traumatic betrayals, immature criteria for
placing trust in self and others are retained or reinstated. Let us now
imagine that the little boy with the superhero fantasy is severely
injured in a car accident. The unconscious traumatic meaning of this

experience might well damage the bonds of trust connecting him to his mirroring selfobjects because his illusion of invulnerability has been shaken.

In order to restore his fantasized relationship to mirroring selfobjects, the boy might intensify his illusions and retain personal invulnerability as a criterion for trust-in-self. For example, when the boy enters adolescence he might feel compelled to confirm his trust-in-self by performing daredevil stunts demonstrating his imperviousness to danger. As an adult, he might resort to other forms of high-risk behavior such as gambling or entering into dubious business deals.

## THE BIDIRECTIONALITY OF SELF-TRUST DISTURBANCES

In the clinical literature, trust disturbance tends to be equated with lowered trust. Patients said to have disturbed trust are usually described as mistrustful of others or lacking in self-confidence. They are rarely described as exhibiting heightened or intensified trust in self or others. Nevertheless, empirical research with trauma survivors reveals that trust disturbance is bi-directional (Brothers, 1982). That is to say, traumatic betrayals may result in intensifications as well as diminutions of trust in one or more of the self-trust dimensions. In response to a traumatic betrayal that threatens a vital selfobject connection, for example, a person may unconsciously attempt to avert psychological catastrophe by intensifying trust-in-others. In Maggie's case, her response to a traumatic rape was the further intensification of trust-in-self.

A person whose trust-in-others is disturbed may become suspicious, hypervigilant, secretive and withdrawn, or so unswervingly trustful even blatent signs of another person's untrustworthiness are overlooked. Disturbed trust-in-self may be expressed either as insecurity, indecisiveness and self-doubt, or blind self-confidence. A person for whom self-as-trustworthy is disturbed may become indifferent to the psychological needs of others or, like certain members of the helping professions, so dedicated to providing trustworthy care, the satisfaction of their own needs is neglected. Disturbed others-as-self-trusting may result in disillusionment and cynicism in authority figures, or lead one to join a cult or other organizations in which allegiance to a self-trusting leader is stressed.

Diminutions and intensifications of self-trust are responsible for the dissociative nature of PTSD symptoms. Ulman's (1984) descriptions of the disturbances in self-experience associated with depersonalization, derealization, and disembodiment supports this assertion.

In other words, trust disturbance produces a lack of familiarity and confidence in the survivor's experience of self and other. For example, among child incest survivors whose survival depends on relationships with relatives who betrayed them, memories of their abusive sexual experiences are often dissociatively split off from consciousness as they intensify trust in their abusers. When memories of abuse are retained or recovered, certain survivors may dissociate all affective connections to them or disavow their meaning (Basch, 1983). As a result, their experiences of self and other tend to lack sharpness and conviction.

In a research study involving rape and incest survivors (Brothers, 1982), the self-trust organization of the most severely traumatized subjects was marked by greatly diminished trust-in-self and greatly intensified trust-in-others. Moreover, their criteria for placing trust in self and in others tended to be highly immature. It is a self-trust organization of just this kind that is most likely to lead to sexual revictimization among incest survivors.

## THE SELF-TRUST ORGANIZATION OF INCEST SURVIVORS

Children sexually exploited by trusted relatives are often desperate for the selfobject functioning of others. These children may require the calming, soothing presence of an idealized parental figure to combat the terror of self-disintegration or they may require mirroring responses to assure then that they are still worthy of love and esteem. In fact, the psychological survival of child victims beset by the dissociative symptoms of PTSD often depends on their ability to trust, on an unconscious level, that these vitally needed selfobject functions will be provided. But, how is trust possible in the face of such profound betrayal?

If children acknowledge that the responsibility for the incestuous abuse was solely that of a trusted relative, they are faced with a terrifying loss. Moreover, they would have little reason to expect that anyone else would serve as a selfobject without also being abusive. Because the preservation of self is at stake, such massive distrust is intolerable. For many child incest survivors, the only way out of an otherwise insoluble dilemma is to disavow the betrayal and absolve the adult relative of blame for the incest. To further protect the trustworthiness of their abusers, these children may fault themselves for provoking the incest. As a consequence, their trust in their own capacity to elicit selfobject functions from others is greatly compromised. Hence, in the service of psychological survival, trust-in-others is greatly intensified and trust-in-self greatly diminished.

Tragically, it is just when incest survivors are once again threatened with betrayal that they are most likely to heighten their already intensified trust-in-others and further diminish their trust-in-self. Because an anticipated betrayal once again poses a dangerous threat to self-preservation, incest survivors are likely to experience a resurgence of disintegration anxiety. Desperate for relief, they may blindly place their trust in a potential betrayer.

Since incest often occurs in childhood or adolescence, the criteria used by many survivors for placing trust in self and in others usually remain immature. Mistaking aggressive, controlling, abusive behavior for protective strength, they may place themselves at great risk. At the same time, their diminished trust-in-self compromises their ability to evaluate the danger they are in. All too often this situation contributes to revictimization.

It is hardly surprising that issues related to trust tend to play a crucial role in the treatment of incest survivors. Transference and countertransference configurations often reflect the self-trust organizations of patient and therapist (Brothers, 1989). The following vignette from a self-psychological treatment case illustrates how the trust disturbance of an incest survivor deepened in the transference, thus setting the stage for sexual revictimization.

## MARGE: A CLINICAL EXAMPLE OF REVICTIMIZATION

Marge, a 29-year-old incest survivor whose self-psychological treatment is described in *The Shattered Self* (Ulman and Brothers, 1988), was raped during the termination period of her four-year, once-weekly treatment. Naturally, plans to terminate the treatment were postponed until the effects of the rape could be worked through. In the course of exploring the unconscious traumatic meanings of the rape, it became apparent that disturbances in self-trust resulting from her incestuous experiences and manifested in the transference had contributed to her sexual revictimization.

Marge originally entered treatment with me for relief from symptoms of PTSD that had accompanied her sudden recollection of having been sexually abused by her brother, Victor, 11 years earlier. Memories of her incestuous experiences had overwhelmed her as she watched a television drama about incest. She recalled awakening one night with her hand on her naked brother's penis. Reconstructive work during treatment revealed that he had initiated sexual contact with her on numerous occasions and had unsuccessfully attempted intercourse with her.

Dissociation had kept memories of Marge's incestuous abuse out of her conscious awareness for 11 years. Her reaction to the rape was very similar. Once again she was thrown into a highly dissociated state. It was not until a month later when I questioned her about noticeable changes in her mood and behavior that Marge mentioned the rape in a therapy session. Even then she began her account of this traumatic experience in a rather offhand manner without ever using the word, rape. In the midst of describing the details of her experience, however, she broke down in sobs and repeated, "I was raped, I was raped."

The rape occurred during Marge's first date with a man she had known as a frequent customer in her father's hardware store where she worked on weekends. Marge characterized him as a "fake Mafia tough guy" who spoke in a crude, wise-cracking manner and dressed in cheap, flashy clothes. Noting that he was over six feet tall and overweight, Marge said she had always felt vaguely threatened by his size and belligerent manner. For months Marge had flatly refused his frequent requests for dates. Shortly after he sent her a huge bouquet of long-stemmed roses, however, she accepted his invitation to dinner. Asked why she had changed her mind, Marge said she wasn't sure. "I really didn't like him," she said, "but maybe I felt flattered, special. My social life hadn't been too lively, and here was somebody who seemed to think I was pretty hot." Marge admitted that after receiving the flowers she had wondered if her negative evaluation of the man had been warranted. Perhaps he was more refined and gentlemanly than she had thought. "I began to think, Maybe there's something wrong with me, maybe I'm too picky," she said.

Marge described feeling alternately bored and uncomfortable during dinner. She remembered resenting the way the man let his eyes gaze suggestively at her breasts and feeling repelled by the poor taste of his sexual jokes. Still, she permitted him to walk her to the door of her apartment after he drove her home. Marge said that her memory for the events that followed is somewhat vague. "From the moment he grabbed me and kissed me at the door, everything got murky," she said. "I know that somehow he got inside the apartment and that I struggled to keep my clothes on for what seemed like hours." When he became more violent and threatened to hurt her, Marge stopped struggling. The man attempted intercourse but lost his erection and demanded that Marge make him a cup of coffee. By this time, Marge said, she felt afraid for her life. Yet Marge remembered taking pains with the coffee, even adding cinnamon, as she does on special occasions. "Maybe I was hoping that I could make it just a date again," she said. After drinking the coffee, the man threw her on her bed and this time succeeded in entering her vaginally. "I think it was over quickly," Marge said.

Marge only dimly remembered what happened after the man left. "I probably just sat there in shock," she said. She vaguely recalled showering, douching and going to bed. "I know that by morning I had completely put it out of my mind," she said. Soon after, however, she became aware of feeling depressed and withdrawn. She refused to see friends and neglected her appearance. Several days later, the man phoned to ask her out again. "For some strange reason," Marge said, "I wasn't even angry." Although she refused him, she said she felt "like dirt." "You won't believe this," she added. "I actually felt guilty about saying no!"

After acknowledging that she had been raped, Marge experienced a resurgence of many of the PTSD symptoms that had plagued her at the time she first entered therapy. In addition to a wide variety of numbing and reexperiencing symptoms, Marge also reported the return of a symptom that had been prominent at the beginning of treatment—an obsession with personal cleanliness. Complaining that she felt dirty, she spent a great deal of time in the shower scrubbing herself repeatedly.

Although Marge said she knew, intellectually, that she was not to blame for the rape, she attacked herself bitterly in therapy sessions. "How could I have trusted that creep after what happened with Victor?" she moaned. She connected her poor judgment in dating the rapist with several disappointing relationships she had had with "the wrong men." Each time she had ignored blatant signs of the man's untrustworthiness and had focused only on his strengths. She had even agreed to marry a man she later described as callous and indifferent to her needs. It was only after he exploited her financially and verbally abused her in public that Marge brought herself to end the relationship.

I reminded Marge that just as she had once longed for closeness with and admiration from her brother as a means of attaining a sense of her own value, her intense longings for attachment to these men had overridden her doubts about them. Marge acknowledged that the worse she felt about herself, the more blind she was to a man's shortcomings. "I guess I was feeling pretty worried about being an old maid when that guy asked me out," she said.

Although a number of Marge's PTSD symptoms including her preoccupation with cleanliness disappeared within weeks of her disclosure, she remained haunted by a sense of inadequacy. She complained of feeling unsure of herself at work and pessimistic about her future. She said she felt especially insecure about her appearance and her desirability as a woman. The thought of dating again filled her with a sense of dread. "I just can't seem to figure out who the creeps are," she said.

At this point, Marge mentioned that she would soon receive a copy of *The Shattered Self*, the publication of which she had been anticipating for months. She expressed excitement at finally reading about herself. Earlier in treatment the knowledge that she was participating in a research project that might result in the publication of her story had caused her a great deal of anxiety. She had feared being "robbed of her privacy" if I were indiscreet in using her story. Her worries about exploitation were found to be closely related to her experience of incestuous abuse.

Just before receiving her copy of the book, Marge reported the following dream fragment:

> I am naked in your office. The walls are made of glass. You are about to run a group for men so you don't give me time to get dressed. I wrap myself in a blanket. When I get to the waiting room all the men are leering at me.

Marge's associations to the dream revealed that she experienced the rape as a betrayal of her trust in herself and in me. After her incestuous experiences with her brother, a criterion for Marge's trust-in-self had been that she experience herself as invulnerable to humiliating exposure and abuse by men. Her trust in me as an idealized maternal figure depended, in part, on my ability to protect her from humiliating abuse.

The dream image of Marge naked in my glass-walled office symbolized both her humiliating exposure to the rapist and my failure as a protective presence in her life. The blanket in which she wrapped herself symbolically represented her efforts to disavow the meaning of her experience, an unconscious effort to restore her fantasies. Further associations revealed that, in spite of her seeming pleasure in the book's publication, Marge still worried that I, like the rapist, her brother, and so many men in her life, had betrayed her trust by exposing her to public humiliation. Instead of becoming invulnerable through her participation in the research project, she had been raped. Now she worried that her identity had not been protected in the book.

Asked to reflect on not having been given time to get dressed, Marge responded, "I guess I wasn't ready to end therapy. Maybe I felt you wanted me to leave before I was ready to face the world alone."

When Marge's finally received a copy of the book, her immediate reaction to reading her case study was intense relief that her identity had been well disguised. However, she soon became enraged with me. "I hate the book," she said. "I wish I had never agreed to be in it." At first Marge could not explain her intensely negative reaction. Then she pointed to an inaccurate quote. "I never used those words," she cried. Asked why that seemed so hurtful, Marge responded, "You didn't use my exact words, so its not really me in the book." She added, "First I was scared that I would be exposed and humiliated, but now I feel terrible that no one will know it's me." Further exploration revealed that Marge had worried that once I had finished the book, her value for me would be over. Marge added, "You weren't going to be there for me anymore and there was no man in sight."

I now understood that because termination of the treatment had coincided with the publication of the book, Marge could not believe that my interest in her extended beyond her participation in the research project. Faced with the possibility that I would abruptly stop providing the empathic responsiveness she had come to depend upon, an outgrowth of highly archaic transference fantasies of mirroring and idealized merger, Marge had searched for an idealizable man in whose company she would feel desirable and special.

Unfortunately, since ending her engagement, Marge had been unable to find such a man. In fact, her experiences with men had only confirmed her fear that men could not be trusted. Concomitantly, her trust in her own capacity to obtain what she needed from them was even further reduced. By the time of the rape, Marge's need to restore her trust in men was intense and her trust in herself was very weak.

In addition, because her incestuous abuse had interfered with the maturation of self-trust, the criteria Marge used to evaluate the trustworthiness of men were highly unrealistic. Thus, for example, the rapist's gift of flowers magically betokened the fulfillment of her longing to be treated as irresistibly desirable. His large physique promised safety and protection. In the urgency of her need to find the man trustworthy, Marge disavowed her initial impression that the man's appearance and manner were cause for alarm. As she later explained, "I just needed him to turn out to be the strong man who'd make me feel like an irresistible woman. I guess I just ignored all the scary things my head was telling me about him. Even while it was happening I tried to convince myself everything was okay."

Marge's trust disturbance exerted a powerful effect on the countertransference. Given the organization of my self-trust which is marked by intensified self-as-trustworthy, the resurgence of Marge's mistrust in me during termination threatened a cherished perception of myself as a trustworthy provider of my patients' selfobject needs. Having taken pains to conceal Marge's identity, I felt that her mistrust was unfounded. As a result, I failed to understand that termination, insofar as it coincided with the publication of her book, threatened Marge with another betrayal. It is likely that this unanalyzed transference–countertransference configuration helped to set the stage for Marge's revictimization.

Having experienced the rape as a profound betrayal of trust-in-self, Marge needed my functioning as a mirroring and idealized selfobject more urgently than ever. Yet, she was terrified that the trusting bond between us had been damaged. Because her identity had been disguised in my book, her old fantasies of merger with me as an idealized selfobject and her ongings to achieve recognition as a valued disciple had been destroyed.

Once her fears of betrayal in the transference were explored and painstakingly worked through, particularly insofar as they replicated earlier betrayals by members of her family, Marge's trust in herself and in me was gradually restored. When she came to understand that a contributing factor in her rape was her intense need to experience the rapist as trustworthy as a consequence of her fear that I could no longer be counted on to serve her needs, Marge was enabled to take a more empathic stance toward herself. Her feelings of self-contempt for having "caused" the rape were replaced by a greater appreciation of herself as a "survivor." This new understanding opened the door to a more fruitful exploration of her troubling relationships with untrustworthy men than had previously been possible.

Increasingly, Marge has become better able to sustain a mature sense of trust in herself and in others. That is, her expectations of selfobject fulfillment are based on a more realistic appraisal of other people as well as on her own capacity to obtain these functions. Marge is currently approaching termination with a sense of pride in herself and optimism in the future.

## SUMMARY AND CONCLUDING REMARKS

In this chapter, Kohut's seminal discoveries about self-experience were employed in an effort to understand more clearly the relationship between trauma and trust disturbance. With the introduction of self-trust, the realm of trust involved in self-experience, a refinement in the "shattered fantasy" theory of trauma was proposed. Traumatic betrayals were shown to result in intensifications and diminutions in the four dimensions self-trust and interfere with the maturation of self-trust criteria. It was argued that a specific type of self-trust organization associated with incest trauma, intensified trust-in-others and diminished trust-in-self, plays an important role in the sexual revictimization of incest survivors.

A vignette from a self-psychological treatment case illustrating this type of trust disturbance was presented. In this case, a significant factor in the revictimization of an incest survivor appears to have been a transference-countertransference configuration leading to the patient's further intensification of trust in a potential rapist and a concomitant reduction of trust in herself.

Further investigation of disturbed self-trust, its role in trauma and its importance in treatment may have applications beyond sexual revictimization. For example, disturbed self-trust offers a theoretical perspective from which to understand patients who enter into repetitious and seemingly destructive relationships without invoking such problematic concepts as feminine masochism. An appreciation of the vital psychological need to trust others and to be trusted by them for the provision of selfobject functions that preserve a sense of cohesive selfhood should facilitate the development of more empathic and effective treatment strategies in these cases.

## REFERENCES

Basch, M. F. (1983), The perception of reality and the disavowal of meaning. *The Annual of Psychoanalysis*, 11:125–153. New York: International Universities Press.

Brothers, D. (1982), Trust Disturbances Among Victims of Rape and Incest. Unpublished doctoral dissertation, Yeshiva University, *DAI* No. 1247, vol. 43 (4-B).

———— (1989), Treating trust pathology in trauma survivors: A self-psychological approach. Presented at the 12th Annual Conference on the Psychology of the Self, San Francisco.

———— (1990a), The trustworthy selfobject: Psychological giving and the therapeutic relationship. Presented at the TRISP/SASP Conference: The Selfobject Revisited, New York City.

———— (1990b), The recollection of incest as a consequence of working through trust disturbances in the transference. Presented at the 6th Annual Meeting of The Society for Traumatic Stress Studies, New Orleans.

Browne, A. & Finkelhor, D. (1986), The impact of child sexual abuse: a review of the research. *Psycholog. Bull.*, 99:66–77.

Corazzini, J. (1977), Trust as a complex multi-dimensional construct. *Psycholog. Reports*, 40:75–80.

Ferenczi, S. (1933), Confusion of tongues between adults and child. *Final Contributions to Psycho-Analysis*. New York: Basic Books, 1955.

Frieze, I. (1983), Investigating the causes and consequences of marital rape. *Signs*, 8:532–553.

Herman, J. (1981), *Father–Daughter Incest*. Cambridge MA: Harvard University Press.

Kohut, H. (1971), *The Analysis of the Self*. New York: International Universities Press.

———— (1977), *The Restoration of the Self*. New York: International Universities Press.

———— (1984), *How Does Analysis Cure?*, ed. A, Goldberg & P. Stepansky. Chicago: University of Chicago Press.

Poston, C. & Lison, K. *Reclaiming our Lives:*. Boston, MA: Little, Brown.

Rempel, J. K. & Holmes (1986), How do I trust thee? *Psychol. Today,*    :28–34.

Rotter, J. B. (1967), A new scale for the measurement of interpersonal trust. *J. Personality,* 35:651–665.

Russell, D. E. H. (1986), *The Secret Trauma.* New York: Basic Books.

Selman, R. L., Jaquette, D. & Lavin, D. R. (1977), Interpersonal awareness in children: toward an integration of developmental and clinical child psychology. *Amer. J. Orthopsychiat.,* 44:264–274.

Stern, D. N. (1985), *The Interpersonal World of the Infant.* New York: Basic Books.

Tolpin, P. (1985), The primacy of the preservation of self. In: *Progress in Self Psychology,* Vol. 1, ed. A. Goldberg. New York: Guilford Press, pp. 83–87.

Ulman, R. B. (1984), Traumatic psychosis: A psychoanalytic phenomenological analysis of dissociation. Unpublished manuscript.

_____ & Brothers, D. (1988), *The Shattered Self.* Hillsdale, NJ: The Analytic Press.

# Chapter 6

# The Desomatizing Selfobject Transference: A Case Report

*Bernard Brickman*

This chapter contains a description of the successful psychotherapy of a 52-year-old man suffering from chronic and severe upper gastrointestinal pain accompanied by nausea, anorexia, and weight loss. The therapy took place over 18 months and consisted of mostly once-weekly sessions, with the exception of the first three months, during which the frequency was twice-weekly.

There were several features of this case that may be of interest to clinicians working psychodynamically. First, the chronic and severe somatic symptoms were able to be successfully treated on a mostly once-weekly basis in a relatively short period of time. Second, the establishment and analysis of what I am calling a desomatizing selfobject transference was the basic therapeutic tool. This term refers to a multifaceted transference configuration that embodies idealizing and affect-integrating selfobject functions that are fundamentally tied to the process of desomatization. Finally, an unusual aspect of the case was the fact that the patient had consulted me for similar complaints some 20 years earlier when I was in general practice.

## CASE REPORT

Mr. R was a middle-aged married man, father of two children, working in a responsible administrative position at the time he contacted me for an appointment. He was self-referred. He reminded me that he had been my patient 20 years earlier, when I was in general practice, and said that he did not expect me to remember him. Indeed, I could not at first recall his name. However, his appearance at his first appointment did jog my memory.

Mr. R's initial complaints were about epigastric pain accompanied by nausea and loss of appetite. The description of the pain was a little vague, but it seemed to consist of a dull ache that did not radiate. It seemed to be present mostly in the morning on awakening. In addition, Mr. R reported an eight- or nine-pound weight loss during the previous three months. His internist suggested a psychiatric consultation after all the appropriate and thorough examinations failed to reveal an organic cause. Nevertheless, Mr. R and his family were concerned that there might still be a physical cause that both the internist and the gastroenterologist to whom he had been referred may have failed to detect.

Mr. R's description of the onset of these complaints was rather vague. At first he thought the symptoms went back about four or five years, with a considerable worsening in the preceding several months. Then, upon careful reflection, he and I were both able to recall that he had complained of similar, albeit less severe, symptoms when he consulted me 20 years earlier. I then remembered further details of Mr. R's earlier visit to my office. I had performed the usual procedures in response to his complaints: a history and physical, routine laboratory tests, and an upper gastrointestinal series, which was then the standard practice. Then, after all these investigations proved unrevealing, I recalled sitting Mr. R down in my consulting room and asking him to tell me about his family life. (Even at that time I was interested in the emotional aspects of physical illness and was quite accustomed to making such inquiries in an effort to get the pertinent psychological information.) I remembered vaguely that Mr. R denied having any problems. Twenty years later, however, he was able to tell me that my question panicked him as he felt totally unprepared to talk about his marital difficulties. He left my office feeling ashamed and cowardly, a feeling state that was to come up frequently in our subsequent work.

In response to my inquiry at this time, however, Mr. R was able to describe considerable emotional turmoil in his two most important relationships: with his wife and with his 30-year-old son. He reported with hesitation that his wife was quite a bit older than he, a fact that he anticipated would cause me to judge him in a negative manner. He was very unhappy with how critical she had been of him in a variety of areas; he felt that they had grown apart over the years so that there remained little that they could share together. His son's struggles to establish himself in his work life were a source of great pain to Mr. R, who inevitably blamed himself for his son's shortcomings. He mentioned also that he had suffered from lifelong feelings of inadequacy as a man, a subject that was very painful and difficult to talk about.

I then learned some of the details of Mr. R's earlier life. He reported with evident pain that his mother and natural father had not been married and that his father had abandoned the family, then consisting of himself, his mother, and his older brother, when he was a few months old. Their life was a difficult struggle. His mother tried to make ends meet by working as a cook in various locations. As a small boy, Mr. R was oftentimes called upon by his mother to approach a prospective employer in order to exploit the appeal of a small child whose mother was without work. At those times he naturally had to overcome strong fears of confronting such a daunting situation. When he was unable to muster sufficient courage to do so, his mother would look at him disapprovingly and call him a coward. One of my first interventions was to suggest that it wasn't fair that he was expected to confront a situation at age five or six that his mother had trouble handling and that he was then treated so scornfully when he failed. His response was, I realized in retrospect, rather characteristic: he replied that it was a simple enough thing for him to do and that he had been a coward all of his life.

Mr. R's mother married when he was six years old. This man, whom he called "Pop," was the only real father he had. Unfortunately, Pop left when Mr. R was 13 and never returned or had anything further to do with his two stepsons. Shortly thereafter, Mr. R's mother married a man who did not want any children in the house. The patient was therefore "consigned" (as he put it) to a residential placement for children that included school through the primary grades. He was sent to a nearby high school and lived in the residence until he graduated from high school, at which time he enlisted in the army. Mr. R remembered the five years spent in the residence as the best years of his childhood. He excelled as a student, made several friends, and generally did well.

Mr. R met his wife during the time that he was serving in the army. Mary was 10 years older than the patient and was reasonably attractive and bright. She was interested in him sexually, which he found very reassuring. Above all, Mary appreciated Mr. R's intellect and encouraged him to pursue his education. They were married at the time of Mr. R's discharge from the service, an event that he was to question and regret for years. He began to feel after a period of time that Mary was too old for him and that perhaps he had rushed into the liaison out a sense of insecurity. "Maybe I married the first woman who was kind to me," he groaned. Furthermore, he was ashamed of the age difference and felt that people would think that he had married his mother.

Mr. R came to the second session and reported the following dream:

> I am waiting at a bus stop for the bus to come. It is the bus to Villa Real (the children's residence). It stops in front of me and a lady gets on before me. I then try to get on the bus but am unable to as the steps are too high and I'm too small. The doors close and the bus drives away leaving me standing there, bereft.

His associations to Villa Real revealed that it was a place that gave him an opportunity to grow up with some semblance of mental health, away from his demanding and neurotic mother. His other associations led us to understand that the dream encapsulated his great disappointment 20 years earlier in my general practice office. He had been given an opportunity then to take a step toward greater mental health when I invited him to talk about what was bothering him. It was now clear that he was unable to "get aboard" at that time: it was too big a step to take. During the intervening 20 years he had been able to gather the courage to explore his anguish through the strength he had acquired through his work accomplishments.

I wondered aloud to him whether he might be concerned that he again would be unable to fully take advantage of this present chance for help. He pondered that question and replied that there might be something to that: perhaps there were some things he might not be able to talk about, things that would be too embarrassing or had some connection to his feeling inadequate and cowardly.

## COURSE OF THE THERAPY

The structure of the sessions was initially twice-weekly, sitting face-to-face. At the start of the fourth month Mr. R wanted to reduce the frequency of the sessions to once-weekly both for financial reasons and because he had been feeling better.

The beginning of the therapy was marked by waxing and waning of abdominal pain and nausea, which threw Mr. R into paroxysms of doubt about the appropriateness of pursuing psychotherapy as an answer to his problems. The symptoms tended to coincide with feelings of disappointment in his son's faltering attempts to make his way in the work world. The meaning that he attached to his son's difficulties was invariable: they were consistent reconfirmation of his failures as a father. He believed that this was so because of a basic, irreparable defect or weakness in himself as a man. He regretted that his son had to suffer for his inability to provide him with a good male role model. It gradually became evident also that his wife not infrequently echoed these sentiments.

Mr. R's doubts about psychotherapy receded whenever his symptoms were less intense, only to redouble when there was an exacerbation of pain. He felt at those times that perhaps there was indeed some as yet undiscovered, potentially life-threatening organic condition that was responsible for it. He would usually go on to reiterate that further examination by a specialist might be indicated. My response at those times was similar to that described by Galatzer-Levy (1982–1983) in his work on hypochondriasis: I replied simply that it must be very frightening to think that there might still be some serious condition that the doctors had not found that could yet endanger him and that perhaps further consultation might be wise. His usual response to these comments was to express surprise that I was not trying to talk him into thinking that it was all in his imagination. Along with this reply he seemed calmer and his resolve to pursue further organic studies faded.

Mr. R progressively became more symptom-free during the period between the two sessions each week. The pain would return in reduced intensity during the longer interval between the second session of the week and the first session of the following week. At those times he would again predictably express anxiety about the existence of organic disease that might be passing unnoticed. I thought that the waxing and waning of his symptomatology was probably connected to his experience of alternate disconnection and reconnection to me as a source of calm and confidence in the budding idealizing selfobject transference. However, I refrained from making that interpretation as I believed it premature in the light of Mr. R's entrenched conviction that the problem would turn out to be organic—in spite of which he was permitting himself to "try psychotherapy." Instead, I continued to empathize with Mr. R's fear that some dread disease such as cancer would eventually turn up. Each time that this occurred, however, he seemed less insistent that it might be foolish to waste his time talking about his feelings while the underlying disease process progressed. From my vantage point I found I had to remind myself that the patient really was afraid that there might be a hidden cancer, since I was by that time understanding the crescendos and decrescendos of his pain as manifestations of his feelings of disconnection and reconnection to me.

As Mr. R's somatic symptoms receded, depressive feelings gradually emerged, an observation that I have had occasion to make a number of times with other patients. Mr. R was very hesitant to reveal the depth, the duration, and the extent of his depressive despair. The resistance analysis revealed his fear that I would be overwhelmed by his pain, feel disgust for him, and regret that I had taken him as a patient. There were spontaneous associations to his mother, who inevitably was overburdened by his even occasional complaints of unhappiness. Memories emerged of her calling him "coward" in relation to such feelings on a number of occasions.

The preceding work led to a strengthening of the selfobject bond, and Mr. R felt more encouraged to try to tackle his most severe problem: his unhappy relationship with Mary. His complaints about her were multiple; she had disappointed him in many ways. In the beginning of their marriage she had been his solid supporter. Then he described her as becoming more and more critical of him in the areas that hurt the most: his lack of assertiveness in the outside world, his tendency to allow others to take advantage of him, and his failure to act as a good role model for their son. Of course, these were the very complaints that Mr. R had of himself, and Mary's echoing of them stirred intense feelings of humiliation. Their sex life gradually deteriorated as the mutual dissatisfaction grew, unrelieved by their discussions of the ways that they were making each other unhappy.

By the time that I was preparing to leave on a monthlong vacation three months after the onset of the treatment, Mr. R was practically asymptomatic and had regained five of the eight pounds that he had lost. He looked quite good at the first session after my return from my vacation. He reported a great deal of "nervousness" about resuming treatment. At first he was not able to specify what this was due to. He went on to report that he had been doing relatively well during the separation with the exception of occasional abdominal pains, which he related to angry feelings toward his wife and son. He had little or none of the type of pain that originally brought him into treatment four months earlier. He had obviously maintained his nutrition and, with the exception of one or two brief depressive episodes, had been feeling quite well.

Mr. R reported further that his relationship with Mary had taken a turn for the better. She seemed less disturbed to him, and he expressed the feeling that even *she* had derived some benefit from his treatment. He went on to bring up, with some reluctance, his feelings of inadequacy relative to men in his life. "One of my biggest problems is that I feel inadequate and unimportant around men," he lamented. "I cannot believe that the men that I am with would be interested in me, like me, or genuinely care for me. In social situations I do whatever I need to do to not be alone with men." I suggested to Mr. R that perhaps our recent separation may have had something to do with these feelings coming up at this time; maybe he experienced my going away as an indication that he was not very important to me. His immediate response was to reject that idea, adding that he was, after all, "just another patient" to me. The subsequent material, however, seemed confirmatory. He spoke at some length of the important men in his life who had abandoned or disappointed him: his father, when he was an infant, and his stepfather, when he was 13. They never returned to renew or attempt to maintain a connection with him as a boy. I offered him the suggestion that those experiences could have a lot to do with his feeling uncomfortable, unacceptable, and uninteresting around men. He responded by expressing the feeling that that explanation seemed "too simplistic" and went on to add that these feelings had something to do with his relationship with his mother as well.

At this point he reported that whenever he was upset or angry with his mother for any reason, he would go off and pout. She would then try to soothe him by fondling his penis. He tied this to his great interest in having his penis held by women during lovemaking. He felt that there was a definite connection between this, the abandonment by his fathers, and his sense of inadequacy around men but was uncertain as to what that connection was. He sensed that he was holding back some painful feelings in this regard. He also reported feeling dissatisfied with his tendency to hold back, both in being reserved or aloof with people and in feeling detached from his feelings. I pointed out to him that he behaved like a man who had to protect himself. He agreed. I added that maybe he had been hurt in the past by people who had reacted to his defenses in a personal way (feeling that he was being withholding with them) and that he might be afraid that his holding back feelings would affect me in a similar way.

Subsequent sessions dealt with Mr. R's rageful feelings, which seemed to be aroused in a variety of situations. Sometimes they were related to shame and lowered self-esteem. These feelings had come up during an argument with his son during which Mary backed the son, causing Mr. R to feel betrayed. He saw himself as a man with a reservoir of anger inside and felt that it didn't take much to puncture that reservoir and have the anger emerge.

Later sessions revealed Mr. R's awareness of episodes of depression and somatic symptoms that were traceable to failures of the husband–wife or the father–son "teams" he was a part of. He realized that he saw himself as having to perform for his wife and son in some sort of ideal manner, as he had to perform for his mother. He felt that if his wife or son failed, he was a failure too.

During the Christmas holidays Mr. R became more anxious and depressed. These feelings were traceable to his need to withdraw into himself during social gatherings because of an inner sense of unworthiness. He was unable to really believe that his friends loved and valued him. What he wanted most of all was to have an intimate relationship. But it was also what he feared the most because of the danger of being rejected and hurt. He then reported that about ten years earlier his wife told him, in connection with her social shyness at parties, "You're not worth it" (i.e., worth overcoming the pain she felt at parties). She then told him some time afterward that she felt that his feelings for her had changed following this comment. He couldn't corroborate her perception; he could only say, with considerable sadness, that each had withdrawn from the other and that their love was not the same.

Further work took place in exploring Mr. R's lifelong feelings of inadequacy and cowardice. Aspects of his insecurity were traceable to several factors, including his mother's divorcing "Pop," whom he idealized, and her sending him to the "home" shortly thereafter. "Maybe she got rid of him *and* me because I was inadequate like him" he speculated. He recalled how as a child, unable to feel secure in the world, he periodically found himself running home to his mother in the kitchen, where he felt safe and secure. His conviction that he was not a real man, but a coward, stemmed from his sense of shame about relying on Mary's presence, which revived his earlier feelings toward his mother. When we were then able to connect his sense of shame about relying on Mary's presence to these same feelings, he was further convinced that he was not a real man but a coward.

In subsequent sessions, Mr. R became aware of feeling more open about expressing his feelings of fearfulness and inadequacy to me. The analysis of his reluctance to do so revealed his fear of my disappointment and wrath. He dreaded my damaging him further by shaming him with the epithet so frequently used by his mother: "coward." I interpreted to him that he seemed hopeful that I would ally myself with him and replace Mary, who had failed him, in order to repair the damage and help him move forward in his life. This comment evoked tears and an expression of the painful unmet longings for someone strong in his life whom he could look up to and count on to be on his side.

In later weeks Mr. R found himself feeling more comfortable going places alone for the weekend. Nevertheless, he chided himself for not being able to enjoy himself as well. Still later, he described an area of "maturing," although he thought it presumptuous to describe the change that way. It applied to the experience of taking steps to separate himself from his son Phil, an experience not without conflict. He described fears of letting his son go; he worried that something terrible might happen to Phil and that he would hold himself responsible. During the following session he fell silent. On close examination, he discovered that he felt that I had been impatient with him in the last session around the issue of "extending" himself "through Phil." He was fearful of further disappointing me, which inhibited him in talking more about Phil. I interpreted to him his need to please me to avoid feeling like a failure as a patient and suggested that his inability to meet the needs of his wife, his son, and his mother also made him feel like a failure.

In the following session Mr. R saw that he automatically felt that he was a failure whenever he either failed to meet someone else's needs or tried to get *his* needs met. I was then able to connect this to what had transpired in the preceding session. He needed me to affirm his progress in being able to take an important step in separating himself from Phil. This was evident in his calling it "presumptuous" of him to think that he was maturing in some way. When I focused on his need to hold himself responsible if something bad happened to Phil in this process of "letting go," he experienced me as not only failing to affirm his progress but also expressing my impatience with him for still holding on to Phil.

Two sessions later Mr. R reported the following:

> I had an interesting dream last night. It was unusual and it was about you. I come into your office. It's like in this office. I'm wearing my bathrobe and I'm with Mary, or at least I think I am. She and I lie down on the couch. You're sitting at your desk. There are a lot of little tobacco cuttings on the corner of your desk. I start to sweep them up. You say, "No, you don't have to bother." I say, "No, it's okay. I like to," and I continue doing that. Then somehow I find myself out in the street looking for your office. I can't seem to find it. I never quite get there.

Then, as an afterthought, he added: "Oh yes. Then there are these two dark men who accost me on the way. They call me over. I know that they're out to do me harm. And then there is this other straight man who comes up and calls them on it and they run away and I feel relieved."

His associations went immediately to the tobacco. "It reminds me of Pop (the stepfather who left when he was 13). I used to help him down in the basement, where he made cigars." Then he stopped himself for a moment and expressed reluctance to go on. I asked about this feeling.

> I guess I realize for the first time what a blow it was for me when he left. My mother sent him away. She used to be very unhappy with him. She actually kicked him out. I wanted so much for him to succeed. I really loved him. He was important to me. During the Depression things went from bad to worse. He was reduced . . . [here there was evident pain in his voice] to pushing around an ice cream cart for thirty-five to fifty cents a day in order to make a living. Eventually, my mother sent him away. I could never tell her how full of grief I was—and also angry. How much I loved and needed him. At the time I felt that I had to look after *her* feelings, that she might be disappointed if I showed her how I felt. I had to be on her side or she would feel betrayed.

I asked for his thoughts about being with Mary in the dream and about his wearing a bathrobe. He associated to his being sick, and he recovered a memory of a house call that I had made on him about 25 years earlier. He went on, "I think one of the reasons I was drawn to you is that you reminded me in some ways of Pop. You look like him." His associations to the men who accosted him in the street went to the obstacles that interfered with his getting together with me. "It would be terribly dangerous . . . I would be afraid . . . of being rejected . . . hurt . . . humiliated. This is the way I feel with all men. In fact, all people. That same danger."

I suggested that he was afraid to be more vulnerable with me, to open up more, since I could disappoint him or leave him, as Pop did. He continued by telling about how he had frozen up at a time when a close male friend, Steve, encouraged him to discuss something that was bothering him. "I was touched by that, but of course I couldn't run the risk of the next step." I commented that it was like the time 20 years ago when I offered him a similar opportunity and he was unable to tell me what was bothering him. His face lit up and he said, "Oh yes, that was very, very threatening, that would have been way too scary." He continued:

> Once when I was sick, Mary came to me when I was sitting on the toilet crying. She asked if I was in pain. I said again and again, "I'm no good, I'm no good." She moved away, I know that that was the way *she* would want to be treated when she's in pain, but I wanted her to tell me that I had been a good father and a good husband.

I interpreted to him that his relationship with Mary reminded him of how he had to keep his pain to himself whenever he was around his mother for fear that it would have an adverse effect upon her. He replied, "That's right. I couldn't tell my mother how much it hurt when Pop left. She couldn't have taken it."

Mr. R decided to discontinue his treatment 5 months after that session, about 18 months after his treatment began. He had been feeling much improved in every way, physically and emotionally. He felt that balance had been restored to his life. He mentioned that if he were to proceed further it would be because he "wanted to," not because he "needed to." It was hard for him to find the justification for proceeding. He also felt "quietly elated" at his progress and wanted to take time to consolidate his gains by himself. He was surprised and pleased to discover that he was a whole person *without* his son getting his life in order.

Although I was concerned about the permanency of structural change in so brief a treatment conducted mostly on a once-weekly basis, I nevertheless felt it best to affirm Mr. R's sense of security about his own progress and to do nothing to challenge his decision. I judged that there had probably been sufficient working through of his resistance to therapy so that in the event that he needed to return, the obstacles would not be too formidable.

## DISCUSSION

This case is remarkable in several ways. First I'd like to discuss the fact that a psychosomatic illness of such duration (at least 20 years) was able to be alleviated by an 18-month treatment consisting of mainly once-a-week psychotherapy. In discussing various aspects of this case with some colleagues in an informal manner, one of them remarked that the treatment really lasted 21 ½ years![1] Actually, it should be noted that the self–selfobject bond was in fact established some 25 years earlier, even though one could not claim that the patient was "in therapy." Nevertheless, I could not help but be struck by the comments that Mr. R made about the impact I had made on him so many years earlier during that house call, when I reminded him of Pop.

The handling of Mr. R's doubts about psychotherapy in the very beginning of his treatment, when his symptoms were so prominent, required special care. I agree, as previously mentioned, with Galatzer-Levy's (1982) approach toward hypochondriacal patients. He recommended that the therapist empathize with the patient's fears in order to help promote a bond of trust between patient and therapist. The

---

[1] I would like to thank Dr. Robert Stolorow for this interesting comment.

work of Basch (1988) demonstrated the ways in which therapists can effectively deal with patients' cultural prohibitions against acknowledging the psychological problems behind their physical symptoms.

I did in fact try to empathize with the patient's fears that there might still be a serious undetected organic illness that might require further investigation. This approach was facilitated by the use of empathy and introspection (Kohut, 1959) as the major data-gathering tool. To treat the patient's fears as defensive maneuvers or resistances against painful affect states probably would have provoked a rupture of the early selfobject tie, since it quite likely would have made him feel more isolated, misunderstood, and frightened. Besides, it was of value for me to remind myself that it could yet be possible that some organic condition might have been missed. One can never be too sure.

At this point, I would like to discuss the pivotal role of affect attunement as a selfobject function promoting the process of desomatization in this patient. Much has been written about the relationship between the phenomenon of somatization and the inability to contain and articulate painful affect states. Schur (1955) associated somatization with ego regression and posited that verbalization of affects could counteract the ego regression. McDougall (1974) presented the idea that psychoanalytic processes are the antithesis of psychosomatic processes. She believed that the psychoanalytic process reestablishes separated links and forges new ones, thereby transforming a life-threatening biological illness into a psychological illness, which is then treatable psychotherapeutically.

The term *alexithymia* was coined to denote the inability of some patients to put their feelings into words. These individuals show a poverty of affective awareness and tend to describe their experiences in purely functional terms, devoid of any affective components (the *pensée opératoire* of the French authors). It is widely held that these patients present formidable obstacles to psychodynamically oriented treatments. It is believed by several authors (Marty and de M'Uzan, 1963; Sifneos, 1967, 1973, 1975; Nemiah and Sifneos, 1970; Nemiah, 1975, 1977) that alexithymia is particularly characteristic of those who suffer from psychosomatic states. In his development of an outline of a self-psychological theory of somatization, Rickles (1986) considered alexithymia to be a form of self disorder; he linked the intrapsychic deficiency in alexithymia to the narcissistic personality disorders. This connection has important implications for the role of affect-integrative selfobject transferences in the treatment of somatized states.

It should be noted that Mr. R did not present the typical features of alexithymia. This may help explain why he did not present some of the formidable obstacles to treatment that alexithymics ordinarily manifest. In fact, unlike alexithymics, he was psychologically minded and capable of fantasy formation and extensive symbolization. This suggests that his pathology was largely conflict-linked rather than deficit-linked and could account for the success of such a brief treatment. Specifically, Mr. R experienced his own painful affect states as potentially endangering the narcissistic balance of vitally needed caretakers. Consequently, these affects endangered his own precariously established narcissistic equilibrium, and they required the establishment of defensive structures designed to protect him from intense feelings of shame and humiliation. Thus, fears of being shamed inevitably signaled the emergence of feelings of anxiety, inadequacy, anger, or grief. A pivotal therapeutic task was the identification of these conflicts and associated affects in the context of the transference and their subsequent working through.

The work of Stern (1985) details the emphasis that various researchers in the field of child development placed on affect attunement as an essential caretaker function in the establishment of the child's core subjective sense of self. As Basch (1985) has additionally pointed out, "from the beginning of life, affective reactions are the basis for the ordering function of the brain" (p. 34). "Through affect attunement," says Basch,

> the mother is serving as the quintessential selfobject for her baby, sharing the infant's experience, confirming it in its activity, and building a sensorimotor model for what will become its self concept. Affect attunement leads to a shared world . . . If . . . affect attunement is not present or is ineffective during those early years, the lack of shared experience may well create a sense of isolation and a belief that one's affective needs generally are somehow unacceptable and shameful [p. 35].

Krystal (1974, 1975) viewed affect development as consisting of the evolution of affects from early somatic states into experiences that could be verbally expressed. Stolorow, Brandchaft, and Atwood, (1987) describe the fundamental role of affectivity in the organization of self-experience. They point out that selfobject functions relate basically to the affective dimension of self-experience. In this light, they view Kohut's (1971) original concepts of mirroring and idealizing as special selfobject functions relating to affect integration.

Accordingly, the acquisition of self-soothing and other self-regulating capacities depend largely on the availability of an idealized figure with whose calm, confidence, and strength the child can merge. Such an experience was clearly lacking in the childhood of Mr. R. Pop was available for only a relatively short period of time. He was devalued and rejected by Mr. R's mother; in leaving her he essentially abandoned Mr. R. The connection to an idealized male figure was able to be reinstated many years later, in latent form, when I made that critical house call. The idealized transference then became mobilized more fully in the early phases of psychotherapy.

According to Stolorow and associates (1987):

> The importance of empathically attuned verbal articulation is not merely that it helps the child put his feelings into words; more fundamentally, it gradually facilitates the integration of affective states into *cognitive-affective schemata* — psychological structures that, in turn, contribute significantly to the organization and consolidation of the self. The caregiver's verbal articulations of the child's initially somatically experienced affects thus serve a vital selfobject function in promoting the structuralization of self-experience. . . . The persistence of psychosomatic states and disorders in adults may be seen as remnants of arrests in this aspect of affective and self-experience [p. 73].

The analysis of Mr. R's resistance to experiencing various painful affect states within the transference bond revealed a repetitive fear that his anxiety and depression would be regarded as shameful and cowardly by me. Further inquiry led to the understanding that Mr. R was repeating with me in the transference his response to the expectation that he fulfill idealizing selfobject functions for others, originally with respect to his mother, and later to his wife and son. This led to a fear of retraumatization, that is, fear of the rejection and abandonment that took place originally with both parents. It became clear that practically all affectivity on his part was infiltrated with the fundamental conflict between its expression and fear for the well-being of his caretakers and, consequently, fear of a rupture of these vitally needed ties.

A fundamental facet of the therapeutic bond was the establishment of a "holding environment" (Winnicott, 1965) in which Mr. R's affective experiences of anxiety, depression, anger, and intense grief could be safely contained and articulated. This process was able to take place fairly rapidly, given the unusual circumstances of Mr. R's history with me. It led to sufficient strengthening of his weakened underlying self-structure to enable him to become asymptomatic and to take steps to allow his son to separate more completely.

The use of the expression *desomatizing selfobject transference* in the title of this chapter is meant to denote the multiple selfobject functions encompassed in the bond between me and Mr. R. In addition to the aforementioned idealizing aspects, affect differentiation and affect articulation, self-delineation, and affect containment and tolerance were all functions that furthered the process of affect development and desomatization.

Each step along the way in the resistance analysis, it became necessary to confront Mr. R's dread of being shamed and rejected in the transference, since he had been shamed and rejected by his mother whenever he experienced feelings of fear, depression, inadequacy, anger, affection, or grief over the loss of his stepfather. There was the ever-present danger that I would echo the dreaded epithet "coward" that fell altogether too easily from mother's lips. Furthermore, Mr. R clearly feared that my narcissistic equilibrium was potentially threatened whenever these affects were experienced by him.

I find it interesting to note that it was not until I had arrived at this point in the writing of this chapter that I could truly understand just how impossible it was for Mr. R to accept my invitation to tell me what was bothering him 20 years ago in my family practice office! This experience renews my appreciation that Mr. R's response was certainly not out of cowardice but, rather, out of a valid inner sense of the enormous risk he would have exposed himself to with a well-intentioned but unsophisticated family physician.

## CONCLUSION

It has been my intent to illuminate through this case study some of the essential ingredients of a successful psychotherapy of a psychosomatic condition. The most important component of the treatment was the spontaneous establishment of what I am calling a desomatizing selfobject transference. This concept denotes a transference configuration that developed out of the patient's unmet developmental needs for merger with an idealized figure who could assist him in various aspects of affect integration. These included affect differentiation, delineation of self-boundaries, and, above all, the containment, tolerance, and articulation of painful affect states that furthered the process of desomatization.

This particular patient did not present the characteristics that are ordinarily associated with alexithymia. Although a part of his pathology consisted of serious structural deficits, the rapidity of the improvement and the relative brevity of the treatment reflected the presence of significant underlying conflict with respect to the identification and articulation of various painful affect states. These included anxiety, depression, anger, and grief, emotions that were experienced by the patient as likely to threaten the precarious narcissistic equilibrium of his caretakers, who were dependent on the patient for their selfobject requirements.

## REFERENCES

Basch, M. F. (1985), Interpretation: Toward a developmental model. In: *Progress in Self Psychology, Vol. 1,* ed. A. Goldberg. New York: Guilford Press, pp. 33–42.

———— (1988), *Understanding Psychotherapy.* New York: Basic Books.

Galatzer-Levy, R. M. (1982–1983), The opening phase of psychotherapy of hypochondriacal states. *Internat. J. Psychoanal. Psychother.,* 9:389–413.

Kohut, H. (1959), Introspection, empathy, and psychoanalysis. *J. Amer. Psychoanal. Assn.,* 7:459–483.

———— (1971), *The Analysis of the Self.* New York: International Universities Press.

Krystal, H. (1974), The genetic development of affects and affect regression. *The Annual of Psychoanalysis,* 2:98–126. New York: International Universities Press.

———— (1975), Affect tolerance. *The Annual of Psychoanalysis,* 3:179–219. New York: International Universities Press.

Marty, P. & de M'Uzan, M. (1963), La pensée operatoire. *Rev. Franc. Psychoanal.,* 27:Suppl.

McDougall, J. (1974), The psychosoma and the psychoanalytic process, *Internat. Rev. Psycho-Anal.,* 1:437–459.

Nemiah, J. (1975), Denial revisited: Reflections of psychosomatic theory, *Psychother. Psychosom.,* 26:140.

———— (1977), Alexithymia: Theoretical considerations. *Psychother. Psychosom.,* 28:199–206.

———— & Sifneos, P. (1970), Affect and fantasy in patients with psychosomatic disorders. In: *Modern Trends in Psychosomatic Medicine, Vol. 2,* ed. O. Hill. London: Butterworths.

Rickles, W. H. (1986), Self psychology and somatization: An integration with alexithymia. In: *Progress in Self Psychology, Vol. 2,* ed. A. Goldberg. New York: Guilford Press, pp. 212–226.

Schur, M. (1955), Comments on the metapsychology of somatization. *The Psychoanalytic Study of the Child,* 10:119–164. New York: International Universities Press.

Sifneos, P. (1967), Clinical observations on some patients suffering from a variety of psychosomatic diseases. *Proc. 7th Eur. Conf. Psychosom. Res.,* 13:339.

———— (1973), The prevalence of "alexithymic" characteristics in psychosomatic patients. *Psychother. Psychosom.,* 22:255–262.

———— (1975), Problems of psychotherapy of patients with alexithymic characteristics and physical disease. *Psychother. Psychosom.,* 26:65–70.

Stern, D. (1985), *The Interpersonal World of the Infant.* New York: Basic Books.

Stolorow, R. D., Brandchaft, B. & Atwood, G. (1987), *Psychoanalytic Treatment: An Intersubjective Approach.* Hillsdale, NJ: The Analytic Press.

Winnicott, D. W. (1965), *The Maturational Processes and the Facilitating Environment.* New York: International Universities Press.

# Chapter 7

# Dissociative Anesthesia and the Transitional Selfobject Transference in the Intersubjective Treatment of the Addictive Personality

*Richard Barrett Ulman*
*Harry Paul*

Atremendous interest exists on the part of mental health professionals as well as the general public in the topic of addiction in all its many and varied forms. It is surprising, therefore, and somewhat distressing, that until recently self psychology has been slow to follow Kohut in applying the principles of self psychology to addiction.

Scattered throughout Kohut's writings are numerous references to, passages about, and fuller contributions to the topic of addiction (see, e.g., Kohut, 1987, pp. 113–132). For instance, Kohut wrote the preface to a National Institute of Drug Abuse monograph entitled *Psychodynamics of Drug Dependence*, a fact unknown even to most self psychologists. This volume included contributions on addiction from leading psychoanalytic investigators such as Edward Khantzian, Herbert Wieder, Henry Krystal, Eugene Kaplan, William Frosch, and Harvey Milkman. In that preface Kohut (1977a, p. vii) wrote that the potential "explanatory power of the new psychology of the self" is particularly significant in the area of "the addictions." We believe that our work (Ulman and Paul, 1989, 1990, forthcoming), and especially this present contribution, constitutes an important step in more fully realizing Kohut's vision of self psychology as contributing to a better psychoanalytic understanding of and approach to treating addictions.

Our present contribution consists of three parts: first, we review and update both our self-psychological theory of addiction and intersubjective approach to treating the addictive personality; second, we provide two necessarily abbreviated treatment case histories—

109

Travis, a heroin and cocaine addict who was also addicted to using women as sexual playthings, and Errol, a compulsive gambler and sex addict—and, third, we summarize our main findings.

## REVIEW AND UPDATE: A SELF-PSYCHOLOGICAL THEORY OF ADDICTION

In our earlier work (Ulman and Paul, 1989, 1990) we defined what we call addictive trigger mechanisms, or ATMs, as specific substances, behaviors, or persons (e.g., alcohol, drugs, food, sexual partner, or gambling) that are used on a habitual and compulsive basis to arouse archaic narcissistic fantasies and accompanying moods of narcissistic bliss, which in turn provide desperately needed antianxiety and/or antidepressant relief from dysphoric affect states.

We have revised this definition and now speak of ATMs as an animate or inanimate thing or activity that arouses "selfobject fantasies" and moods of narcissistic bliss. In line with the recent work of Ulman and Brothers, as explicated in *The Shattered Self: A Psychoanalytic Study of Trauma*, we (Ulman and Paul, 1989, 1990) view archaic narcissistic fantasies, or what we now call selfobject fantasies (see Bacal, 1990, for discussion of what he calls "fantasy selfobjects") as

> affect-laden mental images symbolically depicting one or more of three prototypical scenes or scenarios: the first is that of mirroring, in which the person unconsciously experiences himself or herself as grandly exhibiting or displaying before an admiring, affirming, and approving other or audience; the second is that of idealization, in which the person unconsciously experiences himself or herself as safely and securely merged with an omnipotent object or thing; and the third is that of twinship, in which the person unconsciously experiences himself or herself as accompanied or joined by an alterego companion [Ulman and Paul, 1990, p. 2].

ATM-induced selfobject fantasies and moods of narcissistic bliss together create an intensely pleasurable experience based on alleviating painful affect states of self-dysphoria. Although an ATM may be, and often is, an inanimate thing, it is not therefore inert. On the contrary, an ATM is an active mind- and mood-altering agent that dissociatively alters self-experience by psychopharmacologically, biochemically, physiologically, or behaviorally arousing selfobject fantasies and accompanying moods of narcissistic bliss.

ATMs alleviate a variety of self-dysphoric affect states. Such states are caused by disintegration, depletion, or hypomanic anxiety (see Kohut, 1968, p. 487; see also Ulman and Paul, 1990 for a discussion of hypomanic anxiety), empty and depleted depression, feeling in-human and alone, and chronic narcissistic rage caused by frustration, deprivation, and impotence. ATMs temporarily alleviate these dys-phoric affect states because the archaic narcissistic fantasies and moods of narcissistic bliss that they arouse mimic certain antianxiety, antidepressant, humanizing, and/or pacifying selfobject functions.

In another important modification of our original theory, we have revised our previous view of the use of ATMs to induce a state of self-anesthetization (see Corssen and Domino, 1966, for the original use of this concept in the field of anesthesiology), or dissociated state of anesthesia (see Grinspoon and Bakalar, 1979, and Good, 1989, for a discussion of "dissociative anesthetic" and "substance-induced" dissociative states, respectively). The numbed state of anesthetization is based on the dissociative alteration of self-experience (including conscious awareness) through the ATM-induced activation and in-tensification of very potent selfobject fantasies. These fantasies of mirrored grandiosity, merger with an idealized and omnipotent source of strength, or twinship with an alterego are accompanied by moods of narcissistic bliss, characterized by feelings of euphoria, elation, ecstasy, communion, satiation, and nirvanaic obliviousness. As stated in our second paper on addiction (Ulman and Paul, 1990):

> The activation of archaic narcissistic fantasies and arousal of moods of narcissistic bliss by ATMs temporarily buffers against, anesthetizes, and provides dissociation from (1) painful and chronic states of self-fragmentation and anxious feelings of falling apart, going to pieces, and disintegrating and (2) painful and chronic states of self-collapse and depressive feelings of emptiness, depletion, and deadness [p. 3].

We have now added the selfobject functions of humanization and pacification to those selfobject functions of alleviating depression and anxiety. We view humanization, that is, the developmental process of coming to feel human, as a selfobject function of twinship. In humanization the selfobject—or, later in life, the selfobject in a mutant form as an ATM—functions on an unconscious fantasy level as a twin or alterego that provides the person with a "selfobject experience" (Lichtenberg, 1989) of alikeness and kinship.

We view pacification, that is, the intersubjective process of quelling narcissistic rage, as a selfobject function of idealization. Initially, the selfobject (or, later in life, an ATM) functions on an unconscious fantasy level as an idealized and omnipotent pacifier that provides the person with a selfobject experience of being assuaged, placated, and mollified. In other words, in humanization and pacification, selfob-jects and ATMs function as doubles or pacifiers, respectively.

In some important ways, therefore, an ATM mimics the functions of a selfobject in providing the self with an experience of relief from dysphoric affect states; however, it is not a genuine selfobject. Unlike a selfobject, it lacks the inherent capacity to add structure to and hence transform the self. On the contrary, an ATM functions as an ersatz selfobject. As such, it only mimics the structure-building functions of genuine selfobjects. However, although lacking the capacity to transform the self, an ATM possesses the often deadly power to deform and, in some cases, to destroy the self through trapping a person in addictive ritual and habit.

In our previous conceptualizations (Ulman and Paul, 1989, 1990), we viewed ATMs as taking over the psychological functions of archaic selfobjects. We have revised this view: we now conceive of ATMs, whether things or activities, as taking over for the addict the functions of a "transitional selfobject." On the basis of our continuing and extensive clinical experience with a wide variety of addicts, we realized that what we had previously referred to as an archaic selfobject transference was, in fact, a therapeutic revival of the relationship between the self and a transitional selfobject. A distinctive feature of the transitional selfobject is that it involves a relationship between self and thing or activity as selfobject rather than between self and a person as selfobject.

We find support for our concept of the transitional selfobject and its transference revival in the self-psychological work of Kohut (1971, 1977b), Marian Tolpin (1971), and Stolorow and Lachmann (1980). We have also found additional support for this concept in the psychoanalytic work of Winnicott (1951, 1959), Greenacre (1970), Modell (1970), Volkan (1973), and McDougall (1985).

At this juncture we need to discuss a critical issue concerning the transitional selfobject. Stated simply, we do not believe that the concept of a transitional selfobject represents what Goldberg (1988) calls an error of translating a concept rooted in one particular psychoanalytic theory to another. According to Goldberg (personal communication), "Heinz and I had long talks about transitional objects and he felt they were from an entirely different frame of reference. . . . He would never include the term in his work."

We do not doubt that Kohut may have viewed the concept of a transitional object as incompatible with self psychology. However, we contend that the concept of a transitional *selfobject*, as an intermediate form of narcissism, would, in all likelihood, have been accepted by Kohut. We believe that he would have found it compatible with his self-psychological theory of the different developmental phases of what Wolf (1980) refers to as "selfobject relations."

At the various points in both *The Analysis of the Self* (1971) and *The*

*Restoration of the Self* (1977b), Kohut either explicitly or implicitly addresses the topic of a transitional form of selfobject or selfobject experience. In *The Analysis of the Self*, Kohut (1971) refers to an "archaic, transitional selfobject" (pp. 28, 33), to a "transitional form of narcissism" (p. 34), and to the selfobject transference as an experience of the "analyst as a transitional object" (p. 275).

Although Kohut never explicitly pursued his idea of a transitional form of narcissism, he again implicitly alludes to it in *The Restoration of the Self*. For example, in discussing the underlying dynamics of "exhibitionistic or voyeuristic perversion," Kohut (1977b) indicates that such perversions originate in the breakup of an originally healthy selfobject constellation that "was . . . *transitionally* subject-oriented (selfobject) in one instance and *transitionally* object-oriented (selfobject) in the other" (p. 173, italics added).

Kohut's reference to the shifting and changing subjective experience of a selfobject from "subject" to "object-oriented" is consistent with and parallels Winnicott's (1951, 1959) description of transitional objects and phenomena. According to Winnicott, these objects and phenomena are subjectively experienced as existing in a psychological space of illusion and fantasy between "me" and "not me," that is, between subject and object. In fact, Winnicott (1966, p. 177) often referred to transitional objects and phenomena as "subjective object[s]."

Although Kohut clearly toyed with the idea of what we call the transitional selfobject or transitional selfobject experience, it is equally clear that he did not view the idea of a transitional form of narcissism as equivalent to Winnicott's transitional object or phenomena. For instance, in *The Analysis of the Self* Kohut (1971, p. 33, footnote number 17) distinguishes, on the basis of different observational stances, his theoretical viewpoint regarding transitional objects or phenomena from that of Winnicott (1951, 1959). Winnicott arrived at his conclusions about these phenomena from the direct observation of infants and children, whereas Kohut (1971) came to different conclusions on the basis of the "reconstruction and extrapolations from the analyses of adults with narcissistic personality disorders" (p. 33, footnote 17).

In *The Restoration of the Self* Kohut (1977b), in describing the developmental origins of Mr. W's hypochondriacal symptoms, states the following: "*Fantasies*, for example, of a yearning to take in the absent selfobject through the eyes and anus might at first have been *transitionally experienced* by a still cohesive self during the precursor stage in childhood when the hypochondria first occurred" (p. 156, italics added).

In the bibliography of *The Restoration of the Self*, Kohut cites

Volkan's paper "Transitional Fantasies in the Analysis of a Narcissistic Personality," which appeared in 1973 in *The Journal of the
American Psychoanalytic Association*. This citation clearly indicates that
Kohut was familiar with an important clinical discovery made by
Volkan, namely, the existence of a specific type of transference
fantasy, or what he called a "transitional fantasy," that occurs in
certain narcissistically disordered patients. According to Volkan, such
a patient may unconsciously create, as part of the transference, a
fantasy of the analyst as an inanimate transitional object. Volkan
states that this transference fantasy constitutes a therapeutic revival
of an early developmental relationship with a transitional object or
phenomenon.

In addition to finding support for our concept of the transitional
selfobject in Kohut's work, we also cite the works of Tolpin (1971),
Stolorow and Lachmann (1980). In addition, many recent psychoanalytic infant and child observation studies have documented the
importance of transitional phenomena in psychological development
and psychopathology. (See Sugarman and Jaffe, 1989, for a review
and discussion of this literature and its relevance to clinical work; see
also Sugarman and Kurash, 1981, 1982, for a discussion of the relation
between transitional phenomena and bulimia and marijuana abuse,
respectively.)

Following Kohut's reference in *The Analysis of the Self* to an
"archaic, transitional selfobject" and his allusion to a transitional form
of narcissism, Tolpin argues that as part of normal psychological
development the child creates through fantasy and the magic of
illusion a sustaining relationship with a "transitional selfobject" such
as a blanket. A transitional selfobject relationship facilitates, Tolpin
states, a developmentally significant and unconscious "transference-
like process." Through this process, the soothing and calming functions of the mother, functions that the child is as yet unable to
adequately provide for itself, are unconsciously transferred from the
mother to the blanket, which is then experienced by the child as
providing maternal selfobject functions.

In normal psychological development, the anxiety-relieving functions of the "transitional selfobject" are, according to Tolpin (1971),
transmutingly internalized as part of the unconscious process of
building psychic structure. Having developed sturdier internal psychic structure, the older child is more capable than the toddler of
self-regulation and hence is less dependent than the toddler on
"transitional selfobjects" to provide this function. In normal and
healthy development, the human qualities of transitional selfobjects
are, in part, passed back to human selfobjects, who once again
become important as the toddler continues to mature psychologically.

In a statement of particular relevance for our work, Tolpin (1971) indicates that the "personality is *addicted* to the functions of an external regulator" (p. 331, footnote 7, italics added) in those instances in which the unconscious process of transmuting internalization and psychic structure building becomes developmentally arrested. She refers to this psychic state as the "Goldilocks experience." We understand this phrase as a metaphor for the addicted person who, like Goldilocks in the fairy tale, frantically tries out a series of different things or activities in order to satisfy the painful craving for narcissistic nourishment and sustenance. And, anticipating our work, Tolpin contends that the "clarification" of the role of the "transitional selfobject" and the transmuting internalization of its psychic functions "may assist in understanding disorders like *addiction*" (p. 331, footnote 7, italics added).

In discussing the origin, function, and fate of what she refers to as the "transitional selfobject," Tolpin consistently distinguishes her position—and, by implication, that of self psychology—from Winnicott's British object relations position. Tolpin agrees with Winnicott concerning the central role of fantasy and illusion in the creation and functioning of transitional phenomena. However, differing from Winnicott, Tolpin (1971) proposes that the functions of the transitional object [or "transitional selfobject imago"] "do, in fact, 'go inside' as mental structure; and precisely because of this the treasured possession is neither missed, mourned, nor forgotten. It is no longer needed" (p. 320). Tolpin concludes: "The special case of the blanket as a *transitional selfobject imago* thus illustrates the general psychic tendency to preserve the lost psychic effects and functions of an imago needed for inner regulation" (p. 330, italics added).

Tolpin's distinction between her self-psychological view of the fate of the "transitional selfobject" and Winnicott's similar yet different view of the transitional object is critical to our argument. We believe that it supports our contention that in all probability Kohut would have found our concept of the transitional selfobject compatible with self psychology.

As further evidence of our claim, we point to Kohut's (1977b, p. 56) allusion to the different types of relationship existing between self and "nonhuman selfobject" and "human selfobject" (see also Abrams and Neubauer, 1975, for a discussion of the observed difference in infants between those exhibiting "human-orientedness" and those displaying "thing-orientedness"). Adumbrating our concept and in line with Kohut's distinction, Stolorow and Lachmann (1980), in their discussion of the therapy case of the patient James, discuss the nature and function of a tape recorder that he used during his sessions:

This use of the tape recorder as a *transitional selfobject,* which signaled a partial internalization of the analyst's mirror function, enabled him to regain a sense of conviction about his own substantiality and helped him to restore self-cohesion in the wake of narcissistic injuries (p. 139, emphasis added).

As evidence of a transitional selfobject transference, we discuss, in our two treatment case histories, the extensive and important use patients made of the telephone and telephone answering machine (see Lindon, 1988, for a discussion of the use of the telephone to conduct analysis).

Following Tolpin, we want to emphasize that the capacity of transitional selfobjects to transform self-experience is originally derivative. In marked contrast to the capacity of an ATM merely to alter self-experience dissociatively and temporarily, *nonhuman* selfobjects (things or activities) originally derive a capacity for transforming self-experience from the infant's or toddler's unconscious "transference" (see Tolpin, 1971) to them of the self-transformational power of early and original *human selfobjects.*

The transitional selfobject transference, in which the therapist is initially and unconsciously fantasized by the patient as a nonhuman selfobject (thing or activity) that replaces an ATM or ATMs, is therefore a therapeutic revival of a normal, early childhood relationship between self and a nonhuman selfobject. By working through the transitional selfobject transference, the addicted patient is helped to experience the therapist as more of a human selfobject and less as a nonhuman selfobject. Therefore, the addicted patient completes therapeutically the developmental cycle of transferring back to a human selfobject (in this particular instance, the therapist) the functions previously provided by nonhuman selfobjects—and provided later in life, as deformed versions of these things or activities, by ATMs.

As the addiction-prone person grows older, the original human qualities of transitional selfobject things and activities become progressively more faint. Later in life such a person attempts to develop a nuturing and sustaining relationship not with another human being but, rather, with addictive things and activities. These ersatz selfobjects become for the addict the basic and only means of regulating self-experience and, more precisely, self-image and mood.

In fact, instead of the normal developmental process involving the imbuing of things or activities with human qualities, other people are imbued with the quality of things in the arrested psychological development of the addiction-prone person. Therefore, rather than things becoming more human, humans become more thinglike. This psychological fact helps to explain why certain addicts experience and use both themselves and others as if they and others were nonhuman things.

From our retrospective clinical vantage point, we have discovered in the course of analytic reconstruction that many of our addicted patients were as children overattached to and overreliant on the transitional selfobject functioning of things and activities. Apparently, early disturbance in the child–parent relationship led to overdependence on things and activities to the virtual exclusion of human beings. In these cases, the normal developmental process, whereby the transitional selfobject functions of things and activities are, in part, passed on to human selfobjects, has gone awry. Instead, the transitional selfobject functioning of things and activities are passed on to potentially addictive trigger mechanisms or ATMs, creating the psychological basis for later full-blown addictive disorders of the self.

However, before leaving this brief and necessarily retrospective explanation of the etiology of addiction, we want to make the following point. We are offering what amounts to a partial and "retrodictive explanation" (see Von Wright, 1971, p. 59, on *ex post facto* or "*ex post actu*" reasoning as a valid logic of explanation in the human sciences as contrasted with predictive explanations in the natural sciences; see also Ulman and Zimmermann, 1985, 1987, for an application of the logic of the "retrodictive explanation" to psychoanalysis) of only one possible etiological cause of addiction. More specifically, we are suggesting that one factor that may contribute to addiction is the emergence of an ersatz selfobject relationship with one or more ATMs. We are hardly claiming, however, that this admittedly partial and retrodictive explanation constitutes a full account of the etiology of addiction. On the contrary, we recognize that there are many other significant biological, psychological, and social determinants that are crucial to a full explanation of the etiology of addiction.

In the logic of what Von Wright (1971) called the "practical syllogism," the reasoning behind our retrodictive explanation is as follows: Our major premise (based on extensive and intensive clinical experience in treating addicts) is that an addict's primary selfobject relationship is to an ATM (that is, a nonhuman thing or activity) rather than to another human being. Our minor premise, which follows logically from our major premise, is that an addict suffers from a developmental arrest that expresses itself in a very limited psychological capacity to form an emotionally sustaining and mature selfobject relationship with another human being. Our conclusion, following logically from our two premises, is that during childhood those who later become addicts are overattached to and overdependent on certain things or activities that function emotionally and psychologically as selfobjects.

In our conclusion we are not implying that every child who becomes attached to and dependent on the selfobject functioning of special things or activities will therefore necessarily become an addict. Rather, we are only concluding that many of the addicts whom we have treated were overattached to and overdependent on such special things or activities. And, on the basis of this conclusion, we infer that later in life these attachments devolve into ersatz selfobject relationships to an ATM or ATMs. In other words, we contend that an addict's early relationship to nonhuman things and activities is an important area for further clinical investigation into the determinants and etiology of addiction.

We view things and activities, serving as either transitional selfobjects or ATMs, as forming a functional continuum ranging from the healthy to the pathological. At the healthy end of this continuum is a special class of things or activities that function throughout life in relation to the self as healthy transitional selfobjects. As such, they perform genuine selfobject functions. As they provide the self with antidepressant, antianxiety, humanizing, and pacifying relief from dysphoric affect states, they are internalized and transmuted, or psychically metabolized, into healthy self-structure. As part of this process, they transform the self by adding psychic structure bit by bit to the self.

Early in life the transitional selfobject may be an infant's or toddler's special blanket, doll, or toy, an old baby bottle or other type of pacifier, a piece of clothing, or a part of the body, such as the thumb in thumbsucking. Later in life the transitional selfobjects may be an adolescent's or an adult's special pet; good-luck charm, ring, or other piece of jewelry; exercising, writing, drawing, or singing; watching television or listening to the radio, stereo, cassette, or compact disc player; or working at a computer.

At the pathological end of the continuum are ATMs that, as ersatz selfobjects, only mimic and give the illusion of functioning like structure-building transitional selfobjects. ATMs involve an addiction to things or activities; unlike genuine transitional selfobjects, they do not involve an incorporation of the selfobject functions of things or activities into the organization of the self in the form of new or renewed skills, capacities, or abilities that increase self-reliance and self-sufficiency. An addictive relationship between the self and the thing or activity does not add anything new to the self; rather, it weakens the self by creating a dependency on a foreign entity that ultimately decreases the capacity for self-regulation and self-realization.

In contrast to things or activities functioning as ATMs, some things and activities function as genuine transitional selfobjects, which, by definition, possess a derivative *self-transformational* power. Along the theoretical lines suggested by Freedman (1985), we distinguish self-object-based transformation of the self from an ATM-induced dissociative and purely temporary alteration of self-state. The former entails the creation and addition of psychic structure in the form of new capacities for self-regulation, self-actualization, and self-realization whereas the latter involves an anesthetizing process of blocking psychic pain. An ATM and a transitional selfobject differ as they function in relation to the self in the same way that taking medication to alleviate chest pains differs from surgically implanting a mechanical valve to assist the faulty functioning of the heart.

Let us give examples of these two very different types of relationship between self and a thing or activity. Writing, for instance, may serve as a healthy transitional selfobject activity. The self is strengthened as the individual struggles to master the difficult art of writing. Such strengthening of the self occurs in at least two ways. First, the individual gains an increased power of communication; second, in the process of learning to write, the individual transforms what may have originally been archaic grandiose fantasies of the self as a great writer like Tolstoy or Faulkner into a more realistic and useful image of the self as a skilled but not necessarily world-renowned writer. In developing a more realistic image of the self, the process of transforming archaic narcissistic fantasies of the self creates the psychic strength necessary for the often difficult and painful task of actualizing and realizing cherished goals.

In contrast, to continue the example of the art of writing, using highly addictive substances serves only as an addictive trigger mechanism (ATM) by which archaic grandiose fantasies of the self as a gifted and famous writer are artificially stimulated and intensified. Such powerful and enthralling fantasies may trap a person in a world of magical illusion, where wishing becomes a poor substitute for performing. Trapped in an ATM-induced world of fantasy, magic, and illusion, a person is likely to avoid going through the often difficult and painful process of moderating and tempering archaically organized and fantasy-based visions of the self and others. The failure on the part of an individual to undergo such a necessary developmental process seriously interferes with the transformation of fantasy into structure.

In order to make our point still clearer, let us draw an analogy from outside the field of individual psychology to demonstrate the difference between a healthy transitional selfobject relationship involving the strengthening and empowerment of the self and an addictive relationship in which the person is captivated and trapped by the illusions of strength and empowerment of the self. It is like the difference between increasing America's oil reserves through the discovery of oil fields at home and attempting to compensate for the absence of such reserves through reliance on foreign oil. Such dependence creates the illusion of greater supplies and strength; however, as we have now once again painfully learned, America is left in a vulnerable and precarious position. A foreign nation such as Iraq may arbitrarily and capriciously withhold or cut off oil altogether. Unfortunately, past and more recent painful experience with oil embargoes has taught Americans that without the oil of a foreign nation such as Iraq we are forced to deal with a serious fuel crisis based on the absence of sufficient known domestic oil reserves.

There are several illustrative examples from popular culture of different relationships between the self and a thing or activity. Linus, the "Peanuts" comic strip character, and his blanket are a well-known example of what we would describe as a relationship between childhood self and inanimate thing that functions as a transitional selfobject.

Another example is found in *Fantasia*, the classic Walt Disney animated feature. In this full-length cartoon, Mickey Mouse, playing the part of the sorcerer's apprentice, gets into serious trouble because of his relationship to a broom. In this tale the broom, originally an inanimate thing, magically comes to life (that is, it is anthropomorphized) as a willing and eager worker. At first the broom helps Mickey in completing his task of drawing and carrying water in a bucket from a well. Gradually, however, Mickey loses control of the once-friendly and cooperative broom. The broom begins to multiply itself uncontrollably, and soon it and its clones threaten to drown Mickey in a flood of water. We interpret this story as an allegory warning us about the dangers of establishing overdependent relationships on things that originally are useful to us but that later enslave us. We do not believe it is stretching the meaning of the story too far to interpret it as a powerful illustration of one of our major points. It beautifully illustrates that transitional selfobjects and ATMs exist on a continuum whereby an initially healthy transitional selfobject relationship between the self and a thing, in this case between Mickey and the broom, may turn into an unhealthy and life-threatening relationship to an ATM.

As the example of *Fantasia* demonstrates, certain things or activities, functioning as either transitional selfobjects or ATMs, are imagined as endowed not only with magical powers but with human qualities as well; they are anthropomorphized and personified. From an early psychoanalytic perspective, the fantasy-based experience of things or activities as endowed with human qualities is reflective of what Freud (1913) and Ferenczi (1913) described as the animistic stage in the development of a sense of reality.

Furthermore, in our modern technological society, a whole range of machines with human qualities and capacities has been created. These machines have voices that speak to us, ears that listen to us, and a form of artificial intelligence and memory that thinks with us. This group of humanoid and robot-like machines includes the television, telephone, answering machine, radio, cassette and CD player, computer, and other so-called "smart machines." All of these sophisticated and complex devices have the built-in capacity to provide the user with the experience of relating to a robotic entity that functions, in many important ways, like another human being. The capacity to function in such important respects like a human being empowers these machines with the ability to serve as transitional selfobjects.

Anthropomorphism, personification, animism, or robotics is involved in the fantasy-based experience of a thing or activity as a transitional selfobject. In fact, we contend that as we continue to move into an ever more technologically advanced society, we as individuals will develop transitional selfobject relationships with an ever-increasing array of highly sophisticated mechanical and electronic devices that function more or less like robotic humanoids. In other words, as exemplified by the main character from the popular movie *Robo Cop*, the boundaries separating the nonhuman from the human are increasingly blurring and disappearing both in reality and in the human imagination.

## REVIEW AND UPDATE: THE INTERSUBJECTIVE APPROACH TO ANALYTIC THERAPY WITH THE ADDICTIVE PERSONALITY

Our approach to the analytic therapy of addictive personality disorders, or APDs, is based on a therapeutic process that we have called intersubjective absorption. Intersubjective absorption involves the transfer or unconscious mental translocation of the mimicked selfobject functions of ATMs to the therapist, and the transmuting internalization of these selfobject functions into healthy self-structures that contribute to a mature self-image and reliable self-esteem regulation. As part of intersubjective absorption, the addicted patient transferentially experiences the therapist as an absorbent therapeutic sponge (that is, as a nonhuman and transitional selfobject) that soaks up and transforms dysphoric affect states of self-fragmentation, self-collapse, alienation, and narcissistic rage.

The transitional selfobject transference, as a clinical revival of an earlier developmental relationship, is based on the addicted patient's therapeutic relationship with the therapist as a nonhuman thing or activity. As part of this transference the patient unconsciously fantasizes about the therapist not as, say, an important person from the past but, rather, as a significant thing or activity from the past whose main purpose is to serve as an entity that provides various selfobject functions. (See Searles, 1960, on the patient's transference to the therapist as part of the nonhuman environment.)

The addict's ersatz selfobject relationship with an ATM may be replaced in therapy by a mirroring, idealizing, or twinship transference fantasy of the therapist. Under the influence of these fantasies, the addicted patient experiences the therapist, functioning transferentially as a nonhuman selfobject (that is, thing or activity), as providing antianxiety, antidepressant, humanizing, and/or pacifying relief from dysphoria.

Intersubjective absorption occurs therapeutically in the context of four paradigmatic transitional selfobject transference relationships, corresponding to four types of APD. In the first paradigm the mood of the manic and/or rageful addict who develops a transference relationship with the therapist, unconsciously fantasized about as a nonhuman thing or activity that provides the idealizing selfobject functions of sedating, tranquilizing, or pacifying, shifts from one of agitation, irritability, and tenseness to one of calmness, relaxation, and tranquility.

In the second paradigm the mood of the depressed addict who develops a transference relationship with the therapist, unconsciously fantasized about as a nonhuman thing or activity that provides the mirroring selfobject function of stimulation, inflation, and elation, changes from one of depletion, deflation, emptiness, apathy, lethargy, and boredom to one of euphoria, excitement, and satiation.

In the third paradigm the mood of the manic–depressive addict who develops a transference relationship with the therapist, unconsciously fantasized about as a nonhuman thing or activity that provides both idealizing and mirroring selfobject functions, alternates from one of agitated depletion to one of tranquil euphoria.

The fourth paradigm involves the lonely addict who develops a transference relationship with the therapist, unconsciously fantasized about as a nonhuman thing or activity that provides the twinship selfobject function of humanization. As part of this selfobject transference experience, the lonely addict's mood alters from one of feeling inhuman to one of feeling alikeness to, as well as kinship and communion with, other human beings.

In all four of these paradigmatic transitional selfobject therapeutic relationships, the therapist may need to allow himself or herself to be used by the addicted patient as some *thing* in the transference fantasy that can provide the antianxiety, antidepressant, pacifying, and/or humanizing selfobject functions previously provided by the ATM. We believe that such a clinically based *selfobject provision*[1] is empathic and therapeutic for the following reasons. First, the therapist emphatically understands that in order for the first phase of intersubjective absorption to occur, the addicted patient must establish and maintain a transference fantasy of the therapist as some *thing* that provides the same antianxiety, antidepressant, humanizing, and pacifying relief as an ATM. Second, the therapist also empathically understands that as part of the therapeutic relationship and in order to effectively take over the selfobject functions of the ATM, he or she must be willing and able to clinically provide these selfobject functions.

We are therefore, making, an important theoretical and clinical distinction between an active and passive mode of empathy (see Margulies, 1989, for a discussion of "active empathy"). As conceived in traditional analytic and prevailing self-psychological perspectives, empathy is viewed as a passive mode of listening and understanding that never, or only rarely, entails direct clinical action on the part of the therapist. On the contrary, we view empathy as an at times very active therapeutic mode of providing that which the other—whether infant, child, or patient—is developmentally or clinically unable to provide for himself or herself. In this context, the therapist is, therefore, like the good-enough parent or caretaker who serves as a *selfobject in action*, rather than one merely in thought or fantasy.

Making provision for desperately needed selfobject functions (functions that a patient is often unable to provide for himself or herself) within the necessarily limited clinical confines of the therapeutic relationships does not, we contend, constitute a deviation from the analytic principle of abstinence. Clinically circumscribed provision of selfobject functions involves neither gratifying unhealthy sexual or aggressive needs nor countertransferentially playing the

---

[1]We are indebted to Peter B. Zimmermann, Ph.D., who originally conceived of the idea of clinically based selfobject provisions as empathic and therefore therapeutic.

role of a selfobject. On the contrary, making provisions for the healthy and legitimate selfobject needs of such archaically organized patients as the addict is, we believe, an important self-psychological addition to Eissler's (1953) famous clinical extension of the parameters of classical analytic technique. As our treatment case histories illustrate, our new self-psychological extension of analytic technique meets Eissler's criteria for a legitimate "parameter of a technique" (Eissler, 1953, p. 110); that is, therapeutically derived selfobject provisions are clinically necessary, minimal, and self-eliminating.

Countertransference as well as transference plays an important role in intersubjective absorption. The interaction of transference and countertransference creates what Ulman and coworkers Stolorow (Ulman and Stolorow, 1985), Brothers (Ulman and Brothers, 1987, 1988), and Paul (Ulman and Paul, 1989, 1990) have referred to as a "transference–countertransference neurosis." This intersubjective configuration is based on an unconscious dynamic in which a patient's transference fantasy interacts with a therapist's corresponding countertransference fantasy. As a result, a powerful unconscious mental organizing action is created that influences and shapes the respective subjectivities of the two participants in the therapeutic relationship.

In our necessarily abbreviated report on the therapy case histories of Travis and Errol, we draw special attention to patients' and therapists' shared fantasies (Freud, 1908; Arlow, 1982, unpublished; Blum, 1986, 1988; Lichtenberg, 1989) about drugs and gambling as ATMs.

## THERAPY CASE: TRAVIS

Travis, a stocky, well-built, 42-year-old white married man of average height, works as a benefits counselor. Throughout much of the five-year and still-ongoing analytic therapy, Travis was grave, with little facial expression and a monotone voice. He entered therapy with a history of chronic anxiety and depression; violent, antisocial, and criminal behavior; and alcohol and drug addiction. For the purposes of this presentation, however, we focus on his drug abuse rather than on his alcoholism.

During the early phase of the therapy, the therapist diagnosed Travis as, in our terms, a manic–depressive addict. He was addicted to a potent combination of heroin and cocaine known in street parlance as "speedballs." He also was addicted to using women as sexual playthings. We named this patient "Travis" because he reminded us so much of Travis Bickle, the main character from the

Martin Scorsese movie *Taxi Driver*. Like the movie character, our Travis was a brooding loner, obsessed with violent fantasies, weapons, and sexy women.

It was extremely difficult throughout the early phase of therapy to get a very detailed picture of Travis's early childhood and adolescence. He was amnesic for the details of much of this period in his life. The therapist did learn, however, that he grew up as the only child of middle-class parents who lived in an urban neighborhood in a large northeastern city.

Travis recalled growing up at home in a constant state of fear and terror. He explained that his alcoholic father and emotionally disturbed mother were always screaming and fighting with each other. He described one of his few memories of his early childhood as follows: "I'm lying in my bed at night, listening to my father and mother screaming and brawling in the living room; I'm scared to death that my father will kill my mother and then come into my bedroom and kill me too!"

Travis fled as an adolescent from the violence and terror he experienced at home and sought refuge in the streets with his friends. On the streets, however, he became involved with gangs and even more violence; he also began using alcohol and drugs. Travis went into the military at the age of 18. At this age he had already been involved in violent, antisocial, and criminal activity, including armed robbery and burglary; he had also developed a drug and alcohol problem. After leaving the military and marrying, Travis gradually gave up his life of crime; however, he remained obsessed with violence and guns and resumed his addictive drinking and drug taking.

Eventually, a dream that Travis reported and its interpretation helped to lift the amnesic veil shrouding in darkness important details of his childhood, especially those concerned with significant transitional selfobject relationships. In the dream Travis shot and killed an ex-lover and her current male companion. In discussing Travis's associations to this dream, the therapist learned an important fact, namely, that the gun in the dream was a .357 Magnum revolver, a powerful handgun that Travis had actually used in the past during the commission of his crimes and that he had kept in his possession over the years.

In talking about this particular gun and his attachment to it, Travis remembered that as a child he had been similarly attached to a tripod-mounted toy machine gun that fired rubber bullets. He recalled that as a youngster he spent hours lost in his own private fantasy world as he played with his toy machine gun. Travis fantasized that he was a brave soldier fighting off and killing the enemy, like John Wayne in a classic war movie.

In our terms, Travis had developed a transitional selfobject relationship with his toy machine gun. This relationship was instrumental in fueling a grandiose fantasy in which he experienced himself as a heroic and powerful figure who, like John Wayne, was larger than life. This fantasy-based experience of himself helped Travis find a measure of pleasure and enjoyment in an otherwise emotionally desolate and painful environment at home.

Later, as an adult, Travis used the .357 Magnum revolver as well as the ATMs of speedballs and female sexual playthings to function in a capacity similar to that made possible by his earlier transitional selfobjects; that is, all these objects served to temporarily make him feel strong and powerful. Serving in this capacity, they anesthetized and dissociated him from the pain of feeling powerless, impotent, deprived, and frustrated, a dysphoria that had plagued Travis ever since childhood. More specifically, these ersatz selfobjects provided antianxiety, antidepressant, and pacifying medicinal functions.

In the context of talking about his .357 Magnum revolver, Travis revealed that he used it as part of his drug-taking ritual. High and in a drug-induced stupor, Travis played with and fondled his .357 Magnum. Consistent with this phallic and masturbatory image, he described his getting high on speedballs as similar to an orgasm. He explained the similarity as follows:

> First, I slowly build up tension as I "cop dope" and ready my "works" [that is, the syringe and other drug paraphernalia used in preparing and injecting drugs]; then I experience an explosive release of the built-up tension as I inject the drugs into my veins and they rush through my body and hit my brain; and finally, I have a sense of serenity and obliviousness as the drugs take effect.

An initial transference–countertransference dynamic had emerged during this early phase of the therapy. Travis repeatedly and profusely expressed his gratitude to the therapist for having agreed to work with him. His sense of indebtedness was part of a spontaneously emerging transference idealization. We believe that as part of this selfobject transference, he unconsciously fantasized about the therapist as some *thing* with which he could merge as an omniscient and omnipotent source of strength.

We infer that Travis imagined that his close emotional proximity to the therapist would enable him to magically *absorb* what he experienced as the therapist's strength and power. Apparently, Travis imagined that absorbing these qualities and capacities would magically imbue him with the strength of character and willpower to overcome his drug addiction. In an important sense, therefore, and as part of the first phase of intersubjective absorption, Travis had transmitted the idealizing selfobject functions of the ATM speedballs to the therapist, whom he experienced transferentially as providing these functions.

The therapist had a twofold countertransference reaction to serving for Travis in the transference as some *thing* similar in function to the toy machine gun and the speedballs, both of which had provided Travis with a selfobject experience of relief from dysphoria. On one hand, the therapist accurately read—without, however, interpreting—the unconscious meaning of the transference idealization. As part of the intersubjective absorption, his empathic understanding of this dynamic facilitated the transfer of the idealizing selfobject functions from the speedballs to the therapist.

On the other hand, however, the therapist failed to appreciate the emergence of an important mirroring dimension to the selfobject transference. Travis, in a subtle yet significant shift in the content of his therapy sessions, spoke less about his gratitude and indebtedness to the therapist and more about his daily struggle to resist the temptation to use Speedballs. With the advantage of hindsight, the therapist later came to understand that Travis had unconsciously and transferentially fantasized about the therapist as a mirroring audience before whom he exhibited himself.

As part of his fantasy-based transference experience, Travis imagined himself as a valiant and heroic Odyssean figure locked in mortal combat with an evil and deadly nemesis—drugs. Like the Sirens from Greek mythology, Travis's nemesis tempted him with a bewitching and alluring yet fatal song. In fact, Travis reported a dream to which his associations were similar in thematic content to this mythological description of his fight against drugs.

Travis fantasized about the therapist as an inanimate thing that served as a mirror reflecting back an exhalted image of himself. He was, therefore, transferentially using the therapist as some *thing* similar in function to his childhood John Wayne fantasy. In other words, both his childhood grandiose fantasy and its current transference replica contained an image of himself as a larger than life figure who, like his matinee idol John Wayne, performed heroic feats before a depersonalized audience mirroring back awe and amazement.

Understanding this particular transference dynamic helped the therapist appreciate an underlying dynamic in the therapy that he had previously misunderstood. He had previously thought that

Travis defensively intellectualized in an attempt to rationalize and excuse his repeated drug relapses. On the basis, in part, of this misunderstanding, the therapist had responded countertransferenti-ally to these displays with thinly disguised contempt, annoyance, and exasperation. He berated and harangued Travis each time he relapsed and then offered what the therapist felt were defensive and lame excuses. Finally, the therapist understood that these explanations were actually a grand display by Travis of verbal and intellectual prowess, which he imagined would recapture a positive image of himself as reflected in the eyes of the therapist.

Session after session the therapist listened to Travis describe in minute detail each of his many drug-taking episodes. Travis also reported numerous and extremely pleasant dreams involving drugs. For example, in one such dream, Travis noted: "I'm at a party. I impulsively eat heroin and then I snort it. I feel a warm glow pass over my body."

Countertransferentially, the therapist, who himself had a previous history of alcohol and drug addiction, found himself having dreams of getting drunk and high. In his dreams the therapist fantasized about alcohol and drugs as magic potions that had the power to endow him with special powers of perception. In other words, the therapist shared with Travis the unconscious fantasy that intoxicants could enable one to magically escape the confines of daily existence and the limits of conventional reality.

Sharing this fantasy with Travis helped the therapist in empa-thizing with him about the powerful allure of drugs. However, it also led to a countertransference reaction formation. The therapist at-tempted to counteract his own reactivated cravings for alcohol and drugs by unconsciously acting toward Travis like a strict disciplinar-ian; acting countertransferentially in this self-appointed role, he sternly lectured Travis about the absolute necessity of maintaining his abstinence from drugs.

The therapist's countertransference reaction formation interfered with his ability to empathically understand Travis's desperate need for mirroring. As a result, the antidepressant selfobject functions of the speedballs was not being intersubjectively absorbed through the transitional selfobject transference. The therapist's stern warnings to Travis about the danger of continuing to use the speedballs had a paradoxical and unintended effect.

The admonitions contributed not only to Travis's continued use of the speedballs but to a series of addictive relationships with women functioning as sexual playthings. As a result of the first of these relationships, Travis dropped out of therapy for a year. A second relationship, following his return to therapy, was preceded by a near-fatal overdose on speedballs.

As a result of this traumatic incident, Travis agreed that before using drugs again he would first call and speak to the therapist. This agreement thus formalized what had already been an informal yet important selfobject provision of the therapeutic relationship. The therapist actively encouraged Travis to use the phone and the therapist's answering machine as a means of continuing between sessions his transference relationship with the therapist as a transitional selfobject. In other words, the therapist did not simply and passively exercise his empathic understanding of Travis's selfobject needs by interpreting them to Travis. Instead, on the basis of his empathic understanding, he extended the parameters of analytic technique by providing, albeit in a limited manner, for these selfobject needs.

Both the phone and the answering machine were part of a vital emotional lifeline connecting Travis to the therapist. In exploring this aspect of the therapeutic relationship, Travis revealed that he imagined the therapist on the phone as a disembodied yet soothing and calming voice emanating from a machine that he controlled. As vital parts of the therapy, the phone and the answering machine were concrete manifestations of the transference relationship that Travis had developed with the therapist—that is, *things* that were taking over the selfobject functions of ATMs.

We arrived at this clinical inference on the basis, in part, of Travis's description of his fantasy of the therapist "injecting" him with a "magic potion" that dulled and numbed all of his emotional pain and simultaneously transformed him into a heroic and larger-than-life figure. In this sense, therefore, the therapist was serving as a transitional selfobject that had effectively taken over the antianxiety, antidepressant, and pacifying functions previously provided by the injection of speedballs.

During a more recent phase of the therapy Travis reported a series of dreams. The interpretation of these dreams was critical in providing clinical evidence of intersubjective absorption and, with it, the transmuting internalization of the therapist as some *thing* that was taking over the selfobject functioning of ATMs. At this juncture in the therapy Travis had been abstinent from drugs for several years; he was, however, in the emotional throes of his second addictive sexual relationship. The dreams revealed that Travis had unconsciously equated his latest sexual playmate with speedballs. In associating to these dreams, Travis recalled that as active drug addicts he and his junkie pals used to brag about "scoring woman" just as they scored (that is, obtained) drugs. In this same context they also spoke about intercourse as "shooting pussy." Therefore, on an unconscious fantasy level Travis's mistress existed for him as only a thing, like speedballs. As such, she functioned as an ATM, providing needed dissociative and anesthetizing relief from unbearable dysphoria.

On a more positive note, the dreams also revealed a steady progression in the evolution of Travis's transference relationship with the therapist. The therapist, no longer imagined by Travis as merely a disembodied voice emanating from an inanimate machine, had assumed a more personal and human presence in the therapeutic relationship and was appearing in Travis's dreams as a benign and admired paternal imago. An example of one such dream is the following:

> I'm in a room talking with a male friend about the difficulty in establishing a daily exercise program despite its health benefits. As I'm talking, I notice that the door to the room is open. Standing outside in a crowded shopping mall is a naked man with a clip board. I'm struck by the fact that the man doesn't seem to be bothered at all about being naked in the middle of a crowd of people; instead, he seems very relaxed and at ease. I also notice that the man has a big cock. I think to myself in the dream that I wish that I had a big cock like the naked man.

In associating to the dream, Travis connected the naked man with the therapist, whom, he said, he sometimes experienced in therapy sessions as unabashedly exhibiting his cockiness. In working with the dream, Travis and the therapist moved beyond the manifest oedipal level of its unconscious meaning. The dream was interpreted at a latent level as follows: It symbolically indicated that Travis had internalized and transmuted the therapist, whom he unconsciously fantasized as endowed with impressive phallic attributes and power, as an idealized paternal imago. Moreover, Travis's dream wish to possess a "big cock" like the therapist's was interpreted self-psychologically as a symbolic expression of his desire to transform himself into a phallically endowed and hence more potent version of his former self, a self he had subjectively experienced in the past as weak and impotent.

On the unconscious fantasy level the dream also revealed that for Travis the internalized and transmuted imago of the therapist was functioning as a phallic ideal that psychically replaced the .357 Magnum revolver as well as the ATMs of speedballs and female sexual playthings. All of these *things* had served in the past as "functional equivalents" (Adler and Goleman, 1969) for his earlier transitional selfobject relationship with his toy machine gun.

Clinical evidence of the therapist serving in the transference as a phallic ideal by which Travis measured himself emerged in another dream that Travis reported. In the dream Travis said:

> You and I are standing together in a bathroom and are pissing in urinals. As we're pissing, I look down at a mirror located in-between the two urinals. I can see our two cocks. I notice that yours is larger than mine, but I say to myself that mine is big enough.

The dream can also be interpreted as revealing that Travis, in looking into the intersubjective mirror created by the therapeutic relationship, now saw himself as "big enough."

## THERAPY CASE: ERROL

Errol, a strikingly handsome and debonair foreign-born 36-year-old, entered therapy 3 ½ years ago. He had been married three times and worked as an office machine salesman. We named this patient after Errol Flynn because he shared with the movie idol a swashbuckling bravado and reputation as quite the ladies' man. When Errol began therapy, he was dually addicted to gambling and a variety of sexual activities, including the habitual use of peep shows, massage parlors, and prostitutes, and compulsive masturbation. During this still-ongoing analytic therapy, Errol has been seen once or twice a week, depending on changing clinical circumstances.

The following picture of Errol's early life emerged during the initial phase of the therapy: As a youngster, and later as an adolescent, Errol followed a pattern of compulsive masturbation involving the use of his penis and a Hoover vacuum cleaner as transitional selfobjects. As part of his masturbatory ritual, Errol inserted his penis into the Hoover vacuum cleaner nozzle and then, with the machine turned on, reached orgasm through the sucking and vibrating motion of the nozzle on his penis. Errol's masturbatory use of the Hoover is a good example of a transitional selfobject relationship to an inanimate thing and activity that together provided an intensely pleasurable selfobject experience.

Errol used masturbation as a transitional selfobject activity that aroused archaic narcissistic fantasies and moods of narcissistic bliss. We conjecture that Errol, in a masturbation-induced state of dissociation, experienced anesthetizing relief from what he described as a depressive and lonely feeling of being an odd creature unlike the other members of his family, all of whom he was convinced were normal human beings. Errol said that while masturbating he fantasized about himself as a superhuman male surrounded by beautiful and adoring females, all of whom were irresistibly attracted to him because of his phallic endowments and orgasmic prowess.

We infer that the antidepressant and humanizing functions of Errol's childhood and adolescent transitional selfobjects were passed on to the ATMs of gambling and sex. Later, as an adult, Errol used both of these ersatz selfobjects to stimulate fantasies of himself as surrounded by and connected to others who he imagined worshipped and adored him. In this ATM-induced dissociated state, Errol experienced anesthetizing relief from the dysphoria of feeling depressed, all alone, and unconnected to others.

Early in the therapy Errol reported a self-state dream that seemed to symbolically express his characteristic experience of himself as living in a world populated by inanimate things and devoid of other human beings: "I am walking *alone* down the street. There are no other people around. I'm just surrounded by tall skyscrapers. I'm scared. No one else is there." In associating to this vivid dream image of the inner void of his emotional world, Errol spoke about feeling like a psychological version of the Elephant Man, that is, an oddity and freak of nature.

During this early phase of the therapy Errol initiated a pattern that lasted throughout treatment: he asked the therapist, "What do you think?" after making an observation or offering an explanation. The therapist was puzzled about the underlying meaning and function of Errol's recurring question. As the therapy progressed, however, it became clear that Errol, in order to feel more human and hence less alone, needed to feel that he and the therapist saw eye-to-eye about everything. In other words, the question gave expression to the twinship and humanizing function of the selfobject transference.

The therapist's empathic understanding of this transference dynamic facilitated intersubjective absorption and more specifically, the transmuting internalization of the humanizing function of the ATM gambling. Errol gave up his dependence on gambling as an ATM and replaced it transferentially with the therapist as a transitional selfobject.

Evidence of Errol's transference relationship with the therapist as a transitional selfobject emerged in the context of his use of the therapist's telephone answering machine. No longer using gambling to combat his painful feeling of being a lonely loser, Errol called the therapist on the telephone and left long messages on his answering machine. Apparently, he used the therapist's voice as a stimulus for an elaborate fantasy scenario in which he imagined himself speaking to the therapist just as if he were in session. Always being able to speak with the therapist via his telephone answering machine was important to Errol because he felt continuously connected to the therapist and hence did not feel as alone or inhuman as before. In an important sense, therefore, Errol's childhood transitional selfobject relationship with the Hoover vacuum cleaner was transferentially replicated with the therapist's telephone answering machine. As a transitional selfobject, this inanimate thing (with the human voice of the therapist) was instrumental in helping to take over the human- izing function of the ATM of gambling. Allowing for direct and indirect telephone contact between sessions is an example of a selfobject provision that was critical in facilitating intersubjective absorption.

Although progress was made during the middle phase of the therapy in treating his gambling addiction, Errol remained actively addicted to compulsive sexual activity, which continued to function as an ATM. Obviously, neither the therapy nor his life was providing Errol with the needed "selfobject experience" of being mirrored as part of exhibiting his archaic grandiose self. As part of enacting such a grandiose fantasy and as an expression of a transference twinship, Errol tried unsuccessfully to purchase an expensive home in the therapist's well-to-do suburban neighborhood. Errol's inability to buy his dream home plunged him into a dysphoric state of loneliness and emptiness; he complained of not only feeling deflated but also of having lost his feeling of identity with the therapist. As a result of this disturbance of his transference fantasy of mirrored grandiosity and twinship, Errol continued to use sex as an ATM; he also resumed his use of compulsive gambling as another ersatz selfobject. He used both of these ATMs to dissociate from and anesthetize himself against the painful feeling of being a lonely loser.

At this critical juncture in the therapy, Errol reported the following dream: "I'm with a group of people and we're all gambling. Everyone is winning. We're all happy and excited." Errol associated to the dream with the observation that it depicted his need to feel like a "winner among winners." As ATMs, gambling and sex apparently provided Errol with the comforting illusion that he was a winner surrounded by other winners instead of a freak like the Elephant Man.

In the last phase of the therapy the therapist was better able to understand previously obscure dynamics of the transference–coun- tertransference neurosis, which had interfered with the progress of the therapeutic process of intersubjective absorption. He came to understand that a primary feature of the transference–countertransference neurosis involved sharing a fantasy with Errol about gambling as an ATM.

In the course of listening empathically to Errol's vivid and detailed descriptions of his latest gambling adventures, the therapist found himself responding countertransferentially with his own daydreams of winning the lottery. In fact, the therapist countertransferentially acted out his fantasies by buying lottery tickets; he imagined himself as the lucky winner of a fabulous fortune that would guarantee him and his family a lifetime of leisure and pleasure.

In hindsight the therapist understood that he had shared with Errol an unconscious fantasy of gambling as an activity that temporarily engendered an experience of feeling more human, less lonely, and hence less depressed. The therapist, who himself had just recently bought his new and expensive home, had been feeling all alone in dealing with his recent and considerably increased financial responsibilities. The gambling fantasy of winning the lottery was the therapist's magical way of solving all his financial woes. As part of this magical solution, he imagined himself elevated to the exalted status of a wealthy and powerful multimillionaire.

The therapist's ersatz selfobject relationship with the ATM of gambling, a relationship which he shared with Errol, temporarily dissociated and anesthetized him against his own dysphoric state of aloneness and depression. However, in such an ATM-induced dissociated state, the therapist was countertransferentially less available to Errol in the transference as a transitional selfobject that provided him with humanizing and antidepressant relief from his dysphoria. In other words, the therapist's countertransference fantasies of gambling had seriously interfered with Errol's transference fantasy of the therapist as a thing that he used and controlled totally according to his own wishes and needs. For example, lost in his own countertransference fantasies, the therapist was less available to Errol not only in session but also on the phone. He realized that in the past, as an expression of his transitional selfobject transference relationship, Errol had maintained between-session contact with him by means of the phone and answering machine. Previously, the therapist had listened patiently to Errol's telephone conversations and long phone messages left on the answering machine. When speaking directly to Errol over the phone, he had always answered Errol's question "What do you think?" with the mirroring and twinning response "Absolutely."

However, during the phase of therapy when countertransferential difficulties arose, the therapist had responded impatiently to Errol's phone calls and messages. He disturbed Errol's transference fantasy by becoming emotional and, in the process, too animated and too human. As a result, he was no longer experienced by Errol as an inanimate thing that was totally under his control. As part of this countertransference reaction, the therapist made predictions of catastrophic doom ensuing from Errol's gambling relapse and continued sexual addiction. Of course, the therapist's unavailability to Errol in the transference as a transitional selfobject served only to exacerbate Errol's dependence on the ATMs of gambling and sex.

With the help of peer supervision, the therapist understood that his countertransference fantasies of gambling served as a magical solution to his own financial pressures. This enabled him to resume functioning in the transference as a transitional selfobject that Errol could experience as a thing to be used as he saw fit. As a result, Errol was able to resume the therapeutic process of intersubjective absorption and, more specifically, the unconscious process of internalizing and transmuting the therapist's selfobject functions. Resuming this therapeutic process permitted Errol to gradually give up his dependence on gambling and sex as ATMs used to engender a dissociative experience of anesthetizing relief from dysphoria.

## CONCLUSION

Let us summarize our major findings: First, we stated that a transitional selfobject relationship to things or activities is part of a normal, age-appropriate intermediate phase in the unconscious organization of self-experience. During this intermediate phase of development a sense of self is unconsciously organized through a relationship between self and nonhuman things or activities that are experienced by the person on an unconscious fantasy level as providing selfobject functions. As such, these things and activities constitute transitional selfobjects that provide antianxiety, antidepressant, humanizing, and/or pacifying relief from the respective dysphoric affect states of fragmentation, collapse, aloneness, and/or narcissistic rage.

Second, we made an important distinction between genuine transitional selfobjects and ersatz selfobjects, or ATMs. We argued that through developmental transmuting internalization the former add psychic structure to, and hence transform, the self whereas the latter, which only mimic the functions of genuine selfobjects, add nothing new in the way of psychic structure to the self. Rather, they only dissociatively and temporarily alter self-experience. We stressed that relationships to things or activities functioning as transitional selfobjects, unlike addictive relationships to ATMs, may last throughout life as a healthy part of the self's relation to its "non-human environment" (Searles, 1960).

Third, we offered a retrodictive explanation of one determinant in the etiology of addiction. We argued that this determinant consists of an arrest in the psychological development of the addict based on an overattachment and overdependence on nonhuman things or activities that are experienced on an unconscious fantasy level as functioning as transitional selfobjects. Moreover, we further explained retrodictively that later in life such an overattachment and overdependence may interfere in the life of the potential addict with the normal development of mature selfobject relationships with other human beings. The addiction-prone person creates instead an ersatz selfobject relationship with one or more ATMs. In other words, the self of the addiction-prone person remains emotionally related primarily to the nonhuman environment rather than to the human world.

Fourth, we argued that an active addict uses ATMs to dissociatively alter self-experience by engendering selfobject fantasies and the accompanying moods of narcissistic bliss. We referred to this addictive process as dissociative anesthesia. In such an ATM-induced dissociated state, the addict experiences anesthetizing and intensely pleasurable alleviation of dysphoric and painful affect states.

Fifth, we demonstrated that the addicted patient can develop a therapeutic relationship with the therapist based on a transference fantasy of the therapist as a thing or activity that functions as a transitional selfobject. Such a transference relationship can effectively replace a functionally similar relationship with ATMs by taking over the antianxiety, antidepressant, humanizing, and pacifying selfobject functions of these ATMs. We pointed out that the assumption of these functions in the transference is often facilitated by an active mode of empathic engagement characterized by allowing for limited selfobject provisions within the therapeutic relationship. We highlighted this type of transference and provision by reporting on our addicted patients' transitional selfobject relationship to their therapist's telephone answering machine.

And sixth, in the context of the analysis and working through of the transitional selfobject transference, we pointed out that unconscious fantasies shared by patient and therapist alike may serve antithetical clinical purposes: they may either enhance or interfere with a therapist's empathy and therefore may either advance or impede analytic cure of the addicted patient, which we defined as the intersubjective absorption and transmuting internalization of the selfobject function of ATMs (see Kohut, 1984, for a discussion of the centrality of transmuting internalization in the self-psychological theory of analytic cure).

## REFERENCES

Abrams, S. & Neubauer, P. D. (1975), Object orientedness: The person or the thing. *Psychoanal. Quart.*, 45:73–99.

Adler, N. & Goleman, D. (1969), Gambling and alcoholism; symptom substitution and functional equivalents. *Quart. J. Study of Alcohol*, 30:733–736.

Arlow, J. A. (1982), Unconscious fantasy and political movements. In: *Judaism and Psychoanalysis*, ed. M. Ostow. Hoboken, NJ: KTVA Publishing House.

_____ (unpublished), Unconscious fantasy.

Bacal, H. A. (1990), Does an object relations theory exist in self psychology? *Psychoanal. Inq.*, 10:197–220.

Blum, H. P. (1986), Psychoanalytic studies and Macbeth: Shared fantasy and reciprocal identification. *The Psychoanalytic Study of the Child*, 41:585–599. New Haven, CT: Yale University Press.

_____ (1988), Shared fantasy and reciprocal identification, and their role in gener disorders. In: *Fantasy, Myth, and Reality*, ed. H. P. Blum, Y. Kramer, A. K. Richards & A. D. Richards. Madison, CT: International Universities Press, pp. 323–338.

Corssen, G. & Domino, E. F. (1966), Dissociative anesthesia: Further pharmacologic studies of the first clinical experience with Phencyclkidine derivative CI-581. *Anesthesia & Analgesia*, 4:29–40.

Eissler, K. R. (1953), The effect of the structure of the ego on psychoanalytic technique. *J. Amer. Psychoanal. Assn.*, 1:104–143.

Freud, S. (1908), Creative writers and day-dreaming. *Standard Edition*, 9:141–153. London: Hogarth Press, 1959.

_____ (1913), Totem and taboo. *Standard Edition*, 13:1–161. London: Hogarth Press, 1955.

Ferenczi, S. (1913), Stages in the development of the sense of reality. In: *Sex in Psychoanalysis*. New York: Brunner/Mazel, 1950, pp. 213–239.

Freedman, N. (1985), The concept of transformation in psychoanalysis. *Psychoanal. Psychol.*, 2:317–339.

Goldberg, A. (1988), Translation between psychoanalytic theories. In: *A Fresh Look at Psychoanalysis*. Hillsdale, NJ: The Analytic Press, pp. 30–43.

Greenacre, P. (1970), The transitional object and the fetish with special reference to the role of illusion. *Internat. J. Psycho-Anal.*, 51:447–456.

Good, M. I. (1989), Substance-induced dissociative disorders and psychiatric nosology. *J. Clin. Psychopharmacol.*, 9:88–93.

Grinspoon, L. & Bakalar, J. B. (1979), *Psychedelic Drugs Reconsidered*. New York: Basic Books.

Kohut, H. (1968), The psychoanalytic treatment of narcissistic personality disorders. In: *Search for the Self, Vol. 1*, ed. P. H. Ornstein. New York: International Universities Press, pp. 477–509.

_____ (1971), *The Analysis of the Self*. New York: International Universities Press.

_____ (1977a), Preface. In: *Psychodynamics of Drug Dependence*, ed. J. D. Blaine & D. A. Julius, National Institute of Drug Abuse Monogr. 12. Washington, DC: U. S. Gov. Printing Office, pp. viii–ix.

_____ (1977b), *The Restoration of the Self*. New York: International Universities Press.

_____ (1984), *How Does Analysis Cure?* ed. A. Goldberg & P. Stepansky. Chicago: University of Chicago Press.

_____ (1987), Addictive need for an admiring other in regulation of self-esteem. In: *The Kohut Seminars on Self Psychology and Psychotherapy with Adolescents and Young Adults*, ed. M. Elson. New York: Norton, pp. 113–132.

Lindon, J. A. (1988), Psychoanalysis by telephone. *Bull. Menninger Clin.*, 52:521–528.

Lichtenberg, J. D. (1989), *Psychoanalysis and Motivation*. Hillsdale, NJ: The Analytic Press.

Margulies, A. (1989), *The Empathic Imagination*. New York: Norton.

McDougall, J. (1985), *Theatres of the Mind*. New York: Basic Books.

Modell, A. H. (1970), The transitional object and the creative act. *Psychoanal. Quart.*, 39:240–250.

Searles, H. F. (1960), *The Nonhuman Environment in Normal Development and Schizophrenia*. New York: International Universities Press.

Stolorow, R. D. & Lachmann, F. M. (1980), *The Psychoanalysis of Developmental Arrest*. New York: International Universities Press.

Sugarman, A. & Jaffe, L. S. (1989), A developmental line of transitional phenomena. In: *The Facilitating Environment*, ed. M. B. Fromm & B. L. Smith. Madison, CT: International Universities Press, pp. 88–129.

_____ & Kurash, C. (1981), The body as a transitional object in bulimia. *Internat. J. Eating Dis.*, 1:57–67.

_____ & _____ (1982), Marijuana abuse, transitional experience and the borderline adolescent. *Psychoanal. Inq.*, 2:519–538.

Tolpin, M. (1971), On the beginnings of a cohesive self: An application of the concept of transmuting internalization to the study of the transitional object and signal anxiety. *The Psychoanalytic Study of the Child*, 26:316–352. New Haven, CT: Yale University Press.

Ulman, R. B. & Brothers, D. (1987), A self-psychological revaluation of posttraumatic stress disorder (PTSD) and its treatment: Shattered fantasies. *J. Amer. Acad. Psychoanal.*, 15:175–203.

_____ & _____ (1988), *The Shattered Self*. Hillsdale, NJ: The Analytic Press.

_____ & Paul, H. (1989), A self-psychological theory and approach to treating substance abuse disorders: The "intersubjective absorption" hypothesis. In: *Dimensions of Self Experience: Progress in Self Psychology*, Vol. 5, ed. A. Goldberg, Hillsdale, NJ: The Analytic Press, pp. 129–156.

_____ & _____ (1990), The addictive personality disorder and "addictive trigger mechanism" (ATMs): The self psychology of addiction and its treatment. In: *The Realities of Transference: Progress in Self Psychology*, Vol. 6, ed. A. Goldberg. Hillsdale, NJ: The Analytic Press, pp. 129–156.

_____ & _____ (forthcoming), *Narcissus in Wonderland: The Self Psychology of Addiction and Its Treatment*. Hillsdale, NJ: The Analytic Press.

_____ & Stolorow, R. D. (1985), "The transference–countertransference neurosis" in psychoanalysis: An intersubjective viewpoint. *Bull. Menninger Clin.*, 49:37–51.

_____ & Zimmermann, P. B. (1985), Psychoanalysis as a hermeneutic science and the new paradigm of subjectivity: A prolegomenon. Presented at the Eighth Annual Meeting of the International Society of Political Psychology, George Washington University, Washington, DC, June 18–21.

_____ & _____ (1987), Psychoanalysis as a hermeneutic science and the new paradigm of subjectivity: Evolution of a research tradition. Presented at the Tenth Annual Meeting of the International Society of Political Psychology, Cathedral Hill, San Francisco, California, July 4–7.

Volkan, V. (1970), Transitional fantasies in the analysis of a narcissistic personality. *J. Amer. Psychoanal. Assn.*, 21:351–376.

Winnicott, D. W. (1951), Transitional objects and transitional phenomena. In: *Through Pediatrics to Psycho-Analysis,* New York: Basic Books, 1975, pp. 229–242.

―――― (1959), The fate of the transitional object. In: *D. W. Winnicott: Psycho-Analytic Explorations,* ed. C. Winnicott, R. Shepard & M. Davis, Cambridge, MA: Harvard University Press, pp. 53–58.

―――― (1966), On the split-off male and female elements. In: *D. W. Winnicott: Psycho-Analytic Explorations,* ed. C. Winnicott, R. Shepard & M. Davis. Cambridge, MA: Harvard University Press, pp. 169–188.

Von Wright, G. H. (1971), *Explanation and Understanding.* Ithaca, NY: Cornell University Press.

Wolf, E. S. (1980), On the developmental line of selfobject relations. In: *Advances in Self Psychology,* ed. A. Goldberg. New York: International Universities Press, pp. 117–130.

# Chapter 8

# Codependency: A Self-Psychological Perspective

## Jill Cooper

The concept popularly referred to as codependency is a crucial one in psychotherapy. The self-help literature and the 12-step and other recovery movements use a descriptive language that resonates with a large number of people who then seek the treatments offered by these movements. Recently, articles in the press have been critical of the term and how it has been defined. Codependency appears to be so universally applicable that it is beginning to lose credibility as a phenomenon. Yet the number of people who feel understood by the language of the self-help and recovery literature continues to grow. Simultaneously, patients frustrated with the treatments provided by these movements are showing up in our offices in increasing numbers, feeling injured, disappointed, hopeless, and confused. In following the treatment steps that initially spoke so empathically to their experience, patients are exerting more effort with less improvement in self-esteem or quality of relationships. Rather than dismiss these movements as trite or simplistic, as the press has done, self psychologists can become more empathically attuned to the language these patients find so descriptive, can seek to understand and explain how this cultural movement readies patients for our help, and therefore can become optimally responsive to the treatment needs of this rapidly growing population.

We must convey to these patients that we know they once felt understood and then were let down by the self-help movement; but

I gratefully thank Douglas Detrick, Jane and John Jordan, Dvora Honigstein, Deborah Cooper, and Susan Sands for their guidance and help with this chapter.

we must take care not to dismiss the community that originally helped (and may still be helping) them, lest we lose the opportunity to explore the unconscious parts of the self that remain to be discovered within the transference relationship. We must develop and increase our sensitivity to the language and metaphors our patients use after involvement in the self-help movement. By obtaining a grounding in the many conceptual and historical uses of this terminology, self psychologists gain an advantage in pursuing more detailed individual elaboration and meaning. Our patients must know that we recognize their symptoms as indicative of disorders we can successfully treat.

In this chapter I attempt to demonstrate that the concept of codependency, rather than losing its meaning because of its universal applicability, continues to speak to so many because the grass-roots self-help movement has inadvertently stumbled on descriptions of the self-selfobject matrix and its many pathological manifestations. This chapter reviews the history of the concept of codependency and traces the shift from a conception of codependency as a situational issue based on an adaptation by those who are chemically dependent to a recognition of the childhood roots of the problem, which involve the flawed and narcissistically vulnerable personalities of the early caretakers.

Self-psychologically redefined, the early self-selfobject relations are the core of codependent pathology; that is, they are the source and motivation for the replication of the self-defeating bonds formed originally in the nuclear family. It is not the chemical dependencies that caused the codependencies; the phenomenon of codependency includes the symptoms that seem self-descriptive to those who suffer from the underlying pathology of self-selfobject disorders.

The concept of codependency has had limited utility in fostering understanding and treatment of patients because it was defined in connection with alcoholism, and for many patients it is not the chemical dependency treatment approach that is ultimately the most helpful. While recovery clinicians (Cermak, 1986; Brown, 1988) increasingly acknowledge the disorder of codependence without the presence of chemical dependency, they have not rejected chemical dependency as the etiologic agent. Freeing codependency from its historical linkage to chemical dependency allows the application of treatments that address self-deficits more directly. Timmen Cermak (1986) stated that it is reference to theory that explains and treats intrapsychic and interpersonal disturbance that is the necessary step to understand and treat codependency effectively. Psychoanalytic self psychology takes that step with the unique contribution of the self-selfobject matrix. Self psychology offers treatment approaches to codependency that differ radically from those routinely offered today. Treatment can extend beyond the cognitive-behavioral approach and group settings that have been historically applied to both chemical and codependencies to an approach that addresses developmental deficits that are worked through within the establishment and resolution of the selfobject transferences.

Generically, codependency has been defined as a disorder that includes low self-esteem. Self-image and self-worth are highly dependent on one's relation to another person; it is only within the context of a relationship that a codependent has meaning. The maintenance of the relationship is paramount, and codependents will generally go to any length to ensure its continued existence. Codependents need to be needed and place the needs of the other before the needs of the self. They experience great conflict in the areas of dependency and locus of control and are now generally understood to exhibit such symptoms as eating disorders, compulsions, sexualizations, somatic illnesses, affect disturbances, and low self-esteem. Self-psychologically, it is possible to understand these conflicts and symptoms as the *counterdependent self*, which is discussed in this chapter after a brief review of the codependency literature.

## LITERATURE REVIEW AND DISCUSSION

Codependency was first identified in the late 1970s as *co-alcoholism* by those working in the recovery field. It was loosely applied to those associated with the alcoholic: employers, neighbors, relatives, spouses. The term "co-alcoholism," in line with systems theory, implied that the attitudes and behaviors of others affected, and were affected by, the alcoholic. Specifically, the behaviors of enabling, rescuing, and persecuting were highlighted in the hope that the co-alcoholic could identify, label, and thus overcome attitudinal and behavioral patterns learned in response to living with or depending on an alcoholic (Brown, 1985). Co-alcoholics were (and still are) actively enlisted in the alcoholic's treatment because the alcoholic's recovery clearly was enhanced by their involvement and cooperation. In other words, co-alcoholism was first defined as ancillary to alcoholism, and co-alcoholics were treated in response to the recovery needs of the alcoholic. Johnson (1973) a noted alcohol specialist stated, "The only difference between the alcoholic and the spouse, in instances where the latter does not drink, is that one is physically affected by alcohol; otherwise both have all the symptoms" (p. 30); both the pathology and the treatment were defined relative to the alcoholic's need.

Greenleaf (1981) suggested that co-alcoholism could be developmental rather than situational by offering the term *para-alcoholic* to describe children who had cognitive and behavioral symptoms similar to adult co-alcoholics' symptoms but were acquiring these symptoms during their characterological development into adulthood. The distinction is vital: in adult co-alcoholism the disorder is short lived, cognitive-behavioral, and developed situationally in adulthood in response to another's chemical dependency. This situational adjustment parallels the model of addictive thinking used in chemical dependency treatment to describe the personality adjustments and concessions the alcoholic makes to his or her disease. As the alcoholism progresses physiologically, the alcoholic is forced to make cognitive and behavioral adjustments in his or her life that accommodate continued alcohol use in spite of adverse consequences. The alcoholic's problems are caused by the alcoholism rather than the reverse (Brown, 1985). Adult-onset co-alcoholism is an adaptation to the alcohol too, as it alters the cognition and behavior of the co-alcoholic. The alcoholic has a direct relationship to the alcohol through physiology; the co-alcoholic has an indirect relationship to the alcohol through the relationship with the alcoholic. For example, alcoholism may cause the alcoholic to become irresponsible and forgetful and he or she may neglect to pay the bills. It is adaptation to alcoholism that causes the co-alcoholic to assume more responsibility and pay the bills. The problem in adult-onset co-alcoholism is that these responses rigidify and intensify so that the interdependency energies are all flowing one way: from the needy alcoholic to the co-alcoholic. The co-alcoholic's dependency needs are unmet and eventually denied as he or she becomes increasingly self-sufficient and controlling and simultaneously represses needs for others. It is this type of codependency that is treated by Al-Anon and other groups relying on cognitive–behavioral insight and change.

The idea of adult onset co-alcoholism reflects another aspect of chemical dependency theory that distinguishes problem or abusive drinking from alcoholic drinking. Problem drinking is a response to a stressor; it ceases when the stressor is removed or when the problem drinker has adjusted to it. A parallel adult-onset co-alcoholism would be expected to cease after exposure to the alcoholic stops or after relatively brief educational or psychological intervention. However, contrary to this theoretical paradigm, removal of the co-alcoholic from the alcoholic did not usually provide effective relief from co-alcoholic symptoms. Consequently, clinicians began to look elsewhere for possible etiologies of codependency.

Black (1981), Wegscheider (1981), and Larsen (1985) turned to family systems theory and correlated obvious codependency symptom clusters with family roles. Cermak (1986), clarifying existing popular definitions, explained the change in terminology from co-alcoholism to codependency as simply the reflection of a shift in emphasis from alcoholism to the more general chemical dependency and not a conceptual modification. His three levels of definition recognize codependency as (1) a didactic tool that labels observable behavior to the client and, in doing so, creates a pathway to treatment, (2) a psychological concept that can be described and understood metapsychologically, and (3) a disease entity that can be viewed as a distinct pathology and therefore diagnosed. Cermak recognized the difficulty in proceeding with treatment of a disorder lacking a distinct theoretical basis and proposed the diagnosis of mixed personality disorder to be subsumed under a new diagnostic category of codependent personality disorder. His proposal of a new DSM III diagnosis was noteworthy because it reflected the conceptualization of codependency as a unique psychological disorder whose definition no longer required mention of chemical dependency. Cermak's diagnostic criteria were detailed and thorough and suggested that any role cluster evident in codependency (see Black, 1981; Wegscheider, 1981; Larsen, 1985), had these criteria as core issues. The diagnostic problem was that these symptoms did not seem to differentiate health from pathology.

The first developmental model of codependency from the recovery field was presented by Brown (1988), who discussed codependency in adult children of alcoholics (ACAs) while expanding on her theory of recovery development in alcoholics. Brown views alcoholism as a distinct and primarily treatable disorder and not a cluster of symptoms associated with either a borderline or a narcissistic personality disorder as defined by Kernberg (1969) and Kohut (1959, 1971, 1977a, 1987). Legitimating alcoholism as a distinct disorder led to new and effective treatment alternatives such as the use of cognitive-behavioral recovery groups.

Brown's (1985) earlier work demonstrated that an alcoholic maintains a core and primary relationship to alcohol from the onset of alcoholism for the duration of either continued use or recovery. At the point of abstinence the alcoholic's core beliefs—"I am not alcoholic"and "I am in control"—are shattered. As a result, the alcoholic regresses and fragments, and treatment approaches that contain and bind this fragmentation—in addition to furnishing the alternative core beliefs, "I am alcoholic" and "I am not in control"—are required. Psychodynamic work, that is, genetic and therefore transferential interventions, should not be employed until the patient has reconstituted for a significant period of time as a sober alcoholic who experiences this new identity as positive.

This clarification of priority in treatment strategies innocently but unfortunately reinforced the historical separation that existed between psychodynamic and recovery approaches. Today this theoretical split prevents codependents from receiving the psychological help they need. The antipsychiatric bias in chemical dependency treatment history, which is now beginning to be bridged, has kept "codependency" treatment approaches limited to those that proved effective in chemical dependency recovery. In contributing the first major developmental look at ACAs, Brown extrapolated principles from her model of alcohol recovery and began applying them to ACAs. First, she employed family systems theory to illustrate that alcohol is the central organizing principle in families raising ACAs, or future codependent adults. Then she discussed the developmental difficulties of children raised in alcoholic families. Finally, she offered interactional group therapy as the treatment of choice since it replicated a family grouping; the interactional patterns characteristic of alcoholism were expected to be reenacted with group members and, therefore, worked through.

The continued preference for group treatment again derives from traditional chemical dependency treatment. But group treatment is not necessarily the most beneficial treatment for codependency. The idea of replicating family dynamics by placing patients together in a group is unsubstantiated. Moreover, group therapy makes the necessary unfolding of the selfobject transferences impossible. One is unable to experience the special and unique relationship with the clinician that the patient needs in order to establish and resolve early developmental failures that occurred within the parent–child relationship. Within a group setting patients' alter ego needs predominate (i.e., the need to belong with others and be a part of a group), not the need to replicate earlier dyadic relationships (Detrick, 1985, 1986).

Brown's definition of codependency, while in agreement with the descriptive, role-based definitions of earlier contributors, basically recognized it as associated with chemical dependency; it was the other side of the coin. According to Brown (1988), "The connecting link and most important factor is the centrality of alcoholism" (p. 87). While Brown stated that "the all or nothing categories, and cognitive frame that are so characteristic and so problematic for the children of alcoholics also characterize the field of inquiry" (p. 75), her criticism didn't uncover the bias evident in her own work. The flaw in the family, that is, the grandiosity and narcissistic dominance of the alcoholic's needs, is the flaw in the field because codependents are not suffering their parents' struggles with alcoholism.

According to Beletsis and Brown (1981), codependents suffer from a false self, self-disorder, or dissociative disorder, acquired because their primary developmental/maturational needs were responded to in ways that ensure developmental deficits and/or abuses. Deficits are the core of the codependent's disorder and its treatment, not alcoholism. As a patient recently remarked, "alcoholism was my parents' problem, not mine. My problem was that I wasn't getting what I needed to grow myself up right." Alcoholism is neither primary nor necessary for the development of codependency and should not predominate in its treatment.

Wood (1987) attempted to integrate the descriptive definitions of codependency into the larger body of psychodynamic theory. Recognizing that central to its causation is the faulty parental responsiveness with which the child's needs were met instead of the actual presence of alcohol in the household, she discussed and applied to the concept of codependency the work of Klein, Fairbairn, Winnicott, Guntrip, Jacobson, and Kohut, the psychodynamic theorists most cognizant of self–other interplay as the source of pathology. She reviewed the basic principles of Heinz Kohut's psychoanalytic self psychology and concluded that the treatment focus should be on the end product or faulty self. Wood (1987) defined the codependent's central struggle as a failure to separate from the family of origin, stating that as a result codependents suffer from a false self, internalization of the bad object, a weak self-image, fear of dependency and attachment, and psychic splitting. She suggested that "there is much to be gained by viewing their [ACAs'] problems as impairments of core structures in the psyche" (p. 38).

While Wood's conclusion is certainly a beginning, the route that precedes it is a compilation of opposing theoretical constructs. Most importantly, Wood missed the major conceptual shift of psychoanalytic self psychology, which expanded the idea of self and object as separate and distinct to the concept that an object can provide selfobject functions that are experienced as part of the self. It is theoretically unsound to use the idea of selfobject needs to explain an aspect of structure and then state that "much of the self is formed through the alternate introjection . . . of people and parts of people who are outside the self, and the projection onto others of parts of the self that were previously introjected" (p. 54). In addition, because of the unique and ever-present self-selfobject matrix, self psychology does not conceptualize separation as a primary psychological task.

Rather, selfobject functions, when successful, establish a cohesive and vital self with continuing selfobject needs that mature and change form but never cease to influence the self's solidity and vitality.

## THE COUNTERDEPENDENT SELF

Psychoanalytic self psychology has a major contribution to make in resolving the definitional dilemma described by critics within the clinical communities and the media. Its self-selfobject concept explains and distinguishes codependency as a self disorder and as a relational disorder. Early in life selfobject functions are provided by caretaking others; it is the caretaker's general accuracy at assessing and meeting the child's psychological needs and then the gradual untraumatic failure to regulate psychological needs and comfort that bit by bit aid the child in building a firm, vitalized, and balanced self. The self takes over the archaic selfobject functions, becoming self-soothing, self-knowing and accepting, and self-confident or admiring, to build a self that is cohesive and confident and can easily regulate tension states. The selfobject functions become less archaic; they mature to meet the changing needs of the developing self and are a constant, age-appropriate psychological necessity.

For example, in addressing the idealizing selfobject function, Kohut (1971) states:

> The child's evaluation of the idealized object becomes increasingly realistic—which leads to a withdrawal of the narcissistic cathexes from the imago of the idealized selfobject and to their gradual . . . internalization, i.e., to the acquisition of permanent psychological structures which continue, endopsychically, the functions which the idealized selfobject had previously fulfilled [p. 45].

Faulty selfobject responsiveness leads not only to weakness or frailty in the self-structure but to the continued experience of others as archaic and failing selfobject providers: "The child does not acquire the needed internal structure, his psyche remains fixated on an archaic self object, and the personality will throughout life be dependent on certain objects in what seems to be an intense form of object hunger" (Kohut, 1971, p. 45). This is a psychologically accurate definition of codependency. Objects are experienced less as relatively separate others than as necessary early selfobject functions.

Viewed self-psychologically, codependency is, at its core, a self-selfobject relationship that encapsulates and protects the nuclear self from reinjury and yet seeks continued development of faulty self-structures by pursuing the satisfaction of selfobject needs from others in a counterdependent way. For the counterdependent self, relations with others are predominately based on hoped-for early selfobject needs, which creates a desperate quality of connection. This is done paradoxically: First, by covering over a needy yet fearful and protective self with any defense cluster, including those that seem to be relation seeking, and, second, by disavowing the archaic unconscious selfobject needs that are met by focusing on another's more obviously observed or expressed neediness. There is little chance of these needs truly being met since (1) the needs are unconscious and are thus not within the patient's power and control and (2) the needs are remnants of childhood that can only be reexperienced and reclaimed through the regressive experience and working through of the selfobject transferences. This explains the frequently observed enmeshed quality and difficulty of the interpersonal relations of the codependent person: people are seen less as they are and predominately in terms of whether or not they respond to archaic self-structures and the needs of one's self, making truly interpersonal relationships impossible to maintain or continually dissatisfying. The counterdependent self is one possible outcome of the many self-selfobject configurations. While the term counterdependent self may prove to be more useful to the recovery community to distinguish gradations of selfobject experiences, it differs from other self disorders by its aforementioned self-effacing qualities, which serve to disavow one's own neediness yet seek selfobject provisions by meeting others' needs. However, the following distinguish the counterdependent self produced from the chemically dependent family from other self-selfobject disorders:

1. When raised by a caretaker narcissistically involved with the management of a chemical dependency, children can suffer from embarrassment, shame, or humiliation from two sources. First, these feelings can result when a child's need is not met and the child feels that the need and its expression were at fault and caused him or her harm. Second, depending on the developmental stage, the child experiences the selfobject provider as more or less a part of the self. When the selfobject provider is chemically altered, the child can have these feelings with respect to the caretaker as a functional part of the self that is shameful and embarrassing. Some children have already figured out that it is after watching the caretaker ingest drugs (or after the caretaker smells of alcohol) that he or she undergoes a personality change, which they sense, through alter ego connectedness to the caretaker, is aberrant. In treatment these patients can have a greater

need to hold the therapist accountable when they experience transference disruptions because of these complex sources of poor self-
esteem and boundary confusion. Therefore, the part the therapist
specifically or the therapeutic environment in general contributes to
transference replications and disruptions must be simply, clearly, and
firmly acknowledged and neither argued nor defended according to
the therapist's theory or view of reality; otherwise, these patients will
feel reinjured. When the therapist can concede to the patient's
transferential experience of the therapist and/or the treatment, the
patient recovers developmental strivings held in unconscious abey-
ance until the earlier selfobject obstacles that had prevented cohesion
and/or growth could be removed.

These patients may experience alter ego needs with a heightened
sensitivity. Their alter ego needs may be especially disrupted owing
to their inability to bring friends into the home, the embarrassment
and shame they feel when the parent's drunken or mind-altered
behavior is witnessed, and the resultant isolation of and denial in
chemically dependent families. Conversely, the satisfaction of alter
ego needs sometimes serve as a remarkable compensatory experience
when these children seek such satisfaction not from the family but
from peers, school, or other activities outside the home, a pursuit that
may underscore their self-sufficiency and denial of more intimate
forms of dependency needs.

2. Children witness the chemically dependent adult responding to
the range of life's joys, sorrows, and tensions by voluntarily ingesting
what they observe to be mind-and mood-altering substances. Children deduce any number of meanings from this behavior, which are
usually false beliefs about adulthood. Frequently, these include the
impression that adults feel they are inadequate or incompetent to
manage life's ups and downs as well as the fluctuations of affects and
inner states without chemical sustenance. Well into a lengthy treatment, a patient once remarked as she began to relate her explanations
of the therapist's most recent wounding responsiveness, "I just
figured out that I've been attributing to your behavior the emotional
maturity of a two-year-old and that that is what I have always thought
was normal adulthood."

3. Counterdependent patients have built up a primitive denial of
their dependency needs. These needs, which are consciously ignored
or avoided, are met, however hurtfully and unconsciously, when
these patients care for or control others. Thus, abstention from these
counterdependent practices can be harmful or impede growth; that
is, some need is being met in the counterdependent pattern.

4. These patients deny their emotional and psychological depen-

dencies with the same rigor that the chemically dependent person denies the substance dependency. The recovering chemical dependent recognizes that the chemical usage is aberrant and is motivated by this knowledge and perhaps by any attendant guilt or shame that may accompany the usage of mind-altering chemicals to abstain. Counterdependent patients feel the same way toward their own necessary dependency needs; that is, they feel the needs are aberrant or useless parts of the self from which they must be freed. This may explain the pull these patients feel toward treatment approaches that encourage abstention from the gratification of their dependency needs, treatment approaches that will only deprive the patient of necessary psychological experience.

## TREATMENT COMPARISONS

Self psychology's unique understanding of the selfobject functions accurately defines the counterdependent self and offers treatment approaches that vary widely from those in use today. Treatment goals and methodology have been adopted from approaches that have proved successful in treating chemical dependency. Membership in recovery groups composed of other chemical dependents and led by a group facilitator has become the treatment of choice for chemical dependents. Since the disease of chemical dependency itself is believed to be incurable, treatment addresses recovery from the damage addiction has wrought and teaches coping skills that enable patients to live free of chemical usage.

Recovery treatment for codependency, as with chemical dependency, involves confronting patients with their codependent behaviors and teaching them healthier alternatives. Codependency itself is the pathology, and the treatment rids the patient of codependent thoughts, feelings, and behaviors. For example, codependency literature considers blaming and externalizing anger as character defects one can and needs to stop (to "let go") in order to develop a more healthy form of anger expression. When the codependent feels failed by another, recovery treatment discourages exploration of the anger some patients experience. Instead, the recovery approach confronts the patient to change the codependent expectations of the other. The patient's angry reclaiming of disavowed dependency needs is pathologized and is restrained from needing the other or holding the other accountable, which frequently causes deprived counterdependent patients to experience additional fragmented anger.

When this type of blame or establishment of accountability occurs within a psychodynamic treatment setting, it is frequently called a negative therapeutic reaction. Psychodynamic and recovery under-standings pathologize the negative feeling as the patient's distorted affect expression and expect confrontation and interpretation of it as such to bring it within the patient's conscious control. Both miss the opportunity to examine more closely the uncovered need or self state that had been met with the faulty responsiveness that caused the rage in the first place. Understood from a self-psychological perspective, so-called "blaming anger" is a regression to an earlier cognitive state in which the fragmented toddler knows no other way to protect the self from threats to its cohesion. While not under one's conscious control, the expression of this anger is essential for developmental repair. The injured, angered, hurt, frightened child would, and should have been able to, hold accountable an emotionally stronger and more mature other who was needed and who failed. Without acceptance of this crucial stage of anger expression and the experience of holding the clinician accountable and making necessary repairs together, counterdependent patients continue to blame themselves for others' failings or continue to express anger, disappointment, and loss as blame toward others. This blame is an archaic form of anger, an anger still trapped within an earlier exchange that has never been acknowledged, righted, or grieved over as an interaction that left a need unsatisfied. One can see the difficult strain this places on any relationship outside the treatment room, and yet it is necessary to reexperience this within the therapeutic process as an expression of anger, at one time age appropriate, that requires affirmation.

Within a recovery model, codependent needs for the other are seen as basically pathological. Healthy needs for another are acknowl-edged but conceptualized as alternative behaviors, not as anything that might be contained within the codependent pattern. One must give up the one for the other; one must abstain. Understood self-psychologically, abstention from troubling relationships in par-ticular and compulsive behaviors in general is not a treatment strategy unless the behavior is presently life-threatening. Health returns the codependent to the deficits to give them another chance. Abstention deprives the codependent of the healthy striving that is being protected in some form by the compulsion. The striving will not be kept alive, much less uncovered and understood, and the original failing will never be reexperienced if the behavior is willed away. The health is thrown away with the then-functional early adaptation because their interrelatedness has not been understood. Health is not an alternative one will find when one abstains from "unhealthy" patterns; it lives within the pattern because the compulsion itself is an earlier adaptation designed to protect healthy strivings from the environment that threatened their existence. An early wound is reexperienced and an aborted healthy striving is reawakened when the codependent can tolerate the time, pain, and expense of re-working the entire earlier experience in the relationship with an individual therapist.

Both confronting these repetitive behaviors and abstaining from them are erroneous and wounding approaches. A confrontation from outside the empathic vantage point, no matter how gentle or tactfully worded, can feel assaultive or blaming to the counterdependent patient because, as in the earlier injury, the patient feels he or she is being held accountable for the other's inability to meet his or her needs. The patient feels as if his or her need and its right to be met are being confronted, and the real issue—why it is not being met and how that feels—is being sidestepped. In early childhood an unmet need and the response it received produced shame about one's needs; confrontation now, in adulthood, risks enhancement of the shame. Furthermore, these regressed and younger emotional parts of the self need a treatment setting in which they are the special center of attention. For example, many patients need to reexperience regressed grandiosity with the attuned emotional response from the therapist of prideful admiration. Slowly, the grandiosity matures through this unique abstraction of the past into mature adult self-esteem and humble dignity. Confronting or humbling developmental grandiosity by not understanding it as an earlier, unmet self-experience recreates an earlier injury (it is still in the patient's character precisely because it was not allowed during childhood).

As discussed earlier, both Brown and Wood expanded the concept of codependency beyond a solely cognitive-behavioral perspective to an object relations developmental one. Since object relations theories, which were originally based on Freud's drive theory and later expanded on by Klein, describe the developing infant as projecting and introjecting destructive pathological drives with respect to early caretakers, and later the analyst, the clinician conceptualizes code-pendency as an inherently pathological relationship as well. This theoretical basis then greatly influences the clinical stance and the nature of the interpretation offered. There is a preference for a mechanistic and reductionistic model in which patients are defined psychodynamically by their drive-based cluster of traits and use of defenses, whereas they are understood within the recovery commu-nity in terms of their role-based use of defenses. Both approaches inhibit the exploration of individual subjective experience and the meaning it has. They undermine the basic premise that it is the faulty care provided by early caretakers who were more narcissistically preoccupied with the regulation of their own tension states and/or the demands of a chemical dependency than in responding to the needs of the developing child that is the source of the patient's difficulties.

Bacal and Newman (1990) point out that regardless of some points of theoretical agreement with self psychology, an object relations perspective (as represented by Kernberg, in this case) places more emphasis "on the contribution made by the subject's constitutional drives and phantasy distortions and a minimization of the specific environmental traumata" (p. 7). Furthermore, since the predominant object relational belief in primary narcissism is objectless, its later use as a defense is "being fueled primarily by a pathologically immature and self-centered psychological organization rather than as an understandable and basically self-protective attitude of the self" (p. 12). One is then tempted to understand codependency as hysteria, masochism, or passive dependency and as primarily self-destructive and to analyze the behavior as a defense against either baser instincts or fears of object ties, rather than help remove developmental obstacles so that the healthy strivings contained within the codependency can continue their development. Thus, the object relations clinician confronts and analyzes defenses, an approach that, ironically, replicates the present technique of the recovery clinician, although the two arrive at the same stance from different theoretical positions.

## SPECIAL CONSIDERATIONS FOR THE SELF PSYCHOLOGIST

It is essential that the self psychologist understand the treatment bias against ties with others that may have previously aided our patients in securing a stance against dependency. Frequently, patients arrive in our offices seeking treatment goals of counterdependent self-sufficiency and control. While self psychologists understand these ideals as the self-protective results of selfobject failures, it is useful to understand not only the family environments that initially created these self-protective defenses but also the treatment environments that may have exacerbated these states of injury and made such treatment goals all the more desirable. Premature interpretation of these goals as disruption products of selfobject relationships that the patient would be loath to admit existed in the first place underestimates the power of the previous (or simultaneous) treatment approaches and environments, which have pathologized or simply missed the various attachment needs that patients employ for self-cohesion and functioning, needs that they will maintain even at apparent great cost to themselves.

Because children raised in chemically dependent families are at risk to develop a chemical problem, the self psychologist must be sensitive to issues of evaluation and diagnosis of the existence of a chemical dependency. It should not be assumed that the existence of a chemical dependency will simply rise to the surface or metaphorically announce its readiness to be treated. Brown's work beautifully demonstrates the rigid, primitive denial and actual ignorance that can camouflage chemical dependency from the patient, and the responsibility this gives the clinician to actively pursue the necessary diagnostic criteria. This knowledge and practice should become as ingrained and routine as assessments for suicidality and medication are today.

The self psychologist must maintain a thorough theoretical grounding in the maturational necessities of self-selfobject functions and in the progressive stages of chemical dependency (alcoholism, in particular). Counterdependent patients, profoundly sensitive to perceiving and responding to the chemical dependent's narcissistic needs and frailties, will transferentially experience the therapist according to deficits acquired at various points in their own personality development, developmental stages paralleled by their caretaker's stage of alcoholism or chemical dependency. These patients will transfer their parent's earlier narcissistic needs to the therapist and then try to fill them. Secondly, they may expect the therapist to respond to their expressed need in a way that is narcissistically neglectful or injurious to them. Both are potential transference obstacles to be experienced, understood, worked through, and explained in order to reclaim the patient's denied need, which is commonly protected by anger or a self-sufficient stance that the therapist is somehow unnecessary. Patients who are especially challenging, as the counterdependent patient can be, sorely test the therapist's ability to maintain an empathically attuned clinical stance. Yet such a stance must be maintained in order to aid the patient through the difficult transference exploration, no matter how fittingly the degree of transference expectation may coincide with the therapist's own narcissistic needs and/or vulnerabilities.

Finally, self psychologists can be sensitive to the lack of necessary learning and the deficits in social or cognitive ego skills that counterdependent patients may present evidence of in treatment. In discussing the complexity of clinical work, Kohut (1971) referred to the "ego distortions . . . [that] . . . temporarily require a bit of educational pressure" and "may during certain periods also occur in the central, most reality-near sector of the psyche" (p. 179; see also Kernberg, 1969). In their upbringing these patients frequently missed exposure to social skills as well as attuned responsiveness to their own readiness to learn rudimentary reality-based social practices. It should not be assumed that because patients may intuitively know they are poorly equipped to manage many of life's tasks, they are thus able to recognize and spontaneously recover the necessary missing skills without professional intervention. A therapist's comments on these deficits, when appropriate, are frequently heard as attuned, experience-near, understanding responses and contribute to the trust building that is necessary for the more dynamically based transferential experiences to emerge. Such salutary results follow particularly when the therapist addresses the misinformation on the nature and progression of chemical dependency that this group of patients frequently has.

## A SELF-PSYCHOLOGICAL TREATMENT

Self psychology breaks the counterdependent patient's unnecessary tie to chemical dependency treatment approaches and prioritizes treatment needs according to the disorder itself and not according to its relation to chemical dependency. Employing the empathic vantage point, the clinician explores and understands the patient's experience, and the treatment experience itself offers affirmation and confirmation of the patient's earlier unmet need, which still attempts satisfaction in the codependent exchange. Thus, the clinician not only understands and legitimizes the suffering the patient experiences but offers an opening for the healthy striving to reestablish itself. The patient's own health directs the treatment and resultant growth, not a predetermined and static behavior hoped for and awaited by the clinician.

Self-psychologically, self help, whether a 12-step program or some other group involvement, serves the function of providing alter ego ties through shared experience and cognitive-behavioral aids and tools, which assist the patient during the difficult reworking of regressed experience that occurs within the therapeutic setting. While primary for the chemically dependent person learning to live drug-free, a group experience is a good legitimizing beginning or a help along the way, but not necessarily the primary form of treatment, for the recovering counterdependent. To force group treatment as the treatment of choice is to deprive the counterdependent patient of the most necessary element of a successful treatment—the establishment and working through of the selfobject transferences so that earlier strivings can be reclaimed from the counterdependent's pathologic interactions and rerouted through more satisfying life experiences. And perhaps most importantly, self psychology, by validating the counterdependent self as another form of archaic self-selfobject functioning, offers the hope and vehicle to provide cure for such patients rather than a life of limited modifications and continued vigilance over one's self, which is what the chemically dependent person achieves in a chemical dependency treatment program.

## Case Material

The case presented here is prototypical of the many patients who attempt and gain some improvement from psychodynamically oriented and recovery treatments and yet ultimately feel injured and impeded by both approaches. By the time I see such patients, they are skeptical of the usefulness of any therapy. They feel defeated and "sicker than ever" because at least two previous treatment modalities have already failed to give them the improved inner sense of self, the vitality, and the competence they sought in order to fully feel, express their affective range, meet previously unattained goals, and acquire the values and kinds of relationships they had always sensed were within their potential.

Ms. L is a 30-year-old woman referred to me by a colleague after a year's hiatus following three years in treatment with a psychoanalytic psychotherapist with an object relations orientation. Before, and at times concurrently with, that treatment she was involved in a 12-step based recovery group for adult children of alcoholics (ACA) that was led by a psychotherapist well trained to work within that model. Ms. L was highly successful in an unconventional and demanding field, an achievement she was not able to acknowledge with any sense of satisfaction or pride. Her reason for seeking treatment was that once again she found herself lovingly attached to a man who, although emotionally involved, was uninterested in a romantic relationship with her. Ms. L reported with great frustration that an unrequited two- to three-year attachment was the only type of relationship she had ever experienced with a man and that there had been three or four previous men. She thought this was because she had grown up in a home with an alcoholic father and as an adult hadn't been able to abstain from relationships long enough to let herself get well. It was too depriving and frustrating for her to be single and love no one, she said, and because she was too needy and codependent, she wasn't strong enough to withstand the deprivation.

Most of this explanation was derived from reading self-help

literature and from the persistent confrontation by members of her recovery group who suggested that she was "getting a fix," had no self-esteem, and didn't like herself when she was single. This hurt and humiliation from her group experience, as well as her analyst's interpretation that her group participation permitted her to avoid total attachment to and involvement in the analysis, led her to terminate her membership in the group. For that decision, group members and the leader labeled her as once again running away from her issues. She felt that she had failed both the group and herself and that it was painful but necessary for her to face the truth about her weak, sick, and needy self.

Ms. L. described her previous psychotherapy as being equally difficult to tolerate. She had not been able to express feelings in any session, a phenomenon that she found frustrating and that the therapist repeatedly interpreted as a defense against both her rage toward and longing for the therapist. Ms. L could not understand why she "just didn't feel safe" with this obviously caring, intelligent, and well-trained therapist who was trying with such well-intended effort to help her. Ms. L continued:

> I simply couldn't trust her. I felt that everything I could think to say about what I was thinking, feeling, dreaming, doing, whatever, wasn't the right answer she was waiting for. Especially when we talked about our relationship, I ended up just trying to guess what it was she wanted me to be feeling since I was always feeling the "wrong" feeling. I wanted so desperately to get better, but she said I was always in my own way, that I needed to experience her as not helping me even though she was. Then she'd remind me of all the helpful things she had previously said and done. What could she possibly gain by my not getting better? We could both acknowledge the times I'd felt understood or helped, so I was really confused. She said that when I could stop feeling stuck and start letting her get close to me by taking in all the help she was offering, I'd get better. I guess I just couldn't let the process happen. Now here I was in two relationships that weren't progressing either inside or outside of treatment . . . I was absolutely stuck. I was just supposed to wait it out. The therapist said that if she agreed that she wasn't safe or had failed me in any way, it would make sense for me to leave and she'd be colluding with my defenses. I knew I didn't feel safe, and even though she said I was safe, I finally had to leave, simply trusting my own self.

Early work centered on affirming Ms. L's feelings and strengthening her trust in them as sources of the perceptual information she needed in order to further explore and eventually determine the cause of her unease. She burst into tears in the first session after I gave her the instruction to pay particular attention to thoughts, feelings, and, especially, criticisms, however slight, she experienced toward me. She left with a great feeling of pride that she had finally cried in front of someone and was shocked that she had done this during an initial session. She both mistrusted and was relieved by my constant curiosity about her feelings, the sense she made of them, her fears about sharing or expressing them in my presence. She began to speculate about how these fears had arisen. She felt angry about her earlier treatments and the fact that others had misunderstood her and yet had held her accountable for their misunderstanding of her. It was a great puzzle to her how she could be so easily misunderstood by people who clearly meant to help her. After all, as her therapist had frequently pointed out, it was in *their* best interests, as well as her own, for her to get better.

As treatment progressed, I asked a variety of questions about her education and use of alcohol and discovered that when she drank with others, which she did infrequently, she drank only small amounts. She was relieved that she was not an alcoholic like her father because she was able, when she wanted to, to drink anyone "under the table," a degree of successful control and unusually high tolerance that signaled the possibility, of which she was unaware, of early-stage alcoholism. We began to talk about the progression of her father's alcoholism and how both he and her mother were preoccupied at first with their ongoing pleasure in socializing and later with the ill effects of his drinking too much, that is, his embarrassing and out-of-control behavior. Ms. L became interested in chemical dependency and started reading material about its etiology and progression.

Ms. L's memories of her father were sparse: he was a prominent professional who was always working or needing rest and quiet when he returned home with the result that he was unavailable for contact; he seemed kind but overburdened or reluctant when Ms. L attempted any involvement with him. Her mother was a competent homemaker who protected the father's need for quiet retreat and explained him and his needs to the children, labeling any complaints against him as "silly whining." For example, Ms. L was told to stop being such a baby and get on with the responsibilities of her own life. Mother was busy running her home, which Ms. L described as "a beautiful, empty museum" and was involved in her school, neighborhood, church, and community. Ms. L was an extremely accomplished child, with a history replete with award-winning scholastic, athletic, and social achievements. The boy she was first involved with was a "buddy" who participated with her in all these activities. Although he said he loved Ms. L as she loved him and although they were occasionally sexually involved, he dated other girls and refused a romantic involvement with her. Ms. L repeated this pattern with two or three other men during her twenties until the current involvement, which had led her to seek treatment.

Ms. L vacillated between anger at me when she sensed I was distant or when I had to cancel appointments and fears that she would want more from me than I could give her. She was afraid to find herself right back in yet another dissatisfying relationship in which she was needy and the other was distant, preoccupied, and self-important. She felt I left her and was then uninterested in her and unable to withstand her anger at me for not tending to her during my absences. Whenever we worked through these ruptures, Ms. L would express a closeness toward me that scared her, especially when she knew how busy I was, because she didn't want to need anyone. She imagined how little she and her needs must seem to me in my big, important universe. As we were nearing a vacation, she canceled an appointment and was tearfully outraged at my charging her for it, which she perceived as my coldness and lack of caring for her. After she yelled at me awhile, the tears took over and she expressed her fears of my leaving and of her new realization that she did indeed need me.

While Ms. L and I discussed her involvement in our treatment relationship, she continued to see her "buddy." Rather than talk Ms. L out of her feelings and involvement with her friend, I began exploring with her the needs he stimulated in her and her reluctance to get them met. She began talking about them with her "buddy" and did her best to romanticize their occasional sexual encounters, something she wanted from him that he consistently rejected. Although her feelings were hurt during these interactions, Ms. L began reporting that "something was different." She described the change as follows: "We are closer in some new way. I can say anything I'm experiencing toward him and neither of us leave. When he's not interested in being my partner, it's not about me." We agreed that it was her improved self-esteem that gave her the vitality to both pursue her needs and withstand the disappointment as a worthy, intact person when they remained unsatisfied. She developed an interest in another man, one with whom she could have a mutual involvement, and enjoyed her new sense of self, which allowed her to get her needs met.

During our work together, Ms. L decided that she was alcoholic, stopped drinking, and started attending Alcoholics Anonymous meetings. It is noteworthy that once her feelings were being addressed and understood within a self-psychological approach, the patient was able to get the educational material and supportive help she needed to resolve the questions she had about her own drinking. Of her participation in AA and another 12-step group she attended for codependents, Ms. L said, "I like knowing I wasn't the only one. I admire these people who have made so much from so little and in them I can see how much I've accomplished in my life. I do what they tell me to: I take what I want and leave the rest, which is most of it besides the people."

The case of Ms. L illustrates the many points made in this chapter. The original recovery group's confrontations further deprived Ms. L and threatened to erode what self-esteem she had rather than support and assist her to improve it. Her previous therapist, unable to tolerate Ms. L's transferential mistrust of her, not only failed to explore a deeper understanding of her subjective experience but missed the opportunity to learn the meaning of the transferential relationship, which was probably a replication of the two unrewarding, distant connections she had previously had with her parents. By working within the empathic vantage point, the clinician is better equipped to understand the obstacles to growth and the needs that must be met in order to stimulate development, once it is safe for it to reawaken. Rather than prevent the outside counterdependent relationship from continuing, the clinician utilizes it as another source of valuable information about the patient's earlier life. Ms. L couldn't tolerate her dependency needs or feel in control of getting them met until the therapist could tolerate, understand, and affirm her fears, her protection against reinjury, and, finally, the dependency needs themselves, openly expressed. Successfully working through the many instances of transferential rupture, Ms. L no longer felt shamed and humiliated by her need for others, as she had as a child in the lonely "museum" with distant, preoccupied, need-shaming parents, and began to honor and respect her needs. As she was able to treat herself with greater respect, it became increasingly difficult for her to settle for the compromised versions of her own satisfaction that her family and romantic history evidenced. Ms. L's new and deeper relationship with her "buddy," in addition to her many transferential experiences, helped her to eventually take her needs to a more satisfying end with another man.

## CONCLUSION

The failings of the recovery community to adequately define and treat the phenomenon of codependency is impossible to ignore. Codependency does not lose its meaning because it is applicable and understandable to so many. The concept of codependency has expanded beyond its origins in the chemical dependency community and has popularized the self-selfobject relationship that many people intuitively recognize as a repetition of early childhood relationships in which their own needs, which still control their present, were inadequately met. To remain a useful concept, codependency must now develop past its original association with chemical dependency and its cognitive-behavioral treatments and be understood in all its complexity as the state of the counterdependent self, a state that is unconsciously based and therefore requires treatment that is not limited to a concern with conscious experience and observable behavior.

The one-to-one transference relationship is the treatment that can respond to the special and unique needs of each patient and mobilize the unconscious needs trapped within the unanalyzed counterdependent self, needs that will cause unhealthy behavior patterns to endlessly repeat until they are freed. Self-psychological theory clarifies the codependent's need for the other as a selfobject, a need unmet earlier in time that continues to strive for responsiveness at incredible cost to the counterdependent self.

Self psychologists and codependency theorists alike are observing and trying to understand the results of impaired parental functioning. Whereas codependent theorists developed their ideas out of descriptive interpersonal models, self psychologists developed theirs from a psychoanalytic model. Both patients and recovery clinicians are increasingly aware that the educational approach, primarily in the form of cognitive-behavioral group treatment, while a useful beginning, falls short of treating codependency symptoms over time. Codependency theorists, at this point, have limited ways to acknowledge the healthy, normal interpersonal relationships and dependency needs contained within codependent relationships, since their focus has been on describing and validating the pathology. As a result, treatment approaches suffer from a tendency to overpathologize dependency needs. Codependency theorists can benefit greatly from psychoanalytic self psychology, whose conceptual base recognizes healthy psychological needs and whose treatment approach is rooted in the goals of uncovering and developing the previously thwarted healthy strivings. Self psychologists, while already versed in treating damage to the self and selfobject relations, can gain an increased sensitivity to diagnosing chemical dependency and utilizing the interventions necessary for working with the counterdependent patient, particularly those whose counterdependency was developed in a chemically dependent family. In conclusion, the counterdependent self can be defined as a regressed self with selfobject needs who was derailed early in life because of a poorly responding environment, whose weaknesses and injuries can be ameliorated or healed, and whose development can be resumed in the safe, knowledgeable, and healthy treatment environment of the self-psychologically informed clinician.

## REFERENCES

Bacal, H. & Newman, K. (1990), *Theories of Object Relations: Bridges to Self Psychology.* New York: Columbia University Press.

Bader, M. (1988), Looking for addictions in all the wrong places. *Tikkun,* 3:13–98.

Beletsis, S. & Brown, S. (1981), A developmental framework for understanding the adult children of alcoholics. *Focus on Women: J. Addictions & Health,* 2:187–203.

Black, C. (1981), *It Will Never Happen To Me.* Denver, CO: MAC.

Blau, M., (1990), Adult children: Tied to the past. *Amer. Health* 9:56–65.

Brown, S. (1985), *Treating the Alcoholic.* New York: Wiley.

_____ (1988), *Treating Adult Children of Alcoholics.* New York: Wiley.

Cermak, T. (1986), *Diagnosing and Treating Co-dependence.* Minneapolis, MN: Johnson Institute Books.

Cooper, J. (1991), Codependency is not an addiction. *Recovering,* 25:  –  .

Detrick, D. (1985), Alterego phenomena and the alterego transferences. In: *Progress in Self Psychology,* 1:240–256, ed. A. Goldberg. New York: Guilford Press.

_____ (1986), Alterego phenomena and the alterego transferences: Some further considerations. In: *Progress in Self Psychology,* 2:299–304, ed. A. Goldberg. New York: Guilford Press.

Greenleaf, J. (1981), *Co-Alcoholic: Para-Alcoholic.* Los Angeles, CA: 361 Foundation.

Johnson, V. (1973), *I'll Quit Tomorrow.* New York: Harper & Row.

Kaminer, W. (1990), Chances are you're codependent too. *The New York Times Book Review,* pp. 25–27.

Kernberg, O. (1969), Factors in the psychoanalytic treatment of narcissistic personality disorders. *Bull. Menninger Clin.,* 33:191–196.

Kohut, H. (1959), Introspection, empathy, and psychoanalysis. In: *The Search for the Self, Vol. 2,* ed. P. Ornstein, New York: International Universities Press, 1978.

_____ (1971), *The Analysis of the Self.* New York: International Universities Press.

_____ (1977a), Preface. In: *Psychodynamics of Drug Dependence,* ed. J. D. Blaine & D. A. Julius. National Institute on Drug Abuse Research, Monogr. Series #12, Washington, DC: U.S. Govt. Printing Office.

_____ (1977b), *The Restoration of the Self.* New York: International Universities Press.

_____ (1987), The addictive need for an admiring other in regulation of self-esteem. *The Kohut Seminars on Self Psychology and Psychotherapy with Adolescents and Young Adults,* ed. M. Elson. New York: Norton, pp. 113–132.

Larsen, E. (1985), *Stage II Recovery.* Minneapolis, MN: Winston Press.

Wolf, E. (1988), *Treating the Self.* New York: Guilford Press.

Wegscheider, S. (1981), *Another Chance.* Palo Alto, CA: Science and Behavior Books.

Wood, B. (1987), *Children of Alcoholism.* New York: New York University Press.

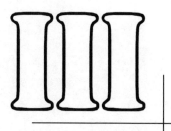

# Applied

# Chapter 9

# Optimal Operative Perversity: A Contribution to the Theory of Creativity

## Carl T. Rotenberg

The study of creativity is an ongoing interest of self psychology. I have discussed how art objects can have selfobject meaning for both the audience and for their creators. Recently, Dr. Howard Baker (1988) explored the contributions of the painter Vincent Van Gogh and discussed the artist's selfobject needs. I think there are a number of reasons why self psychology is congenial, in theory, practice, and in its general spirit, to the development of thinking about creativity. One of these derives from Kohut's early recognition that a direct outcome of the restoration to cohesiveness of a previously fragmented or defensively distorted self-organization was the "uninterrupted flow" toward creative expression in some form (Kohut, 1977, pp. 40, 54). To introduce this chapter, I offer a clinical vignette whose purpose is to illustrate (1) the expression of creative action in the fabric of clinical work and (2) the significant expression of oppositionism as part and parcel of that creative action.

## CLINICAL EXAMPLE

Lydia was a married mother of three children and a professional woman in the health field. She was regarded generally as highly competent in both her professional and personal life. Lydia sought treatment because of persisting depressive symptoms of several years' duration that met the psychiatric diagnostic criteria for a Major Depressive Disorder. In spite of the many successes in her career, her marriage, her growing children, and her community contributions, Lydia felt that there was a great deal missing. Although she felt that she had been successful in many areas of her life, where much was expected of her, and although she felt genuinely proud of herself, she nevertheless felt an emptiness at the center. In her fight to achieve, significant aspects of herself had gone undeveloped—and could not develop within the relationship context in which she was currently living. She did not suffer from a false self organization (Winnicott, 1952), in which existing accomplishments are felt as empty; it is more that she experienced her existing self-organization as dissociated and incomplete.

Lydia indicated that she had been a caretaker to her mother since the age of three. To some extent, her depressive feelings date back to that time. Her earliest memories were those of feeling elated that she was capable of consoling her depressed, depleted, and withdrawn mother. A dream early in treatment conveyed her sense of depression, self-constriction, and her unwanted identification with the object of her early caretaking efforts, her mother: "I was trying to escape from somewhere. I was crawling on my knees through a water pipe. My knees were cut by pieces of gravel. When I awoke, my knee hurt me the whole day." Knee injury in the dream was associated directly with a knee injury and operation that her mother had when Lydia was very young and that caused her mother limitation of movement and feelings of shame.

In the third month of treatment the patient mentioned playfully that she felt an interest in doing photography. She tended to mention this subject in segments of the session she deliberately designated as "time for chatter" (during which her comments were less serious and more like social conversation). I responded with interest to this when she mentioned it and disclosed that it was an area of art with which I was familiar. At various times she would talk in passing about looking for a specific camera, and she wondered if I knew one that would be good. I told her that I didn't know a specific model, that I thought doing photography was about finding the unique way in which one saw things, and that most modern cameras would do the job. I encouraged her to get past the equipment question and take pictures.

In the fifth month of treatment and shortly before a vacation, she brought in her first developed roll of film for me to see. She offered me the pictures with great tentativeness; they seemed to be mostly snapshots of her family, with a few shots of scenery that were picturesque. The images showed that she had a good feeling for composition. These transactions were for the most part transient, and they were enacted in the sessions with an understanding that we were engaged in a kind of play whose meaning was not entirely clear.

In the first session following a three-week vacation period, Lydia started the session by discussing a recent unhappy fight with her mother. She realized that when her mother inflicted pain, this was done mainly out of empathic obliviousness to her rather than out of deliberate cruelty. Shortly thereafter, her mood changed, and she discussed with delight how she had bought a camera. Through this initiative, she had achieved an unexpected affirming response from her husband, an equally dedicated "caretaker." His response helped her to see, somewhat to her surprise, that he did not feel it was disloyal of her to have an interest of her own. As she discussed her purchase, her mood was one of prideful accomplishment and playful excitement. She then asked me to look at a roll of developed pictures but not to say anything about them. I looked through them and was impressed at seeing a number of nicely composed picturesque images of plants, flowers, flowing water, and other scenes. I was impressed that in a single roll of film she had achieved picturesque portrayal so consistently, but I said nothing of this, asking her only what she saw. She replied:

I see very pretty pictures. They look dead. They look black and empty. What I can't understand is whether the deadness I see is in me or in the medium. Maybe I should do another form of art, like getting my hands messy with paint or mucky with clay. Do I need to *patschke*? [The Yiddish word *patschke* connotes repetitive play and fussiness.] Photography is a trick and does not have a lot of humanity. Is it that I feel dead inside and what I see is looking back at me? These are lovely pictures, but they don't speak to me in any way. These pictures should be related uniquely to me, whatever and whoever that is.

Lydia was clear that she wanted to *"patschke"* in a messy material, like clay, paint, or mud, that would introduce elements of disorder and disorganization. I commented that her feelings were understandable in that what one tries to create is related to the core of who one is and what there is about the self that one thinks is good. I affirmed her right to *"patschke"* in whatever field she chose and suggested that the anxiety and dread were inherent in the attempt to create anew and that her feelings were understandable and concerned not only the pictures but, in a larger sense, the shifts and changes in herself that she was trying to accomplish. We laughed over the notion that maybe what she needed to experiment with was finding mess and ugliness to photograph. She thought she might go to her garage and make pictures there; she was not going to find what she was looking for about herself in what was conventional and pretty.

This vignette illustrates important aspects of the created object to themes in the self. In her attempt to find original beauty and uniqueness in herself, Lydia saw empty conventionality reflected back to her in the images she made. To my mind her aesthetic observations about her images were correct, but her expectations for technical originality in her second roll of film were as extravagant and self-punitive as her vulnerability was painful. In her images the patient was not relating so much to the content as to the form. She rejected the conventionality, the deadness of formal repetition empty of innovation, the absence of a departure from accustomed form that would have represented a unique expression of her own.

Developmentally, this tendency to comply with authority repeated the too early thwarting of important sectors of Lydia's own self-development. The stifled formal conventionality of her images mirrored the way her psychological coping skills and adaptive flexibility were in a rut, so to speak. In a rather global fashion, she had maintained a needed relationship with her empathically opaque, depressed, and punitively critical mother through the elaboration of a caretaking self-organization. She was able to govern herself and prevent chaos by being highly attuned to the expectations of others, and she patterned her own behavior along these conventional lines. In the context of her relationship with me and in her attempts to extract herself from the prison of her self-confinement, her images had, individually and as an aggregate, important selfobject meaning for her. They offered the potential—but also the risks—for self-transformation along uncharted paths. Of course, what needs further exploration is whether Lydia's pursuit of photography at that stage in treatment was mainly a defensive repetition in the transference of her customary way of doing things, that is, a dutiful repetition of her accommodation to the expectations of her mother, and not yet her own original medium of expression, but that is a topic for another discussion.

This clinical description will be recognizable to most self psychologists, since the spontaneous appearance in treatment of new ambitions for creative expression is a frequent occurrence in self-psychologically guided treatments. For the purposes of this chapter, where I discuss the relationship of aspects of self-development to the formal aspects of art, it is important to note that it was the formal qualities of Lydia's initial work that were significant. She noticed the absence of oppositionism in herself, the absence of messiness, and, along with those, the absence of her own originality. In this specific manner Lydia both informed me of and invited my validation of the positive significance of delving into her inner psychic "messiness." She was setting the stage for our mutual exploration at a later date of the full extent of her inner "muck."

This case vignette illustrates several additional matters. First, studies of creativity are *not* limited to the realm of intellectual curiosity, as the term *applied psychoanalysis* sometimes implies. Creative initiative is part of the fabric of everyday clinical life (both in the patient and in the analyst), and an appreciation for the forces that generate it is crucial to effective therapeutic action. In this passage I have described a patient's playful reencounter with the long-neglected germs of creativity in the core of her self. Paradoxically, this same playful activity unleashed intense anxieties of potential hazards to her self-experience. The vignette also shows how, even from the outset of creative action, created objects can have selfobject meaning for the creator. Lydia's pictures had mirroring significance for a dissociated core of self-experience felt to be devitalized and void. They also were a concrete clarification of how she hoped to improve in treatment.

## OPTIMAL OPERATIVE PERVERSITY

There is a feature of art work for which I have designated the term "optimal operative perversity." This term condenses attitudes and actions within the creative field whereby the artist creates problems *or* stumbles upon them and then attempts to resolve them. The field in which the artist works may be viewed as being the same field that comprises the relation of self to selfobject. This relationship of artist to product is an intersubjective field, whether the psychological one described by Stolorow, Brandchaft, and Atwood (1987) or the transactional one described by Bruner (1983) and Trevarthan (1980). I will now discuss in detail the meaning of "optimal operative perversity."

### Perversity

The term *perversity* is used here in its dictionary sense of "deviating from what is right or acceptable" or "stubbornly contrary." In this sense perversity is the expression of the artist who consistently, and with technical means, contradicts a previously held principle of organization. In painting, the overthrown principle could well be a formal one, such as the use of the picture plane in painting, or it could involve the narrative content. To take a historical example, noted by Kohut (1984, p. 175), in the Renaissance Brunelleschi introduced the new artistic principle of geometric perspective. Although it was genuinely radical in the early Renaissance, it no longer holds its original revolutionary distinctiveness. What characterizes the artist's initiative is his decision to call into question and reverse a previously held artistic structural assumption. The term *perverse* suggests that this expressive initiative occurs in an artistic field that can be disinclined to accept it or that may resist seeing the merit that gives birth to it.

Perverse expression can occur in a variety of forms. Insofar as we are focusing for the moment on visual art, the perversity (i.e., the stubbornly contrary idea) can be expressed through a novel approach to form, line, composition, color, narrative content, or an aspect of technique that has relevance for significant form.

The language of art is a continuously evolving one, and it moves, like culture in general, through sequences of historical traditions that are forever transformed. Art is ordered but within that structural consistency there is the expectable introduction of disorder, and perverse expression is an agent of this change. Perverse expression in itself, as used here, has nothing to do with pathological sexuality or aggression as such. I think this is evident in the examples that follow. However, the vocabulary of sexuality and aggression may be presented, as in drama, as a means of intensification of new formal expression.

The expression of perversity can cause the introduction of elements that might be regarded as ugly or, alternatively, that might not be recognized as art at all. The introduction of elements that are original or new results in perception whose implications have not yet been assimilated into the order-making structures of the self, either at conscious or nonconscious levels. What is gratifying improvisation for the maker might be unattractive or even hideous for the viewer because it is not yet comprehensible within acknowledged frameworks. For example, until one appreciates that expressionist art involves representational images of what might be felt emotionally rather than "realistic" images, the paintings might be viewed as hideous and repulsive (e.g., Munch, Kokoschka, Picasso). The obtrusive, seemingly gratuitous display of grotesque forms can elicit the violent affective reactions that often accompany the introduction of avant-garde art. Strong emotional reactions of this sort are, of course, not in themselves necessarily evidence of great art. Original art, however, is likely to produce strong affective reactions that express the pain experienced by the self in not being able to either dismiss or assimilate the percepts to which it has been exposed. At the same time, for nonconscious reasons, these same percepts tempt the self.

For example, the public outrage over the photographs of the late photographer Mapplethorpe is an example of this phenomenon. His provocative pornographic works, technically produced with the aesthetic skill that derives from modernist photography, raise serious and probing artistic questions that can neither be visited comfortably nor easily dismissed. Rage, depression, anxiety, and the wish to rid oneself of the percepts in a variety of ways are all potential affective reactions to the originality in his work. Of course, in Mapplethorpe's works the notion of perversity achieves concrete expression in visual form that resembles pornography. The notoriety of Mapplethorpe's images, however, lies entirely in the formal questions they provoke. If his photographs were merely pornographic, they could be easily dismissed, as is most pornography. But precisely because they are executed with the technical skill and the aesthetic standard of traditional modernist photography, Mapplethorpe's images cause us to confront important questions about public imagery and private sensibility, figure and ground, form versus content; they cause a forceful reexamination of the exclusion of human narrative from modernist and postmodernist abstraction (see, by contrast, the exquisite nudes of the modernist photographer Edward Weston, whose aesthetic message from an earlier artistic era is entirely different).

The point of discussing Mapplethorpe's work here lies in the opportunity to examine our own affective reaction to new work of our day. The public outrage in reaction to his work is at least similar in *mood* to the affective reaction that greeted the work of the Impressionists in their day; this contemporary response can give us perspective on a similar response from that historical era.

At this point, I would like to briefly review some aspects of the notion of oppositionism as viewed by psychoanalytic theory. This is significant for our subject since psychoanalytic contributions to art generally have not received widespread intellectual acceptance. Aestheticians and artists express a consensus that their work is reduced in scope, rather than enhanced, by traditional psychoanalytic interpretation. For example, in the recent dialogue between John Gedo (1987) and Theodore Reff (1987) concerning Cezanne, Gedo, the analyst, points out evidence for Cezanne's masochism, symbiotic conflicts, and unconscious homosexuality. Reff, the art scholar, feels Gedo provides a few useful insights about Cezanne's character but does not find these insights useful in understanding either Cezanne's art itself or the strength and resolution that made Cezanne's heroic achievement possible. In a way that I have found to be characteristic, the art scholar objects to the psychopathological emphasis analysts employ in psychobiographical studies.[1] In part, the failure of psycho-analysis to fully apprehend artistic struggles is evident in the perusal of theory about enactments and oppositionism.

A complete review of the theory of oppositional behavior in psychoanalysis would take us far afield, but let me at least mention a few familiar terms that convey the aforementioned psychopatholog-ical tilt to the analytic understanding of contrary behavior. I am thinking of the anal triad of Freud and the recent employment by Nagera (1967) of the concept of anal sadistic regression and uncon-scious homosexuality (as well as his equation of painting and mas-turbation) in explaining the psychodynamics of the artist Van Gogh. By contrast, in my mind the artist engages in perverse expression because it is essential to the process of creativity. The artist's goal is to incorporate information that will transform or expand existing as-sumptions and structures by changing the rules. He achieves this goal within a context of evolving artistic knowledge that has its own traditions and does so in some form that is readily observable. In the course of this activity he creates problems to which he must respond. Hopefully, this series of initiatives and subsequent responses will result in an integrated aesthetic that expresses the artist's individual style.

In theory and in practice traditional psychoanalysis emphasizes the notion of psychic structure and the predictable, ordered behavior that arises from intact structures that lead to adaptation and reality testing. The notion of psychic structure, as Goldberg (1988) points out, "directs our attention to the forms and patterns by which the composite elements connect and relate to one another" (p. 129); he uses the analogy of a railway schedule on a particular line as a way of illustrating this. Thus, normative behavior tends to be viewed as that which is consistent with a given set of forms, rules, and expected sequences of events. Behavior that seeks to call existing forms into question as a matter of principle is then viewed with suspicion as "unstructured" and therefore potentially pathological.

Similarly, since reality relationships have traditionally been one of our most accustomed clinical criteria for the assessment of psychic well-being, that which asserts the necessity of being "stubbornly contrary" to existing ways of organizing and experiencing reality may

---

[1]Gedo (1987) the accomplished psychobiographer of artists, gives a partial expla-nation for the psychopathological emphasis of psychoanalysts when he notes that the more deeply Gedo immersed himself empathically into the artist's private life and his "human isolation," the more difficult Gedo found it to keep Cezanne's stature in mind (p. 187).

be assumed to have suspicious potential for psychopathology. Even within the framework of self psychology, which in theory asserts the primacy of psychological reality, however "unrealistic" it may be, there reigns an academicism that feels traditional—there still exists a set of rules. Self psychology, however, at least asks how parts of the structured self-system come to be organized and how it relates to the communicative context of which the self-structure is a part. The nature of the relationship to reality is, to some extent, an unresolved debate within the structure of self-psychological theory, as illustrated in the debates during the 1989 Self Psychology Conference.

The act of oppositional expression may be driven to some extent by aspects of the self that deserve elucidation. One of these is the feeling of grandeur, which is often seen by others as pathological grandiosity. Creating anew requires the assumption of one's capacity to surpass predecessors who are socially idealized. The expression of one's capacity to achieve this might be received as sacrilege within the context of uncritical idealization. The Canadian artist Jack Bush (personal communication, 1970) expressed this notion firmly but disarmingly when he said, upon returning from an initial viewing of Matisse's European paintings, "I expect to outdo Matisse—I don't think he'll mind."

Much has been written about the grandiosity of the artist, the ostensibly inflated self-esteem. Kohut was the first analyst, to my knowledge, to recognize the regular occurrence in the creative self of feelings of heightened grandeur necessary to confront the experience of anxiety inherent in original expression. He reported the labile shifts in self-esteem and narcissistic tensions inherent in the anticipation and then the completion of the creative act. "During creative periods, the self is at the mercy of powerful forces it cannot control . . . it feels itself hopelessly exposed to extreme mood swings which range from severe precreative depression to dangerous hypomanic overstimulation" (1976, p. 818). It is as if the artist is saying, "I am sufficiently great to meet this challenge. I can go where no person has gone before!" And this entails both feelings of isolation and exhilaration. These elevations of self-esteem are often accompanied by the manifestation of other personality traits in the artist, such as stubbornness, rigidity, defiance, and iconoclasm.[2] One can recognize in the formal

---

[2]For example, Henri Matisse was described by Picasso's ex-wife, Francoise Gilot (1990), as follows: "Matisse, the benevolent patriarch, was endowed with an impish spirit. The word 'impossible' was not part of his vocabulary. He needed to overstep the bounds, to experience how far he could carry things so as to test his own forbearance, as well as the potential adverse reactions of his friends" (p. 191).

elements of art qualities that seem to say, "How do you like this?" or even "So there! Stick it in your ear."

Developmentally, such attitudes draw on attributes that originate in the earliest stages of development. Bollas (1978) has sensitively described "the aesthetics of maternal handling." Originality can be traced to experimentation in play and to the developing infant's earliest experiments in researching the puzzling world around it (Stern, 1985). Oppositionism can be seen in the stage described by Spitz (1957) as the "third organizer of the psyche," in which a toddler learns to say no out of identification with the aggressive aspects of its mother. The hauteur, grandeur, defiance, and stubbornness of the artist's self are reminiscent of Kohut's original description of the bipolar self, particularly the grandiose pole of the self. While this description of the artistic personality is reminiscent of narcissistic psychopathology, it is important to understand that this exaggeration of apparently pathological personality traits reflects the experience of an anxiously vulnerable self that first anticipates the anxieties inherent in improvisatory thinking and, secondly, buttresses itself to meet the anticipated challenges in this area.

Artistic creativity does not necessarily reflect the primacy of conflicts and deficits retroactively determined. Oppositional expression, insofar as it determines creativity, is not negativism; it is not reaction formation; it is not the symptomatic defiance through which persons guard their autonomy against external forces felt to be threatening; it is not the experiential pole of ambivalent paralysis. It may, of course, include elements of all of these.

In describing the attribute of perversity, I am only describing one of the many elements in a person's capacity to produce independent ideas. Perversity in this sense facilitates the opportunity to be original, separate, and spontaneous, but it is not synonymous with originality. The choice of the individual's particular mode of original expression (visual in painting, auditory in music, tactile in sculpture), the determination to be creative, and the ability and talent to participate in the larger context of culture and art are all issues I am not considering at this time.

### "Optimal"

*Optimal* as a term carries the meaning of "most desirable or satisfactory." It is synonymous with *optimum*, which means "the most favorable or most conducive to a given end." Thus we speak of optimal temperature for growth, an optimal dose of medication for a desired therapeutic effect, and optimal timing and tact in analytic interpretation. While I have used this word in its generic sense, it is not intended to refer to the notion of "optimal responsiveness" (Bacal, 1985), a term that has a more specific delineated meaning within the theory and language of self psychology. What is optimal in the sense I mean is easier to illustrate than to describe. Insofar as it refers to the perversity of artistic enactments, optimal refers to the quality and degree of unusualness that also achieves an integration with the rest of the pictorial field of which it is a part. *Optimal* is a term that indicates that the proposed perverse enactment does not stand by itself. Rather, it inevitably asserts itself within a field it seeks to integrate and with which it interacts. Perverse expression that is not optimal is that which cannot achieve integration and so, in a sense, falls out of the picture; in other words, it leads to fragmentation of the experience of the picture. Synthesis, harmony, and pictorial integration are not achieved; the failing effort may appear as little more than idiosyncrasy or personal quirk.

Often, it is easier to distinguish the disintegrated quality of a picture than to actively identify how it may be unified; the *experience* of the viewer would be of disintegration rather than integration. Obviously, the optimal quality of perverse expression is a quality that inheres in the picture but at the same time is relative over time to the audiences' assimilation of the pictorial truths expressed. To pick an example, the aesthetic modes expressed in Van Gogh's paintings are far more sought after in 1990 than they were a century ago, when they were viewed as unacceptably bad art. This acceptance derives from the public's learning to appreciate over time how Van Gogh's technique established harmony and order and contrasts with the initial reaction to his work as disorder generated by storms of unusual color in combination with vigorously textured and coarse brush strokes, seen by many as vulgar at first.

To appreciate the importance of pictorial synthesis and overall unity, it might be helpful to review the concepts of self and selfobject. I incline here toward the succinct yet comprehensive definition of the self offered by Basch (1988): the self is the experience (at all levels of consciousness) of how the brain makes order. This not only describes the self as an abstraction referring to the core of the personality but it says something of how this happens. Basch once mentioned that the self might be better expressed as a verb (i.e., as "selfing"), which would refer actively to its ordering functions.

Selfobjects are objects that are experienced as part of the self. Selfobjects are noteworthy in that they function in a variety of describable ways to maintain the cohesiveness of the self and the experience of competent selfhood. Among their various active functions, selfobjects serve to "delineate" (Stolorow, 1989) the self and to "transform" the self (Rotenberg, 1988). An overview of the numerous potential functions of the selfobject informs us that each one refers to the specific way in which it has organizing potential for the self or facilitates the achievement of order and/or continuity. Since the self is not static throughout life but continuously evolves, there arises the paradox that maintaining order requires transformational evolution. Participating in the experience of art assists this process. Artistic experience, whether of the creator or spectator, is not only pleasurable but can transform the participating self to different levels of functional order. Elsewhere (Rotenberg, 1988) I described how the art work has selfobject significance both for the artist and the viewer. In each art work, noise, disorder, chaos, or disorganization is introduced by the perverse expression described in earlier paragraphs. As a consequence, there arises a struggle between the organizing and disorganizing principles as seen at that point in time. Art works are "syntactically dense" (Goodman, 1973); in saying this, the constructivist philosopher Goodman refers to the multiplicity and variety of struggles and dialectics—formal, iconic, moral—that are set up with or without conscious purpose within the context of any given work. Art works are felt to be successful insofar as these struggles are resolved in the work, both individually and in relationship to each other. For example, for Monet, confluent expressive color and blurred linear draftsmanship are separate but interrelated formal issues, and their individual resolutions reinforce each other. Pictorial unity is the hoped-for artistic result. The more highly ordered structuralization of the self is the hoped-for result of the experience of "transient coextensiveness" with the work. To quote Milner (1957), "Are we not rather driven by the internal necessity for inner organization, pattern, coherence, the basic need to discover identity and difference, without which experience becomes chaos?" (p. 103).

To summarize this section, *optimal* refers to the extent to which the perverse expression is integrated syntactically and aesthetically with the whole work of art and each of its details. Less than optimal perverse expression would represent the extent to which fragmentation in the work is manifested, as represented by disorder, disorganization, or a lack of synthetic unity.[3]

---

[3]I am reminded of Matisse's felicitous statement: "Expression, for me, does not reside in passions glowing in a human face or manifested by violent movement. The entire arrangement of my picture is expressive: the place occupied by the figures, the empty spaces between them, the proportions, everything has its share" (quoted in Flam, 1978, p. 36).

## "Operative"

I shall limit my remarks in this section to a few observations. Art work can be viewed simultaneously as product and process. Insofar as art work is material product and more than fantasy, its substantial properties are significant in that it leaves a record for judgment over time. While the object has its origins in the conscious and unconscious psyche of its creator, it achieves materiality through technical methods and modes of execution, and the record of those enactments is part of the aesthetic experience. As Kuhns (1983) has pointed out, "Enactments are cultural events, objects, actions that are used, presented, and honoured; they have a cultural status not unlike that of persons, though they are made things that can be classified in terms of their media." (p. 53) Culture in general is, then, a "tradition of enactments" (p. 53). It is a long way from fantasy, however imaginative and complex, to its realization as a cultural enactment. One of the requirements for a successfully enacted art work is that it is functionally whole. This integrated quality is not a requirement of fantasy, transference activity, or symptomatic acting out. In this light the tendency of psychoanalysis to intermingle concepts of artistic expression and symptomatic acting out without distinguishing between them is untenable. Self psychology has taken a different view of activity within the clinical realm by differentiating enactments from "acting out" as described traditionally. As used here, *operative* refers to the enacted quality of the art work and to the technical skill that makes it possible.

At this point, I will illustrate some of the principles of "optimal operative perversity" by discussing two paintings. The paintings are by Darryl Hughto and by Susan Roth, both contemporary American painters whose work is widely known and publicly exhibited. I have selected these paintings because their abstractness facilitates the vivid demonstration of specific formal and material issues through which the artists express their originality.

### *Brunett* by Darryl Hughto (Figure 1)

Although Hughto's reputation has been solidly built on his achievements in abstract art, in 1986 he brought his hard-won facility and knowledge to a renewed study of one of the classical themes in art, the human figure. Since then, he has also worked on figures in groups, and still lifes. In *Brunett*, a recent painting of this genre, I shall identify several perversities that represent enduring aspects of Hughto's artistic self, as expressed in his style and in his content. Hughto's perversity in style is most immediately felt in the virtuoso

FIGURE 1. Darryl Hughto, "Brunett," 1990, 30 inches by 24 inches. Courtesy of the artist.

manner with which he makes the complex look simple and the technically arduous look easy. How does he accomplish this?

First, let us pay attention to color.[4] Hughto's "perversity" lies partly in his ability to select colors that in themselves might be offensive or colors that do not ordinarily seem like they belong together and use them harmoniously in the same pictorial space. For example, in *Brunett* the small crimson triangle (at two o'clock), the deep blue, and the green on either side seem by themselves unattractive; however, in the overall context of this picture, they seem to be natural neighbors. Another example lies in the different areas of the figure, where the khaki breast and right arm are set off against different hues and textures in the back, hip, and leg. In this relatively small picture, color is articulated with elegance.

Hughto is also innovative in the way he uses original materials, for example, iridescent paint alongside transparency, again to achieve harmonious contrasts within the picture. As we examine the painting, we can see that it is analogous to an essay in its expressiveness about the interrelationship of colors and the materials that contain them; the analogy might be to the give-and-take of personal conversation. Note also the entrancing variety of ways in which paint is handled within one picture, both in the technical mastery of choice of materials and the bravura quality of the draftsmanship. We see here the effect of the master's hand in the way he controls paint on canvas.

Another noteworthy element consists of the many forms in Hughto's painting. There is no outline as such; Hughto frequently uses line that changes color along its length. Drawing is also evident in his masterful use of the gel, and his facility with gel is one of his strongest features. The thickness of the gel as set against its transparency is one of the noteworthy push-and-pull dialectics we see. The rugged gel work in the apricot area (lower right) breaks up the continuity of the color surface in that area, which causes it to contrast with, yet exist comfortably alongside, the pink smooth-surfaced translucent area in the lower center. The counterpoint of textures yields a vibrancy to the surface. The vigorous drawing texturally balances the apricot area by creating simultaneous contrasts with the silver ground and the smooth lime green area above.

Finally, the translucency of the gel over the lower half of the body demonstrates the new ways in which color can be viewed and experienced. Gel is used in the painting to give thickness and texture as well as to lend translucency to color and to allow us to experience

---

[4]Hughto's use of color is entirely his own, although he follows in the tradition of Matisse, Hofmann, and Bush.

color emerging, as it were, from the depths of the canvas. The painting is flat, but the various uses of colour, texture, and surface take us both behind and in front of the painting, setting up dynamic spatial tensions.

Next, the perimeter of the painting bears consideration. To Hughto, the perimeter of the painting becomes an essential artistic decision. He crops the canvas to locate the painting and decides whether or not the interior painting calls for a rectangular perimeter, as in *Brunett*, or an oddly shaped perimeter, as in *Crosstown* (Figure 2). This is a technique that was Hughto's innovation, although it draws on the historical initiatives of Manet. The goal of this technique is to see the perimeter of the painting as part of and responsive to the formal aspects of the painting. Rather than being a preconceived and arbitrary rectangular shape, the perimeter coexists with the inner area of the painting with formal integrity. This is an inversion of traditional thinking.

Lastly, regarding content, let us turn to Hughto's place in the history of painting. Hughto's reexamination of the figure has elicited opposition from the academicism of the modernist group of which he is a part. His departure from pure abstraction to reexamine the figure has been regarded as heretical within his peer abstract expressionist group. Among his peers there has been a lag in recognizing that "it matters little what you paint; what matters much is how well you paint it" (Hughto, 1987, p. 1). Hughto brings to the figure the insights of modernism and has thus taken a major step forward. These insights include spontaneity of color, pliability of materials, and flexibility of technique, as well as the primacy of pictorial flatness. Hughto's defiance has given him a unique place in modern art. Many artists in the postmodernist tradition have forsworn modernist abstraction to reintegrate the representational because modernism had seemed aloof, sterile, and irrelevant to contemporary life. Some of these artists—Jasper Johns, for example—have caricatured modernism rather than reintegrate the truths it discovered.[5] In a sense, Hughto is calling for reexamination of artistic questions whose tradition goes back at least a century, when Monet's impressionist rendition of the Giverny gardens and his images of haystacks first led to the abstraction of Kandinsky, Mondrian, and others. Hughto's pictures represent a pictorial paradox that informs the viewer that the abstract art revolution can be creatively advanced through the repre-

---

[5]Each of the technical and stylistic issues mentioned here have potential denotative and symbolic significance, although these may not be articulable from a vantage point so close in time to the painting's production.

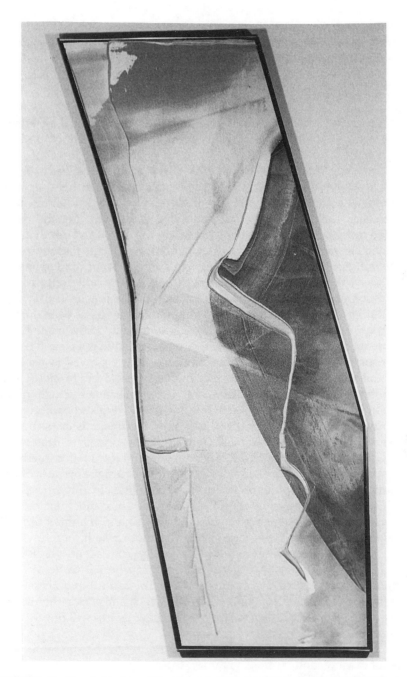

FIGURE 2. Darryl Hughto, "Crosstown," 1986, 81 inches by 39 inches. Private Collection.

sentational idiom. Paintings such as *Brunett* combine the best of these two worlds. To my mind, this superb picture is representative of an oeuvre whose greatness is yet to be apprehended.

### *Sugar Cookie* by Susan Roth (Figure 3)

In Susan Roth's *Sugar Cookie* I shall point out some formal aspects of the artist's originality that bear upon this discussion of optimal perversity.

Cropping the canvas to locate the picture is not original to Roth. However, her manner of shaping the canvas is uniquely her own. Her manner of drawing and her use of materials create formal tensions that elicit their own contours. In this particular painting the right-sided indentation is determined in part by the shape and depth of the folded canvas on the right, re-directing our eyes to the flatter area on the left. At the same time, it stands as a statement of draftsmanship on its own, aggressively challenging the viewer's adherence to the tradition of the rectangle and also to traditional methods of drawing.

Roth's most outstanding and original contribution has been the use of the folded canvas as a means of drawing and, at the same time, representing color dynamics. This formal technique is a clear illustration of optimal perversity. The painted, folded canvas is used to produce sensations that are at once highly physical and luscious. The folding technique becomes drawing and establishes fluctuations in the hue and intensity of color. While line in drawing and painting has always conveyed a physical sense of how the image is constructed, the use of varying materials creating folds brings to the work interplays of depth and flatness that are unique to this method. Giacometti's use of clay and physical form were unique because of the particular way he brought us to appreciate line. In this sense, the folds of Roth's material, the space they occupy, and their overall shape are formal elements producing surprise and requiring assimilation to her tough expression. Roth does not make it more inviting for us by suffusing her work with pretty colors and traditional materials. Her use of variegated surfaces can be felt to be at once smooth like silk (see, for example, the pink ground) and abrasively defiant, as in her use of concrete paint, which she also is the first to use. The undulating folds in the canvas draw us inward, but the use of other materials seem to push us away.

The formal elements of Roth's work are perverse from an artistic point of view, and, as in all great art, the optimal aspect of it not only makes the painting work but raises still broader questions. The application of canvas to canvas, in itself singular, asks intriguing

FIGURE 3. Susan Roth, "Sugar Cookie," 1990, 30 inches by 23 inches. Private Collection.

questions about orientation to the picture plane. The nature of her technique, which contains a large measure of spontaneity, asks us to ponder the nature of the random act. Her work forces us to consider pictorial flatness versus depth, the surface tactile qualities, sculpture versus painting, separation versus unity, painting versus drawing, and the reciprocal influences of color and shape. Moreover, in asking oneself what unifies her paintings, we may be brought to consider the physics of randomness and chaos. Any of these formal issues might be analogized to broader contemporary social or philosophical dilemmas.

In summary, I have explored the significance of "optimal operative perversity" as an important element in creative expression. I have reviewed briefly its implications for psychoanalytic thought, with particular reference to some of the issues in self psychology. I have given a clinical vignette that illustrates the tentative beginnings of creative expression in an adult patient. Finally, I have used two paintings to illustrate optimal operative perversity as an active principle in creative work.

## REFERENCES

Bacal, H. (1985), Optimal responsiveness and the therapeutic process. In: *Progress in Self Psychology. Vol. 1*, A. Goldberg, ed. New York: Guilford Press, pp. 202–227.

Baker, H. (1988), Vincent van Gogh and his selfobjects. Workshop given at the 11th Annual Conference on the Psychology of the Self, Washington, DC.

Basch, M. (1988), *Understanding Psychotherapy*. New York: Basic Books.

Bollas, C. (1978), The aesthetic moment and the search for transformation. *The Annual of Psychoanalysis*, 6:385–394. New York: International Universities Press.

Bruner, J. (1983), *Child's Talk*. New York. Norton.

Flam, J. (1978), *Matisse on Art*. New York: Viking.

Gedo, J. (1987), Paul Cezanne: Symbiosis, Masochism and the struggle for perception. In: *Psychoanalytic Perspectives on Art, Vol. 2*, ed. M. Gedo. Hillsdale, NJ: The Analytic Press, pp. 187–202.

_____ (1987), Interdisciplinary dialogue as a "Lutte d'amour." In: *Psychoanalytic Perspectives on Art, Vol. 2*, ed. M. Gedo. Hillsdale, NJ: The Analytic Press, pp. 223–236.

Gilot, F. (1990), Friends and foes. *Art and Antiques*, Oct., p. 123.

Goldberg, A. (1988), *A Fresh Look at Psychoanalysis*. Hillsdale, NJ: The Analytic Press.

Goodman, N. (1978), *Ways of Worldmaking*. Indianapolis, IN: Hackett.

Hughto, D. (1987), Introduction to *Exhibition Catalogue*. Elca London Gallery.

Kohut, H. (1976), Creativeness, charisma, and group psychology. In: *The Search for the Self, Vol. 2*, ed. P. Ornstein., New York: International Universities Press, 1978, pp. 793–843.

_____ (1977), *The Restoration of the Self*. New York: International Universities Press.

_____ (1984), *How Does Analysis Cure?* ed. A. Goldberg & P. Stepansky. Chicago: University of Chicago Press.

Kuhns, R. (1983), *Psychoanalytic Theory of Art*. New York: Columbia Universities Press.

Milner, M. (1957), *On Not Being Able To Paint*. New York: International Universities Press.

Nagera, H. (1967), *Vincent Van Gogh.* Madison, CT: International Universities Press.

Reff, T. (1987), John Gedo and the struggle for perception. In: *Psychoanalytic Perspectives on Art, Vol. 2,* ed. M. Gedo. Hillsdale, NJ: The Analytic Press, pp. 237–244.

Rotenberg, C. (1988), Selfobject theory and the artistic process. In: *Learning from Kohut: Progress in Self Psychology, Vol. 4.* ed. A. Goldberg. Hillsdale, NJ: The Analytic Press, 193–213.

Spitz, R. (1957), Some early prototypes of ego defenses. *J. Amer. Psychoanal. Assn.* 9:626–651.

Stern, D. (1985), *The Interpersonal World of the Infant.* New York: Basic Books.

Stolorow, R. (1989), Discussion of "Beyond the written word," by Estelle Shane. At the 12th Annual Conference on the Psychology of the Self.

_____ Brandchaft, B. & Atwood, G. (1987), *Psychoanalytic Treatment.* Hillsdale, NJ: The Analytic Press.

Trevarthen, C. (1980), The foundations of intersubjectivity. The development of interpersonal cooperative understanding in infants. In: *The Social Foundations of Language and Thought,* ed. D. Olese. New York: Norton. 1980.

Winnicott, D. (1952), Psychoses and child care. In: *Collected Papers.* London: Tavistock, 1958.

# Chapter 10

# Subjectivism, Relativism, and Realism in Psychoanalysis

## Donna M. Orange

In his recent book *A Fresh Look at Psychoanalysis: The View from Self Psychology* Goldberg (1988), has addressed some crucial conceptual and philosophical questions embedded in our field. Specifically, my interest was piqued by chapter 4, "The Tension Between Realism and Relativism in Psychoanalysis," and chapter 5, "Self Psychology and External Reality," where Goldberg wrestles with such basic and perennial philosophical questions as the nature of the real and the limits of human knowledge as they affect psychoanalysis and psychoanalytic theory. Goldberg's chapters prompted me to consider again these basic philosophical issues and their salience for questions of psychoanalytic theory. In particular, recent thought about these questions bears on the nature of transference and countertransference and has supported the development of intersubjective and relational perspectives in psychoanalysis.

Philosophers have long made distinctions their stock in trade. In that tradition, I attempt here a modest and limited task: to draw three distinctions and to point out aspects of their relevance for psychoanalytic theory. Specifically, I distinguish between subjectivity and subjectivism, between subjectivism and relativism, and between objectivism and realism. A related but larger task, the consideration of the implications of various versions of philosophical realism for psychoanalytic theory, must await a future and more extensive treatment.

Today the concept of subjectivity roughly replaces Freud's psychic

189

reality. The equivalence is not precise because psychic reality tends to imply the existence or significance of external reality and subjectivity does not. Subjectivity most commonly refers to the individual organization of experience. Atwood and Stolorow (1984) borrow the term from Husserl's transcendental phenomenology and enrich it with the views expressed in Kohut's (1959) seminal paper "Introspection, Empathy, and Psychoanalysis," in which he stated unequivocally that the domain of psychoanalysis is limited to whatever is accessible via introspection and empathy. Subjectivity includes both process, the activity of organizing experience, and product, the organization of experience, understood as a relatively enduring configuration that shapes and limits a person's future experience and activity.

Subjectivity can be distinguished from subjectivism and, indeed, must be so distinguished. Subjectivism, as an epistemological view, holds the Cartesian view that truth and knowledge are accessible only via individual subjectivity. As an ethical theory, subjectivism means that actions are good or evil depending on the individual's view of them, that moral values are radically individual. Subjectivism as, for example, embraced by Husserl—but not by all those inspired by his project—ends in a radical solipsism, where the knowable is limited to the contents of one's own mind. For Atwood and Stolorow (1984), "the practice of transcendental phenomenology [Husserl's project] presents a spectacle of thought detached from social life, circling inwardly upon itself and mistaking a reified symbol of its own solitude for the discovery of its absolute foundation" (p. 13). Husserl's phenomenology insists on the universality of the reduction or epoche—taking nothing for granted—and refuses to recognize as valid anything not "intentionally constituted in transcendental subjectivity" (Lauer, 1978). In the words of Herbert Spiegelberg (1960), a historian of phenomenology:

> While it is true that Husserl is the founder and remains the central figure of the [phenomenological] Movement he is also its most radical representative and that not only in the sense that he tried to go to the roots, but that he kept digging deeper and deeper, often undermining his own earlier results; he was always the most extreme member of his Movement, and hence became increasingly the loneliest of them all [xxviii].

In Lauer's (1978) words, the phenomenological project ends with only "Edmund Husserl himself in splendid isolation" (p. 165).

But just as phenomenology extends beyond Husserl's own view, the emphasis on the study of subjectivity inspired by Husserl is not coextensive with Husserl's subjectivism/solipsism. As Lauer (1978) notes, "there can be no question that, historically speaking, phenomenology has in recent times performed the important philosophical function of directing attention more seriously to experience as the only legitimate starting point of philosophizing" (p. 167). Similarly, we might say that phenomenology has pointed psychoanalysis toward its only legitimate starting point, the subject's experience. A phenomenological view of the method and theory of psychoanalysis—the view uncompromisingly espoused by Kohut—requires us to eliminate preconceptions (diagnostic, metapsychological, and otherwise) and to work as completely as possible within the subjective experience of the patient. Only thus, can we, to use Husserlian language, gain insight into the essential structures of the patient's subjectivity. The qualifier "as possible" recognizes the limits on this phenomenological project imposed by our own historically constituted subjectivity, our own organization of experience, limits in which Husserl himself did not seem much interested but that we cannot avoid and that we sometimes recognize under the rubric of *countertransference*. In addition, we now know we must recognize our inevitable influence on the patient's subjective experience.

For Husserl (1960), however, the search for the essential structures of subjectivity had to precede any consideration of intersubjectivity and prevented his philosophy from ever getting that far. The radically ahistorical character of Husserl's phenomenology prevented any consideration of the effects of experience of others on subjectivity, and the complete suspension of preconceptions eliminated any recognition of relatedness from the search for essential structures of subjectivity in the present. A psychoanalytic phenomenology, which must take the past and present experience of others into account in order to be psychoanalysis, must be less philosophically radical than Husserl was. We can leave to philosophers the task of deciding whether a phenomenology embedded in history and relatedness is still phenomenology. My point is that defining the domain of psychoanalysis as the domain of the subjective organization of experience need not commit us to espousing the radical subjectivism or solipsism of Husserl. Subjectivity is inevitably given essence and structure by way of assimilating and organizing past and present experience, especially relational experience.

To proceed to the second distinction, subjectivism is not coextensive with relativism and may not even be compatible with it. Relativism is usually thought of as radical dependency on theory, on social context, on circumstance, or on utility and denies the existence of any universal truth or moral framework. Truth, for the relativist, is purely a function of socially constructed theoretical frameworks and not, as for the subjectivist, a product of the individual's subjectivity. Goldberg (1988) views relativism as a denial of objectivism: "Relativism is a viewpoint that considers the world as a variable thing that need have no inherent composition save as we choose to categorize it" (p. 44). Truth or morality can, in other words, be evaluated only from within a socially agreed-upon system. For a moral relativist, situational criteria external to the moral agent determine the morality of particular actions, whereas a subjectivist understands morality as a function of the individual's preferences or values. Both subjectivists and relativists deny the existence of universal truths or moral values, but they locate differently the truths and moral criteria they do recognize: the subjectivist in the individual, the relativist in the theoretical framework or social context. American philosopher Richard Bernstein (1988) expresses the distinction clearly:

> It should be clear from the way I am using the term "relativism" that it must be carefully distinguished from "subjectivism." A relativist need not be a subjectivist, and a subjectivist is not necessarily a relativist. Husserl is a subjectivist, as least insofar as he claims that there are a priori structures of transcendental subjectivity that can be apodictically [with absolute certainty] known—structures of transcendental subjectivity that ground both our scientific objective knowledge and the pregiven Lebenswelt of everyday experience. However, there is nothing relativistic about Husserl's conception of transcendental phenomenology; it is intended to be the definitive answer to all forms of relativism, skepticism, and historicism. Even if we think of subjectivism in its more common and mundane sense—using the term to call attention to whatever is "merely" a matter of personal opinion, taste, or bias, and consequently idiosyncratic—a relativist is not necessarily a subjectivist. As I have characterized the relativist, his or her essential claim is that there can be no higher appeal than to a given conceptual scheme, language game, set of social practices, or historical epoch. There is a nonreducible plurality of such schemes, paradigms, and practices; there is no substantive overarching framework in which radically different and alternative schemes are commensurable—no universal standard that somehow stands outside of and above these competing alternatives. But the relativist does not necessarily claim that there is anything subjective about these schemes, paradigms, and practices [pp. 11–12].

Relativism here appears not as Husserlian subjectivism but, rather, as a Protagorean epistemology and as a moral position rejecting universals. Protagoras's "man is the measure" does not mean that individual subjectivity is ultimate reality or moral court of last appeal. Protagorean relativism means, as Bernstein says, that "there can be no higher appeal than to a given conceptual scheme, language game, set of social practices, or historical epoch." It is perhaps this meaning intended by Fosshage (1990) when he contrasts relativism with a scientific positivism and suggests that relativism makes better sense of the psychoanalytic situation and especially of the forms of relatedness we call transference and countertransference. But relativism continues to be vulnerable to the traditional critique of self-contradictoriness: in order to compare positivism and relativism, one must take a nonrelativistic epistemological position that can in turn be evaluated from another external position and so to an infinite regress. To choose relativism one must take a nonrelativistic position. Indeed, one must be a nonrelativist even to choose among theories. Psychoanalysis, therefore, needs alternatives to relativism as well as to positivism, to scientific empiricism, and to naive realism. It is precisely this need that my third distinction, between objectivism and realism, addresses.

Distinguishing relativism from subjectivism prepares the way for consideration of so-called "objective reality" and its bearing on the exclusive concentration on experience in psychoanalysis. An exclusive focus on the experiential world of the patient may seem to neglect what interpersonalists would call "problems in living" and to restrict, even eliminate, the analyst's access to data to be gained through normal perceptual processes. As European thinkers like Gadamer and Habermas might ask, What good is a world of meanings detached from praxis, that action which proceeds from practical wisdom?

To avoid the conceptual problems inherent in subjectivism, and in self-contradictory relativism, as well as to avoid neglect of practical realities, we need to distinguish between objectivism and realism. There are many objectivisms whose exact definitions and history need not concern us here. What they have in common—in contrast to all forms of subjectivism and of relativism—is the claim that there are fundamental and universal criteria for judging truth and falsehood, right and wrong. A common form of objectivism, also known as empiricism, claims that the ultimate court of appeal is something called "objective reality" or "the facts." In midcentury philosophy of science, as represented by Popper (1959) and Hempel (1951), this empiricism took the form of a demand that any theory had to meet the test of falsifiability to qualify as scientific. That is, the proponents of the theory had to specify what experimental results would lead to the rejection or falsification of the theory; the human sciences (Geisteswissenschaften), including psychoanalysis, could thus be easily excluded, along with religion, metaphysics, and astrology. Any theory that could not be falsified by experimental evidence had no cognitive significance. In this spirit, psychoanalytic objectivists, wanting to be scientific, have claimed that transference consists in distortions that can be seen by the observer-analyst to be distortions when compared with the facts. A major criterion of psychological health, for objectivists, has been access to the facts, or reality testing.

The postempiricist philosophy of science of Kuhn, Feyerabend, Hesse, and others, has almost universally rejected these forms of empiricist epistemology. British philosopher Mary Hesse (1980) attacks the underlying assumption that there are radical differences between the natural sciences and the human sciences. She details five contrasts often thought to divide the natural and the human sciences:

1. In natural science, experience is taken to be objective, testable, and independent of theoretical explanation. In human science, data are not detachable from theory, for what count as data are determined in the light of some theoretical interpretation and the facts themselves have to be reconstructed in the light of interpretation.

2. In natural science, theories are artificial constructions or models, yielding explanation in the sense of a logic of hypothetico-deduction: *if* external nature were of such a kind, *then* data and experience would be as we find them. In human science, theories are mimetic reconstructions of the facts themselves and the criterion of a good theory is understanding of meanings and intentions rather than deductive explanation.

3. In natural science, the lawlike relations asserted of experience are external, both to the objects connected and to the investigator, since they are merely correlational. In human science, the relations asserted are internal, both because the objects studied are essentially constituted by their interrelations with one another, and also because the relations are mental, in the sense of being created by human categories of understanding recognized (or imposed?) by the investigator.

4. The language of natural science is exact, formalizable, and literal; therefore, meanings are univocal and a problem of meaning arises only in the application of universal categories to particulars. The language of human science is irreducibly equivocal and continually adapts itself to particulars.

5. Meanings in natural science are separate from facts. Meanings in human science are what constitute facts, for data consists of documents, inscriptions, intentional behavior, social rules, human artefacts, and the like, and these are inseparable from their meanings for agents [pp. 170-171].

If these differences between the natural and the human sciences actually existed, psychoanalytic transference could be viewed as mere human science, a distortion, or even a delusion when compared with the objectively verifiable facts provided by the natural sciences, evidence provided by medical tests, say. But every characteristic of the human sciences listed by Hesse is now assigned to the natural sciences as well, calling into serious question such venerable psychoanalytic conceptions as reality testing and transference as distortion. Hesse summarizes the conclusions of postempiricist philosophies of science, which undermine each of the five contrasts:

> 1. In natural science data [are] not detachable from theory, for what count as data are determined in the light of some theoretical interpretation, and the facts themselves have to be reconstructed in the light of interpretation.
>
> 2. In natural science theories are not models externally compared to nature in a hypothetico-deductive schema, they are the way the facts themselves are seen.
>
> 3. In natural science the lawlike relations asserted of experience are internal, because what count as facts are constituted by what the theory says about their inter-relations with one another.
>
> 4. The language of natural science is irreducibly metaphorical and inexact, and formalizable only at the cost of distortion of the historical dynamics of scientific development and of the imaginative construction in terms of which nature is interpreted by science.
>
> 5. Meanings in natural science are determined by theory; they are understood by theoretical coherence rather than by correspondence with facts [p. 171-172].

Rejecting these contrasts does not mean that there are no differences between the natural and the human sciences but, rather, that the differences do not consist in an honorific scientific status accorded to so-called objective facts. The empiricism so soundly rejected in recent philosophy of science remains, however, popular in psychoanalysis (Hanly, 1990), which has remained relatively unaffected by recent university-based ferment in the philosophy of science. Psychoanalysis, starting with Freud, has a long tradition of calling itself a science and of wishing to be a natural science in that honorific and empiricist sense. Perhaps, in addition, working wholly with meanings leads psychoanalysts to yearn for the certainty thought to be afforded by facts and universals. In any case, postempiricist understandings of the nature of science make considerable room for psychoanalysis, even without resorting to "objective reality," and in particular for intersubjective and relational theories.

But the rejection of objectivism, and of its associated scientific empiricism, does not imply relativism and does not imply the falsehood of every form of philosophical realism. Realism is the view that some things are at least partly independent of opinions about them, that there is something to be more fully known, discovered, or articulated. In the words of American philosopher Charles Sanders Peirce (1868), "The real . . . is that which, sooner or later, information and reasoning would finally result in, and which is therefore independent of the vagaries of me and you" (p. 168)—a thoroughgoing process conception of reality. Ironically, the original philosophical meaning of realism (i.e., that universals exist apart from human knowledge of them) originated with Plato, who eschewed every form of commonsense realism. The commonsense realism embedded in empiricism, with its Popperian requirement that proponents of any theory specify those factual conditions that would lead them to consider the theory inadequate—the falsifiability criterion—has been widely criticized as inadequate even in the natural sciences. Correspondence theories of truth are seen as naive. Other forms of realism, especially those that see truth as gradually emergent in a community of inquirers (Peirce, 1868) or in a dialogic community, show more promise. One version of this communitarian or intersubjective (Bernstein, 1988) realism might be a *perspectivalism* that would conceive of reality as a socially understood or socially articulated process in which each participant in the inquiry has a perspective that gives access to a part or an aspect of reality. There could be an infinite—or at least an indefinite—number of such perspectives. (Hoffman, 1983, has recently applied a similar perspectivalism to transference and countertransference). Since none of us can entirely escape the confines of our own perspective, our view of truth is necessarily partial, but dialogue can increase our access to it.

Such an intersubjective perspectivalist realism is not equivalent to the cultural and epistemological relativism mentioned earlier; rather, cultures and theories themselves are perspectives on emergent truth. Nor is such realism reducible to the historical narrative negotiated in treatment (Spence, 1982; Schafer, 1983). Though such negotiation provides a small-scale approximation of the larger process, it can provide only another perspective on "the truth." Such a perspectivalist realism recognizes that the only truth or reality to which psychoanalysis provides access is the subjective organization of experience as understood in an intersubjective context (Stolorow, Brandchaft, and Atwood, 1987). At the same time, such a subjective organization of experience is one perspective on a larger reality never fully attained or known but continually being approached, apprehended, articulated, and shared. In other words, unlike Husserl's phenomenology, an intersubjective theory can admit the importance of social life and of the continuing effect of practical life in the world. It is true that Kohut viewed subjectivity as the entire domain of psychoanalysis and saw "external" events as important only as experienced and organized by the patient. This view does exclude commonsense realisms, correspondence theories of truth, and scientific empiricisms. It does not exclude the possibility of dialogic, communitarian, or perspectivalist realism, in which reality is seen as an emergent, self-correcting process only partly accessible via individual subjectivity but increasingly understandable in communitarian dialogue.

## REFERENCES

Atwood, G. & Stolorow, R. (1984), *Structures of Subjectivity*. Hillsdale, NJ: The Analytic Press.

Bernstein, R. (1988), *Beyond Objectivism and Relativism*. Philadelphia: University of Pennsylvania Press.

Fosshage, J. (1990), Toward reconceptualizing transference: Theoretical and clinical considerations. Presented at American Psychological Association Division 39 Spring Conference, New York.

Goldberg, A. (1988), *A Fresh Look at Psychoanalysis*. Hillsdale, NJ: The Analytic Press.

Hanly, C. (1990), The concept of truth in psychoanalysis. *Internat. Psycho.-Anal.*, 71:375–383.

Hempel, C. (1951), The concept of cognitive significance: A reconsideration. *Proc. Amer. Acad. Arts & Sci.*, 80:61–77.

Hesse, M. (1980), *Revolutions and Reconstructions in the Philosophy of Science*. Brighton, UK: Harvester Press.

Hoffman, I. (1983), The patient as interpreter of the analyst's experience. *Contemp. Psychoanal.*, 19:389–422.

Husserl, E. (1960), *Cartesian Meditations* (trans. D. Cairns). The Hague: Nijoff.

Kohut, H. (1959), Introspection, empathy, and psychoanalysis. *J. Amer. Psychoanal. Assn.*, 7:459–483.

Lauer, Q. (1978), *The Triumph of Subjectivity*. New York: Fordham University Press.

Peirce, C. (1868), Some consequences of four incapacities. In: *Collected Papers of Charles Sanders Peirce, Vol. 5*. Cambridge, MA: Harvard University Press, 1934, pp. 156–189.

Popper, K. (1959), *The Logic of Scientific Discovery*. London: Hutchinson.

Schafer, R. (1983), *The Analytic Attitude*. New York: Basic Books.

Spence, H. (1982), *Narrative Truth and Historical Truth*. New York: Norton.

Spiegelberg, H. (1960), *The Phenomenological Movement, Vols. 1 & 2*. The Hague: Nijoff.

Stolorow, R., Brandchaft, B. & Atwood, G. (1987), *Psychoanalytic Treatment*. Hillsdale, NJ: The Analytic Press.

# Chapter 11

# Quantum Physics and Self Psychology: Toward a New Epistemology

## Maxwell S. Sucharov

As one examines the epistemological consequences of the discoveries of modern physics, one is immediately struck by many parallels to psychoanalysis. These parallels reflect fundamental relationships that penetrate to the very heart of psychoanalysis. This century has witnessed a revolution of our traditional way of thinking about objective reality and of the descriptive framework we use to gather knowledge about that reality. The awareness of these changes was confined to a select group of physicists and philosophers in the period immediately following the discoveries of quantum physics and relativity, and it is only now that this awareness is beginning to spread to a wider segment of the public mind.

Psychoanalysis has been a happy beneficiary of this revolution. Under the old scientific regime it was grudgingly relegated to a position on the fringe of scientific enterprise. The new way of thinking has moved psychoanalysis right into the thick of a now redefined concept of what is science. It is also my contention that the current evolution of our field is itself a reflection of the new scientific epistemology. Encouraged by finding ourselves full-fledged citizens of the scientific community, we are feeling more free to examine our own methodology.

The scope of this chapter is to examine the relationship between the descriptive frameworks of modern physics and of self psychology. It is my view that Kohut was well aware of the epistemological implications of modern physics and that this awareness shaped his views on mental life and allowed him to implicitly incorporate the new epistemology into a new descriptive framework for psychoanalysis. This chapter is an attempt to render that incorporation more explicit. It is my belief that by firmly grounding self psychology in the new descriptive framework of modern physics we will be able to solve some of the problems elicited by the self psychology point of view.

The quantum revolution began with Max Planck's postulate in 1900 that radiant energy is released in discrete discontinuous "packets," which he called quanta. This was a momentous assertion because it was at variance with the notion of energy as a continuous force, a notion absolutely indispensable to maintain the consistency of Newtonian mechanics.

Neils Bohr incorporated Planck's postulate in his model of the atom, which received empirical support through a remarkably accurate capacity to account for the hydrogen spectrum. Thus, Planck's postulate of discrete quanta of energy was accepted as a reality of nature. However, a series of interconnected contradictions began to appear. One was that depending on the experimental arrangement, light would behave as either a wave or a particle. Yet no single experiment could manifest both behaviors at the same time; the experiments were mutually exclusive. This dualism between waves and particles was extended to all matter by de Broglie in his concept of matter-waves.

It was also discovered that one could not, in principle, measure simultaneously and with precision both position and momentum of an electron. This phenomenon received formal expression in the Heisenberg uncertainty principle, which recognizes the impossibility of predicting with certainty the future position of a quantum particle. The reason for this imprecision in prediction is the fact that the process of observation itself generates an uncontrollable interaction between the light photons of the microscope and the quantum particle.

Despite such difficulties and with the aid of sophisticated mathematical techniques, physicists were able to develop a remarkably complete picture of the microphysical world, which was in agreement with experiments. Yet the physical interpretation of quantum theory remained a problematic area. The indivisibility of quanta, wave-particle dualities, and the uncertainty relations were all deeply contradictory to classical physics, which was dependent on assumptions of continuity, determinism, and a sharp separation of observer and object of observation.

In 1927 Neils Bohr (1934, 1963) provided what has become known as the Copenhagen interpretation of quantum theory. He stressed the need to recognize a fundamental shift in our traditional way of thinking. In the world of microphysics, one can no longer neglect the interaction between the observing instrument and the object of observation. This interaction is an *integral part of the phenomenon* and demands that one renounce a causal mode of description.

Bohr introduced the term *complementarity* to denote a novel logical relation between two descriptions that cannot *in principle* be visualized simultaneously, that may appear to be contradictory, and that together form a complete picture of reality. Thus, wave and particle are complementary pictures of matter. In a similar vein, position and momentum are complementary pictures of a particle. The precise measurement of one in principle precludes precise measurement of the other. Bohr emphasized that the framework of complementarity reflects the quality of knowledge we obtain whenever the *interaction between measuring instruments and the objects form an integral part of the phenomenon.* He also commented that this mode of description is most familiar to us from the field of psychology, where the observer and observed coincide, and he recognized that the subject–object separation demanded special attention. He recognized that the capacity for unambiguous communication about the state of one's mind is contingent on a separation between the content of one's consciousness and the background agent of observation ("observing ego"). However, Bohr (1963) specified that "any attempt at an exhaustive description of the richness of conscious life demands in various situations a *different placing of the section between subject and object*" (p. 13). Thus, recognized that both psychology and microphysics were restricted to a framework of complementary descriptions.

In a recent review of Neils Bohr's philosophy (Folse, 1985), it was emphasized that the framework of complementarity retains an assumption of the existence of an objective reality out there that is independent of our observation. The new descriptive framework does specify a fundamental limit on what we can know about that reality. The arbitrary choice of the dividing line between the measuring instruments and the objects implies that the classical presupposition that the description of an observation is equivalent to assumed properties of the object independent of observation cannot be upheld. We are limited to a series of complementary descriptions, each of which refers to a different phenomenal appearance of the object under investigation.

A number of physicists and philosophers (Bachelard, 1934; Heisenberg, 1958; Bohm, 1984) have further clarified and deepened our understanding of the far-reaching changes in our thinking necessitated by the new physics. Newtonian physics, with its associated mechanistic deterministic worldview, is dependent on a descriptive framework that assumes a sharp separation between observer and observed and on the capacity to embrace all of the phenomena in a single description. The empirical discoveries of quantum physics demonstrated that these two assumptions are oversimplified ideals that cannot be upheld in the world of microphysics. Physicists recognized the need to develop a new descriptive framework that took into account the interaction between observing instruments and the objects. They were compelled to accept that nature itself has imposed a fundamental limitation on the kinds of knowledge we can obtain. The framework of complementarity, which renounces the capacity to embrace all of the phenomena in a single description, replaces the mechanistic worldview with a new quantum worldview. This view recognizes that subjectivity, uncertainty, contradiction, and the need to forego causal modes of description are essential elements of science.

With respect to psychoanalysis, it is generally agreed that one of Freud's fundamental empirical discoveries was the importance of the unconscious interaction between analyst (measuring instrument) and the patient as observational data. Of course, Freud did not have the benefits of the new epistemology of quantum physics. He was understandably committed to a mechanistic framework of description that assumed the Cartesian ideal of a sharp separation between observer and object. It is understandable that Freud, using this framework, would not explain this unconscious interaction (transference and countertransference) as an integral feature of the phenomenon but would instead reduce the interaction to two components and treat them separately: transference was a manifestation of the patient's unconscious mental life and arose strictly from within the patient; countertransference was a flaw in the analyst (measuring instrument) that, in principle, could be reduced to zero. Freud's mental apparatus model of the mind was a natural consequence of his scientific method and represents, I believe, the most powerful explanatory model one can achieve within the constraints of the 19th-century mechanistic descriptive framework.

It is my contention that any set of concepts that would expand the explanatory power of psychoanalysis beyond the power of Freud's mental apparatus model, would have to make use of a new nonmechanistic descriptive framework. This is precisely what self psychology has done. Kohut's assertion that the introspective empathic stance defines both the methodology of psychoanalysis and the kind of knowledge that can be derived from this mode of observation demonstrates his recognition that the interaction between analyst and patient is an intrinsic part of the phenomenon. He was certainly aware of the connection of his redefined methodology to the epistemological issues of quantum physics. In the *Restoration of the Self* Kohut (1977) states:

> And there is finally the fundamental claim of modern physics that the means of observation and the target of observation constitute a unit that, in certain respects, is in principle indivisible. This claim finds its counterpart in the equally fundamental claim of the psychology of the self that the presence of an empathic or introspective observer defines, in principle, the psychological field [pp. 31–32].

A new epistemology breeds a new theory. It is therefore inevitable that once Kohut began to apply a method that explicitly recognized observer–object interaction as an integral part of the phenomenon, he would arrive at an explanatory model that would transcend the power of Freud's mental apparatus model. The concept of the experiencing self has features of wholeness and indivisibility that defy its decomposition into simpler parts. The notion of the self as a whole having a separate developmental line from that of its parts (Kohut, 1978), is a wonderful example of how self psychology has transcended the Cartesian notion of complex entities reduced to simple parts in mechanical interaction. It is also inevitable that Kohut (1977) would recognize the need for complementary modes of description to account for the phenomena of mental life:

> In accordance with a psychological principle of complementarity . . . a grasp of the phenomena encountered in our clinical work . . . requires two approaches: a psychology in which the self is seen as the centre of the psychological universe and a psychology in which the self is seen as a content of the mental apparatus [p. xv].

It is my contention that because we are restricted to complementary modes of description whenever the interaction between observer and object form an integral part of the phenomenon, complementarity is an essential feature of self psychology. I therefore propose that the descriptive framework of complementarity be explicitly recognized as the framework incorporated by psychoanalysis as redefined by Kohut. I also suggest that the central feature that justifies self psychology's claim to be a new paradigm is its adoption of this new descriptive framework.

Kohut's ability to embrace contradictory points of view received formal expression in the rules of description specified by the framework of complementarity and allowed him to retain the concepts of Freud's mental apparatus psychology. These concepts are only characterized as mechanistic if they belong to an observational framework that assumes that a sharp separation between observing analyst and patient as object is the *only* observational stance. Within the descriptive framework of complementarity, in which the dividing line between observer and object is *arbitrarily chosen,* Freud's mental apparatus psychology takes on a different non-mechanistic meaning. It refers to that special case of descriptions in which the dividing line between observer and object is sharply drawn between analyst and patient. By applying to a series of complementary descriptions of mental life, corresponding to different dividing lines between observer and object, Freud's mental apparatus model is stripped of its mechanistic meaning.

A corollary to this argument is that the capacity to embrace a nonmechanistic view of mental life does not depend on the removal of mechanistic language from our descriptions. Heisenberg was aware of this problem of language in quantum physics in situations where the experimental arrangements had to be described in the language of classical physics. The introduction of complementary modes of description, each of which must be expressed in classical everyday language, was itself an attempt to transcend this problem of language. In a similar vein, psychoanalysis does not have to preoccupy itself with exorcising all concepts that are couched in mechanistic terms as long as their limited application is recognized by grounding them inside the descriptive framework of complementarity.

The epistemological argument presented here does have clinical relevance. Let us consider an analyst who is confronted with a patient who does not seem to experience the analyst as someone with an independent center of initiative. If the analyst *chooses* to approach the patient from the point of view in which the self is the center of the psychological universe, he will describe a patient with a fragmentation-prone self trying to maintain an archaic tie with a selfobject in order to restore a feeling of cohesiveness to his self-experience. If he chooses to approach the patient from the point of view of the self as a content of a mental apparatus, he will describe a person with pervasive ego weakness who is maintaining an illusion of merger with an idealized analyst in order to defend against primitive feelings of envy and hostility associated with an internalized bad object–bad self relationship.

I am aware that the two sets of explanations are contradictory and cannot be arrived at in the same analytic "moment," yet I assert that both explanations are necessary to account for a more complete understanding of the patient. One can also say that during any one analytic moment one cannot with precision know the state of the experiencing self, as reflected in the reinstatement of selfobject needs, and the state of the mental apparatus, as reflected in the defensive meaning of the transference.

This dilemma is precisely the kind of situation that confronted physicists seeking to understand the wave and particle behavior of light or the relation between position and momentum of the electron. We can solve our dilemma by using the identical epistemological argument: we renounce the possibility of simultaneous description, accept the contradiction, and introduce the concept of complementarity to denote a novel logical relation between the description of a mental apparatus psychology and the description of a psychology of the self in the broad sense.

In the use of ourselves as instruments of observation, we must be prepared during different analytic moments to use different sets of concepts that are mutually exclusive but when taken together form a more complete picture. Furthermore, the necessity to resort to complementary modes of description is directly tied to the fact that in psychoanalysis the interaction between the observer and the object is an integral feature of the phenomenon. It was Kohut who explicitly clarified the existence of this feature in psychoanalysis by his introduction of the introspective empathic mode of observation. It is because of the centrality of this feature that the epistemology of modern physics is intimately linked to the epistemology of self psychology. The descriptive framework of complementarity is the bridge that joins these two fields of knowledge and justifies the placement of psychoanalysis inside the domain of modern natural science.

In the transposition of the framework of complementarity from quantum physics to psychoanalysis I have been oversimplifying in order to introduce my point of view. In quantum physics the measuring instruments are mechanical objects that interact with the quantum particle. The human experimenter is the agent of observation who observes this interaction from outside, and there is no notion of his subjectivity affecting the observation. The element of subjectivity is restricted to the experimental arrangement he chooses to perform. The number of complementary descriptions necessary to embrace the phenomena is restricted to two, and these descriptions can be communicated in a strictly unambiguous fashion in the language of classical physics.

In psychoanalysis the measuring instrument and the agent of

observation are both inside the person of the analyst. The element of subjectivity is a much larger factor, and the interaction between "measuring instrument" and patient as object is clearly much more complex and is not amenable to the unambiguous description in the strict sense that characterizes the experiments of microphysics. In order to observe his interaction with the patient, the analyst must separate off a part of his self-experience to act as an agent of observation (observing ego). If he wanted to include this observing ego in the observation, he would need to designate a new observing ego to make this new observation. We thus generate an indefinite number of observing egos corresponding to different dividing lines between observer and observed (the observed is the interaction between patient and that part of the analyst's self-experience that has been split off from the observing ego). In contrast to quantum physics psychoanalysis thus has a large number of complementary descriptions to embrace the phenomena. Perhaps the need for a larger number of complementary descriptions counterbalances our reduced capacity to communicate these descriptions in a strictly unambiguous fashion.

My characterization of a mental apparatus psychology applied to a situation where the dividing line between observer and observed is sharply drawn between analyst and patient is also an oversimplification. In my illustrative clinical example, there was a clear implication that a description must always take into account the theoretical frame of reference adopted by the analyst because it will contribute to his attempt to shape himself as measuring instrument. Thus, even a description of the patient based on the concepts of a mental apparatus psychology, postulating a sharp separation in the strict sense between analyst and patient, would not allow us to take into account the influence of the analyst's theoretical frame of reference on his observations. It would be more accurate to say that the use of description based on a mental apparatus psychology applies to a situation in which the dividing line between observer and observed is most *sharply* between analyst and patient.

I would therefore suggest that the descriptive framework of complementarity is a complex mode of description that approaches its simplest form in microphysics, where the number of descriptions is restricted to two, communication can be unambiguous in the strictest sense, and the element of subjectivity is restricted to the choice the experimenter exercises with respect to the experimental arrangement. In psychoanalysis we need to resort to a large number of complementary descriptions that cannot be communicated unambiguously in the strict sense; the element of subjectivity plays a much more complex role, and observations always take into account the theoretical frame of reference adopted by the analyst. I would like to introduce a note of caution: it would be a gross misuse of the framework of complementarity to use it as a rationalization to permit any theoretical frame of reference to be used in order to formulate observations. Our theories still need to meet the usual criteria of internal consistency and conformity with clinical observations.

Unfortunately, a lot of confusion and misunderstanding has arisen in connection with the term *complementarity*. In response to Greenberg and Mitchell's criticism (1983), the fact that self psychology in the broad sense may be mutually exclusive with self psychology in the narrow sense is perfectly compatible with defining their relationship as complementary. The term was introduced by Bohr to account for precisely the condition when two mutually exclusive modes of description are necessary to account for a complete description of the phenomenon in question. One can also see that the conception that the complementarity between self psychology and classical theory is a temporary expedient in order to see which model will contain the other (Ornstein, 1983) betrays a profound misunderstanding of the meaning of the term *complementarity*, which should be used to describe a relationship between two modes of description neither of which in *principle* can be reduced to the other.

In an otherwise elegant overview of self psychology, Wallerstein (1983) criticized the use of complementarity because he took it to mean that deficit psychology was being placed in an either–or relationship to conflict psychology. Invoking Waelder's (1930) principle of multiple function, he emphasized the need to think in terms of "both–and" rather than either–or. Once again, we have a profound misunderstanding of the term *complementarity*. Neither the expression *either/or* nor the expression *both/and* describes the meaning of complementarity. In fact, the term was introduced by Bohr as a novel logical relation for which we did not have a linguistic term. Furthermore, Wallerstein's reference to Waelder's principle of multiple function demonstrates a misunderstanding of the new epistemology incorporated by Kohut. Waelder's 1930 paper is grounded in a mechanistic descriptive framework that assumes the capacity to embrace all of the phenomena simultaneously in a single description. His thesis, almost a direct application of a corollary to Newton's third law of motion, is that vectors of force (8 in number) act simultaneously on an object (the ego) to determine a composite vector force (psychic act). One cannot perform an operation of addition between the descriptions of self psychology in the broad sense and the descriptions of a mental apparatus ego psychology.

Modell's (1984) application of Bohr's concept of complementarity to the contradictions of self psychology is similar in spirit to my own. His proposal of a complementary relationship between a one-person psychology and a two-person psychology is similar to my proposal of a complementary relationship between the descriptions of a mental apparatus psychology and the descriptions of a psychology of the self in the broad sense. However, his suggestion of a relationship of complementarity between the epistemology of natural science and the epistemology of historical meaning is inconsistent with the meaning of Bohr's concept. Complementarity is itself an epistemological framework for specifying the relationship between mutually exclusive *descriptions*. It cannot define a relationship between epistemological systems. Complementarity should not be used as a panacea to resolve all contradictions.

Stolorow, Brandchaft, and Atwood (1987) relate the meaning of complementarity to the shifting figure–ground relationship of the selfobject dimension of transference. However, they seem to assume that the selfobject dimension of the transference is sitting there in a position of figure or ground waiting to be observed by the correctly empathic therapist. That kind of knowledge transcends the limitation imposed by the nonmechanical nature of mental life. What they fail to appreciate is that the assessment by a therapist as to the figure or ground position of the selfobject dimension of the transference will depend at least in part on the theoretical frame of reference with which the therapist chooses to approach the patient. Applying the same kind of reasoning used in the clinical example discussed previously, I would view the figure or ground position of the selfobject dimension of transference to represent two mutually exclusive complementary descriptions.

The concept of intersubjectivity of Stolorow and associates does have features that link it to the framework of complementarity. They recognize the dependence of observation on the interaction between patient and therapist, and their statement concerning the paradox that the invariant structures of the patient's psychological organization are illuminated only through the shifting intersubjective context closely resembles the quantum paradox that recognizes that the features of a quantum system are illuminated by a series of complementary descriptions. I do, however, disagree with the proposed divorce between psychoanalysis and natural science, the apparent exclusion of objective reality, and the restriction of psychoanalysis to a hermeneutic discipline.

It has been made abundantly clear that modern science has introduced a richly expanded conceptual framework that has allowed it to move well beyond the restricted mechanical point of view. Psychoanalysis can now be comfortably contained inside this new expanded framework. It should be pointed out that a person's unconscious organizing activity is a form of objective reality that has an existence independent of our observation of that reality. What is relative is the descriptions we use and what we can infer from them. Furthermore, I would characterize the patient's psychological organization as a nonmechanical system without having to specify it being of a nonphysical nature. In the quantum, nonmechanical, worldview the wave-particle duality of matter has given a more expanded meaning to what is physical and has therefore blurred the boundaries between the material and nonmaterial world. Including the invariant structures of the patient's psychological organization within the descriptive framework of complementarity is equivalent to specifying their nonmechanical nature.

Furthermore, once we are inside a modern nonmechanical worldview, the rationale for restricting psychoanalysis to a hermeneutic discipline collapses. It is only when we are restricted to a 19th-century mechanical worldview, where physical is equivalent to mechanical, that it is necessary to sharply separate the world of psychological meaning from the physical, materialistic, world. Defining psychoanalysis as a hermeneutic discipline is therefore applying a 19th-century solution to the problem of mind versus matter and keeps psychoanalysis inside the mechanical worldview from which the authors are trying to emancipate it.

We are thus free to put equal weight to both the meaning of our patient's experiences and to the structure generating that meaning. Furthermore, the limitations to our knowledge of the structure of mental life, specified by the framework of complementarity, reminds us that whether we describe it in terms of superego–ego–id, bipolar self, or invariant structures of psychological organization, we can never know the essence of this structure in the way that we know a mechanical system. In a quantum worldview the structure of mental life becomes a fuzzy entity whose essential nature will always elude our grasp. One can say that the mental apparatus description of this structure represents its separateness or "particle" aspect while the bipolar-self description represents its relatedness or "wave-like" aspect, representing the inseparability of the self from its selfobjects. By renouncing the capacity for simultaneous description and limiting ourselves to a series of complementary descriptions, we are more free to account for the richness and texture of the structure of mental life.

This fundamental limitation to what we can know about mental life was most eloquently expressed by Kohut (1977): "We cannot by introspection and empathy penetrate to the self per se; only its introspectively or empathically perceived psychological manifestations are open to us . . . we will still not know the essence of the self as differentiated from its manifestations" (p. 311).

The notion of a series of phenomenal appearances of a real object (the self) whose ultimate reality remains hidden from us is precisely the kind of situation for which the descriptive framework of complementarity was introduced. If we firmly ground psychoanalysis in the descriptive framework of complementarity, we also leave the door open for a future theory to embrace the physical domain of brain and the psychological domain of subjective experience under one conceptual umbrella. Zohar (1990) suggests a physical explanation for the unity of consciousness in terms of vibrations of neuronal molecules obeying quantum mechanical laws. Although her ideas are still of a speculative nature, I think they do demonstrate future areas of exploration and growth if psychoanalysis maintains its ties with modern science.

In conclusion, it is my contention that a transposition of the epistemology of modern physics to the field of psychoanalysis provides the appropriate logical framework to embrace its unique features. Contradiction and uncertainty are essential strands of the complex fabric of our field. The framework of complementarity is simply the logical tool that allows us to weave these strands into the fabric accounting for its richness and texture. It is therefore my contention that the descriptive framework of complementarity is an essential feature of self psychology. Equipped with this new logical tool self psychology has the means from within its own vantage point to account for the concepts of a mental apparatus psychology. These latter concepts refer to that special case of descriptions in which the dividing line between observer and object of observation is sharply drawn between therapist and patient. However, within the framework of complementarity the description of a mental apparatus psychology becomes merely part of a series of complementary descriptions of mental life corresponding to different dividing lines between observer and object. This feature renders an entirely different nonmechanistic meaning to the concepts of a mental apparatus psychology.

Conversely, one cannot account for the concepts of self psychology from inside the vantage point of an ego mental apparatus psychology alone. The set of concepts of such a psychology is based on a more limited epistemology that does not include the descriptive framework of complementarity. Complementarity is like a one-way mirror linking two worlds. From inside the world of self psychology one can view both one's own world and look outside and see the more limited world of a mental apparatus psychology. If one attempts to look out from inside the world of ego psychology, one simply sees one's own image reflected back.

Self psychology's claim to be a new paradigm is justified by its use of a descriptive framework that is more in conformity to the nature of psychoanalysis and more powerful than the descriptive framework of 19th-century science. It was the discovery of the quantum of action that led to the development of this new framework and the incorporation of this framework by Kohut, as reflected in his rigorous application of the introspective empathic mode, that facilitated our quantum leap from ego psychology to self psychology.

## REFERENCES

Bachelard, G. (1934), *The New Scientific Spirit [Le Nouvel esprit scientifique]* Boston: Beacon Press, 1984.

Bohm, D. (1984), *Causality and Chance in Modern Physics.* London: Routledge & Kegan Paul.

Bohr, N. (1934), *Atomic Theory and the Description of Nature.* New York: Macmillan.

Bohr, N. (1963), *Essays 1958–1962 on Atomic Physics and Human Knowledge.* New York: Interscience.

Folse, H. J. (1985), *The Philosophy of Neils Bohr.* Amsterdam: North-Holland Physics.

Greenberg, J. R. & Mitchell, S. A. (1983), *Object Relations in Psychoanalytic Theory.* Cambridge, MA: Harvard University Press.

Heisenberg, W. (1958), *Physics and Philosophy.* New York: Harper & Row.

Kohut, H. (1977), *The Restoration of the Self.* New York: International Universities Press.

_____ (1978). *The Search for the Self,* ed. P. Ornstein. New York: International Universities Press.

Modell, A. H. (1984). *Psychoanalysis in a New Context.* New York: International Universities Press.

Ornstein, P. (1983), Discussion of papers by A. Goldberg, R. Stolorow, and R. Wallerstein. In: *Reflections on Self Psychology,* ed. J. Lichtenberg & S. Kaplan. Hillsdale, NJ: The Analytic Press, pp. 339–384.

Stolorow, R., Brandchaft, B. & Atwood, G. (1987), *Psychoanalytic Treatment.* Hillsdale, NJ: The Analytic Press.

Waelder, R. (1930), The principle of multiple function: Observations on overdetermination. *Psychoanal. Quart.* 5:45–62.

Wallerstein, R. S. (1983), Self psychology and "classical" psychoanalytic psychology— The nature of their relationship: A review and overview. In: *Reflections on Self Psychology,* ed. J. Lichtenberg & S. Kaplan. Hillsdale, NJ: The Analytic Press, pp. 313–337.

Zohar, D. (1990), *The Quantum Self.* New York: William Morrow.

# Further Contributions

# Chapter 12

# The Latest Word: A Discussion of Three Major Contributions to Self Psychology by Ernest Wolf, Howard Bacal and Kenneth Newman, and Joseph Lichtenberg*

## Estelle Shane

In this chapter three outstanding books, which are major contributions to the widening scope of self psychology, are reviewed: But as it happens, there is something else about these books that makes their being reviewed together especially stimulating and provocative. When Heinz Kohut was alive, he was often in the position of being asked by his detractors to defend what was *actually creative* in his creative efforts; it was argued that he did not identify, or even recognize, the historical psychoanalytic origins of his new ideas or the ways in which these new ideas continued to interdigitate with contemporaneous mainstream and alternative schools of thought. On the other side, there were those enthusiasts of self psychology who were excited by the fact that Kohut's ideas fit better with findings from infant observation and other ancillary disciplines than did the ideas of classical analysis and who encouraged Kohut to pay more attention in his own writings to these newer experimental data. Kohut chose to do neither. To the first group, the critics, Kohut responded that the time and scholarship required to trace either the origins of his ideas or the parallels to his ideas would distract him from the thrust of his own self-defining efforts and deter him from the

---

*E. Wolf, *Treating the Self* (1988, The Guilford Press).

H. Bacal & K. Newman, *Theories of Object Relations: Bridges to Self Psychology* (1990, Columbia University Press).

J. Lichtenberg, *Psychoanalysis and Motivation* (1989, The Analytic Press).

accomplishment of his own established purposes and goals. He acknowledged the importance and value of such efforts but insisted that they must be left to others to complete. To the second group, the enthusiasts, Kohut maintained that while he was pleased with the fit between his findings and those from other fields, such congruence of findings only served to reconfirm for him his own conviction that the best place, indeed the only place, for the discovery of new ideas in psychoanalysis was in the clinical psychoanalytic situation. He had expressed this credo in 1959, when he stated that the domain of psychoanalysis is limited to and defined by the empathy and intro-spection derived from actual practice with patients, and he never wavered from this position. Nevertheless, he both responded to and encouraged these efforts of correlation on the part of others. For himself, however, he continued to the last in the way that he had begun, eschewing findings from related peripheral fields, including not only infant research but also neurophysiology and communica-tions theory as well.

At the end of Kohut's life, therefore, there were three major directions identified for self psychology: the one put forward by Kohut himself and the ones put forward by his friendly and his not so friendly critics. Each of the three books discussed here takes us on a journey in one of these three directions. Ernest Wolf, in *Treating the Self*, remains within the tradition of Heinz Kohut, firmly and exclu-sively anchored in the clinical situation, using the empathic introspec-tive mode to further define, deepen, and expand the field; Howard Bacal and Kenneth Newman, in their book *Theories of Object Relations: Bridges to Self Psychology*, examine the historical antecedents to self psychology found in object relations theory, as well as the extent to which these antecedents can be articulated with and integrated into an expanded and refined object relations–informed psychology of the self. Finally, Joseph Lichtenberg, in his book *Psychoanalysis and Motivation*, uses infant and toddler observational research to concep-tualize for psychoanalysis and self psychology a theory of classical analysis and at the same time to expand the motivational base of self psychology.

Thus, each of these contributions clearly and distinctly widens the horizons of self psychology, using clearly and distinctly different approaches. Therefore, in discussing them, I focus on the question, In what way does each of these contributions widen the horizons of self psychology? I want to emphasize, however, that these books are distinguished by different purposes and that each fulfills its own individual purpose admirably. Whereas Wolf has written a quintes-sentially clinical discussion of the self psychologist in action with his patient, a practical guide in the best meaning of that term, Bacal and Newman, and even Lichtenberg, focus less on the clinical situation and more on their particular and challenging theoretical innovations.

Wolf's identification with Kohut's method of clarifying and expanding the field through introspection and empathy should not surprise us. The spirit of his closely reasoned, insightful survey of normal personality types and pathological character disorders, which he coauthored with Kohut in 1978, suffuses this present work as well. In fact, Wolf writes in his preface to *Treating the Self* that he has avoided delineating in this book the *theory* of self psychology, having accepted the main body of principles, hypotheses, and definitions advocated by Kohut and his followers over the past two decades, and that his focus is on the application of that theory to the conduct of psychoanalytic treatment. In doing so, he operationalizes many familiar concepts and constructs in a way that both disarms the reader and demystifies the process. Avoiding elaborate definitions (he actually states a preference for a certain vagueness of terminology), Wolf illustrates his thesis that the clarity of a concept can best be derived from its application in the clinical situation. For example, Wolf emphasizes that the important but often misunderstood and, in fact, frequently attacked concept of fragmentation is just a metaphor for a subjective state. He explains that one can be said to be fragmented when one no longer feels aspects of one's self-experience to be coordinated or fitted together; he then provides, as he does throughout, a singularly apt illustration. Thus, Wolf's primary intention is to present a demonstration of self psychology in action.

Nevertheless, while it is by no means his chief purpose, I believe that Wolf *has* discovered new ideas to add to the body of self-psychological theory—in the very way that Kohut himself has pioneered, from within the clinical situation itself. To begin with, Wolf, adds to the three known and accepted selfobject types conceptualized by Kohut. Wolf had identified prior to this publication an adversarial selfobject function, which serves to provide an experience with a benignly opposing force who, while continuing to be supportive and responsive, allows, or even encourages, active opposition, thus confirming for the self a partial autonomy. In this current work Wolf once again illustrates the adversarial selfobject function and, in addition, describes another variety of selfobject experience, the efficacy selfobject function, which provides an experience of having an effective impact on the other, thereby revealing a capacity in the self to evoke necessary selfobject experiences from the other. About this selfobject type, Wolf comments first that while efficacy pleasure is a variety of mirroring experience, it is nevertheless best conceptualized as a separate and distinct selfobject type because of the overriding importance of the inborn motivational trend to learn and to do. Wolf adds that this motive is more important in infancy than is sensual-sexual pleasure.

Another important addition made by Wolf to clinical theory lies in his clear elaboration of the psychoanalytic setting. He makes a distinction among the concepts of situation, ambience, and process, describing *situation* as the analytic setting viewed from the perspective of the objective interpersonal vantage point and including such external observables as time, place, fees, and the like. By *ambience* is meant the way in which the psychoanalytic situation is experienced by the participants, that is, from a subjective, intrapsychic perspective. The ambience, says Wolf, may be experienced quite differently by analyst and analysand, but it is upon how the analysand experiences the ambience that the success or failure of the analysis depends. Finally, *process* is defined as psychological changes initiated and maintained in the participants by virtue of their participation in the therapy. Again, two processes, the one in the analyst and the one in the analysand, may be observed; Wolf emphasizes that although there are two such processes, it is upon the analysand that we should primarily focus our attention. Moreover, the process that is begun through the analysis ideally does not end with its termination but continues on in the analysand and, more incidentally, in the analyst as well.

In his discussion on countertransference, Wolf elucidates the self-psychological contribution to this most important aspect of the clinical situation. He notes that the analyst, like the patient, is fearful of narcissistic injury and defines *countertransference* as mainly a fear of and defense against such self-injurious experiences, interfering with the exercise of the analyzing function. Wolf explains that, just as with the patient, there are constraints in the therapeutic situation on the analyst's self-expression and a similar injunction to dismiss what is familiar and customary in ordinary discourse. These very limitations and restraints foster regression, not just in the patient but in the analyst too, and mobilize the analyst's selfobject needs, including a felt need for empathic attunement. While this can be disruptive, it is nevertheless the analyst's need for attunement that facilitates understanding of the patient.

Finally, Wolf takes up the familiar dichotomy of illusion versus reality in the psychoanalytic situation. Self psychology's position of respecting the patient's subjective reality, including the patient's memories of past experiences with significant others, is brought into a dialectic with Kris's classical and widely influential view that memory is significantly distorted by the patient's past and present needs, wishes, and defensive requirements. Giving due credit to Kris's cogent observations, Wolf nevertheless discerns in them a kind of disparagement and moralizing vis-à-vis the patient's need to construct a reality tolerable to the self and reasonably consistent with self-experience. Wolf concludes, with a tolerance and a simple elegance, that "we must accept the analysand's truth, because only by accepting as true what he or she experiences as true, can we begin the analytic dialogue that will determine the *meaning* of this truth" (p. 160).

It seems to me that Wolf and Lichtenberg agree on expanding, in Wolf's terms, the types of selfobject experience or, in Lichtenberg's, the varieties of motivational systems. There is a rough correlation between Wolf's adversarial selfobject needs and Lichtenberg's aversive motivational system, and between Wolf's efficacy selfobject needs and Lichtenberg's exploratory-assertive motivational system. Further, I think there is also some correlation between aspects of those selfobject types discovered by Kohut and included by Wolf, and Lichtenberg's motivational systems of physiological regulation and attachment. For example, the alterego selfobject resonates with vitality affects under the system of physiological regulation, the idealizing selfobject correlates with physiological regulation, and the mirroring selfobject is consistent with the attachment motivational system. It appears that only the sensual-sexual motivational system is slighted. While Lichtenberg includes a sensual-sexual motivational system, which exists on the same basic level as do all the others, Wolf does not appear to make conceptual room for a sensual-sexual selfobject experience. Is this because he formulates such experiences as a part of mirroring, or does he relegate them to a secondary position in the individual's life? More generally, I sense in Wolf's writing a hierarchy in selfobject experiences, some types originating earlier in life than others. Is this an accurate reading?

The next book I consider fulfills most admirably a long-felt need in self psychology, and, in fact, in all of analysis: to elucidate the connections between self psychology and those theories, principally object relations theories, that have not only predated Kohut's insights but may even have preempted them. Howard Bacal and Kenneth Newman have constructed *Theories of Object Relations: Bridges to Self Psychology* by separately writing the individual chapters that make up the whole. Nevertheless, they assume a single authorial voice and thereby give the clear impression that each speaks for both. Thus, as I discuss this book, I refer to "the authors" rather than make specific attribution. The authors, then, supply the historical antecedents either unknown to or unacknowledged by Kohut. They also identify concepts from those object relations theories they survey that in their view can be usefully integrated into an expanded self-psychological model. Finally, they attempt to demonstrate that the basic structure of psychoanalytic self psychology is essentially *relational*, that self psychology is, in effect, an object relations theory, placing, as it does, relationship at its center. I want to emphasize, however, that the authors clearly take the position that despite the antecedents they have uncovered, Kohut created a unique and original theoretical model. They identify for self psychology several aspects that characterize the theory as a distinct shift from classical analysis. These include a movement from a one-body to a two-body psychology; the relegation of instinctual motivation from the center to the periphery of the theory, together with a recognition of significant connections other than the instinctual between self and object; and the emphasis on the central importance of self-experience and the self–selfobject relationship at the core of analytic consideration, thereby transforming the traditional view of narcissism. More to the point, these authors note that while object relations theories also move from a one-body to a two-body psychology and although several of them, notably those of Suttie, Fairbairn, Guntrip, Balint, Winnicott, and Bowlby, move away from the dominance of instincts, none of the object relations theorists reviewed, with the exception of Guntrip, focuses so centrally on the self and none of them reconceptualizes narcissism in the way that Kohut did. Thus, self psychology, in their view, stands as a unique and original entity.

Bacal and Newman provide concise summaries of the central ideas of the major object relations theorists, examining with great skill their similarities to self psychology as well as the potential for integrating their ideas into the body of self-psychological theory. The book is eminently readable, informative, and scholarly, ranging as it does from a review of Suttie, a little-known but remarkably prescient analyst who first published in 1923, through Sullivan, Mahler, Kernberg, Racker and all the major English school contributors. I regret that I will have to limit my discussion to what the authors identify as potential additions and emendations of self psychology derived from their in-depth study of these various object relations theorists and will have to ignore their fascinating and often remarkable critiques of the ideas of these men and women who so closely paralleled in their writings self-psychological attitudes and approaches.

Beginning, then, with Melanie Klein, Bacal and Newman note that in contrast to Kohut, who emphasized the importance of the child's experience of an object insofar as it fulfills selfobject functions, Klein emphasized the child's unconscious fantasies about an object. Bacal and Newman contend that the role of fantasy, ignored in self psychology in both theory and practice, must be considered. They support their contention that fantasy can and does have a role in infant mental life by their own reading of Stern; they contend that the infant's early cognitive capacities are much more sophisticated than had been previously realized, except by Klein and her followers, and argue that Kohut's selfobject and Klein's internal object are comparable concepts insofar as both are internal representatives of the outside world that has had a profound effect upon the individual's self. The difference is that Klein's object is the internal experience of the external object, an experience determined by vicissitudes of unconscious instinctual fantasy, whereas Kohut's selfobject is the experience of that external object as the lived experience, one devoid of fantasy as it positively affects the sense of self. Whether the selfobject is internal or external, and the extent to which it is determined by the self and not by the environment, is not addressed in self psychology because such considerations would require utilizing the concept of distortion of perception, a concept that is ignored in that theory in favor of accepting the validity of the individual's subjective reality. The authors conclude that Klein's unconscious fantasy could add a dimension to the usual understanding of the selfobject experience, with the fantasy either detracting from or augmenting the experience. They contend that one's perception of the selfobject is always influenced by unconscious fantasy generated by the self. Therefore, they say, self psychology would benefit from the theoretical conception of fantasy as an influence in the perception of selfobject experience, the addition of which would effectively emphasize the predominance of the intrapsychic component in selfobject experience, both developmentally and in the analysis. Moreover, a fantasy selfobject could take the place of an actual good selfobject relationship. Thus, while Kohut postulated that in the lifetime of anyone capable of being analyzed at all, some positive selfobject functions must have been provided, these authors postulate a fantasy selfobject that can make up for the absence of a good object. They contend that transferences based on a fantasy selfobject experience rather than on any substantive selfobject experience from the past would be especially prone to disruption in the treatment situation, which would account for the particular vulnerability that some patients seem to have to selfobject failure in the clinical situation. On the other hand, the capacity for elaborating in fantasy a selfobject experience one never had before is a testament to the creative capacity of the self.

In their consideration of Bion, Bacal and Newman believe that a positive contribution to self psychology might be found in his construction of "attacks on linking," as well as in his analyst-as-container concept. Attacks on linking can be understood as a covert manifestation of the analysand's overt narcissistic rage toward the analyst, a hidden attempt to defensively dissociate or delink himself from objects he expects to fail him in providing selfobject function. Should he turn to these objects, they would, he feels, endanger his psychological existence; by attacking the link between them, he hopes to survive. Interpretation of this dynamic, these authors explain, might facilitate understanding of the selfobject transference, the defenses against its establishment, and the defenses against its reestablishment once the transference has been disrupted. The Bionian analyst-as-container concept refers to a clinical situation wherein the patient needs the analyst to contain and detoxify his own unbearable feelings; the patient, in effect, hands these feelings over to the analyst for this purpose. I understand this as a variant of an affect-tuning or affect-attuning selfobject other functioning to modulate affects, making them bearable for the self. Again, the authors see an understanding of the container function as clinically useful.

In their analysis of Mahler's contributions, Bacal and Newman stress the importance that she placed on the role of the mother as the mediator of affect containment and affect integration. They point also to Mahler's concept of splitting as the infant's essential defense against conflictual negative affect experience. Mahler's ideas, according to these authors, can provide a useful corrective to what they see as self psychology's unfortunate tendency to minimize both conflict and the complexities of dealing with negative affect. Bacal and Newman acknowledge Marion Tolpin's work, which they note does address affects but does so essentially by referring to the soothing and self-regulating functions of the maternal selfobject in normal development. Tolpin's insights can be extended to indicate as well the essential part this maternal function plays at times of severe distress in the infant's life, but Tolpin herself did not do this, stressing baseline conditions of maternal selfobject gratification rather than the infant's responses to the disturbing and intensified emotions that arise out of selfobject failure. In this context, as well as in many others, Bacal and Newman point out the highly significant role they feel Stolorow and his colleagues have played in addressing gaps in self-psychological theory. Bacal and Newman view intersubjectivity in general as the bridge between self psychology and object relations theory. In this particular instance, Bacal and Newman contend that the theory of intersubjectivity emphasizes the weakness in the self that derives from the failure of primary caretakers to provide containment and integration of strong affects, with conflict and defense resulting from such selfobject failure as efforts to avoid retraumatization. The theoretical emendation of intersubjectivity thus establishes both conflict and the centrality of affect as concepts integral to self psychology.

Turning to Fairbairn and Guntrip, Bacal and Newman believe that Fairbairn's concept of the schizoid defense, which is further elaborated by Guntrip, can particularize our understanding of lack of self-cohesion. The schizoid defense involves isolating oneself from the outer world of disappointing objects and turning inward. While Kohut described vertical and horizontal splitting, he did not describe the nature of the internal disruption that results from such splitting, except in the broadest of terms. This is because, the authors explain, self psychology follows narcissistic issues, concentrating on the self in its relationship to others, with little attention to the structural condition of the self following traumatic experience. In contrast, the focus of object relations theory is within the self that has suffered the damage. Fairbairn introduces a self split by pathological object relationships, leaving only the surviving essence of a true self. Guntrip describes how, with the advent of further trauma, an even deeper split occurs, what he terms "the regressed ego," (in effect, the regressed self); Guntrip's "living heart of the self" takes flight into more recessed regions of the psyche, culminating in a defensive escape from utter aloneness called the "schizoid suicide." The ultimate wish at this point is to die and to then be reborn. Bacal and Newman claim that an understanding of this construct, "disunited psychic functioning," might permit the analyst to make more effective responses to the patient's resistance to therapy. Such resistance could be interpreted not just as a fear of retraumatization by the selfobject but a fear of intrapsychic splitting within the self.

Finally, I will just mention Bacal and Newman's pointing to Winnicott's familiar and seminal idea that the mother survives the infant's attack, an idea that functions in the therapeutic situation to explain the patient's continuing utilization of the analyst in the face of narcissistic rage; thus, narcissistic rage can be conceptualized as ultimately spending itself so that the therapist can then be used by the patient for other, more development-enhancing selfobject needs. Also, the authors note that Winnicott's false self can enrich self psychology by contributing a view of selfobject failure that recognizes, in addition to the weak and fragile self, a self that has, in some cases, compromised its genuineness.

Bacal and Newman's final chapter embodies a revised view of self psychology, amended and expanded by object relations theory. Their basic arguments are that self psychology is an object relations theory, that what is implicit in object relations theory is the self, and what is implicit in self psychology is a particular type of object relationship. Their argument is with Kohut, who insists that it is the self, not the self and its object, that is at the center of self psychology. The authors believe, in contrast, that by focusing on selfobject function and on the importance of subjective experience, self psychology has inadvertently lost sight of the object that provides that function, so that the distinction is blurred between the characteristics of the external object and the individual's intrapsychic experience of it. Their contention is stated succinctly: the selfobject is best understood as the self's object.

The question I have for Bacal and Newman is the following: In conceptualizing the selfobject as the self's object, are you not in danger of blurring, or even losing altogether, the vital distinction between object and selfobject that organizes self psychology as a distinct theory, as, for example, when you speak of guilt generated by inflicting suffering on the selfobject (p. 241) or when you equate a failed selfobject with a bad object (p. 264)?

I turn now to Lichtenberg's *Psychoanalysis and Motivation*. Lichtenberg's thesis, as he proclaims at the outset, is that psychoanalytic theory at its core is a theory of structured motivation, not a theory of structure. He means by this declaration that human needs are paramount and that, therefore, a full comprehension of such needs is the key to modern psychoanalytic understanding. He postulates a theory of five distinct motivational-functional systems. Each centers around a particular and distinct need, and each includes within it the means for both the fulfillment of that need and its regulation. Lichtenberg includes the concept of "functional" in each separate motivational-functional system to take cognizance of the significant contribution of the environment in determining the person's experience of and expression of needs and wishes derived from within the system self–other. As for the concept of self, Lichtenberg sees the self as developing out of the experience of having needs and having these needs recognized, acknowledged, and fulfilled through affect-laden interactions with the caregiver. The self becomes, then, an independent center for initiating, organizing, and integrating motivation, and the sense of self arises from such experiences.

It is important to note that the evidence for all motivational systems can be discerned in the individual at any given moment.

However, one system, or set of systems, is prominent, based on the need state and the interpersonal context. The significance for the clinician is to determine what motivational system is dominant at any given time. For example, in supporting the importance of postulating a motivational system based on the regulation of physiological requirements, Lichtenberg argues convincingly that anorexia can be misunderstood if it is only viewed as a pathological expression of attachment need. The lack during development of an other who meets the need for satisfactory regulation of the hunger state may be of crucial importance in the makeup of the anorectic patient, but to interpret to that patient exclusively in terms of the need to maintain the selfobject tie may miss the central point in that person's pathology. Some problems in trust in the regulatory efforts of others may derive from the internally recognized failure to be satisfactorily fed, and such problems of trust can only be resolved if this motivational need is understood and explained within the therapeutic situation. It is to the acknowledgment and interpretation of the dominant motivational system that Lichtenberg devotes his own therapeutic efforts, as he illustrates quite effectively throughout his work.

In the body of this book, which I believe will become a classic in psychoanalysis, Lichtenberg details the five motivational-functional systems he has identified as encompassing the whole of conscious and unconscious human motivation. They are the following: the motivational systems based on the regulation of physiological requirements; the attachment-affiliation motivational system; the exploratory-assertive motivational system; the aversive motivational system, and the sensual-sexual motivational system. He includes within each chapter the aggregate yield of psychoanalytic understanding of the particular motivation, assessing that psychoanalytic understanding by applying to it current findings from infant and toddler research. Each chapter thus becomes a compendium of past and present thinking around the topic, together with Lichtenberg's own cogent observations and clinical illustrations. The last section of the book includes, first, a discussion of model scenes, Lichtenberg's original contribution to psychoanalytic reconstruction and, next, Lichtenberg's contribution to the understanding of psychoanalytic cure, in which he argues that the concept of growth, or the resumption of normal development, is inadequate and insufficient to explain cure in psychoanalysis. Lichtenberg identifies two significant innate processes that correct or reverse pathological development: the self-righting tendency, based on a homeostatic psychobiological principle and the later-developing capacity to reorganize symbolic representations, based on the plastic receptivity of symbolic thought to developmental and environmental influences, including the influences of interpretation and explanation in the therapeutic setting. Through the elaboration of these two inborn processes, Lichtenberg resolves the presumed discrepancy between the self-psychological and the classical view of cure. Self psychology's view of interrupted or skewed development moving forward can be understood in terms of the self-righting principle; the classical analytic view of pathological psychic structures resulting from maladaptive responses to a subjectively perceived hierarchy of dangers being corrected through insight can be understood in terms of symbolic reorganization. Both processes taken together, Lichtenberg argues, can explain all of psychoanalytic cure. The book's final chapter is written by June Hadley, who addresses the question of correlates between infant observational findings, Lichtenberg's inferences about motivation as derived from them, and neurophysiology. Hadley does find a reasonable fit among them. This satisfactory fit would seem to predict both an increased receptivity from within the larger community of sciences for psychoanalytic thinking and a productive future for such continued efforts to expand, confirm, and revise psychoanalytic theory from the vantage point of relevant but peripheral disciplines.

It must be clear that Lichtenberg's book is an indispensable addition to self psychology, moving it both forward in the direction of providing an encompassing reconceptualized compendium of motivation and, at the same time, outward to incorporate and integrate a remodeled and redefined classical analysis within its body of theory. I can provide but a few examples from the rich assortment of theoretical additions Lichtenberg offers from the five systems of motivation he has identified.

I begin with Lichtenberg's revised view of aggression, which in classical analysis represents one of the two major instinctual drives that constitute human motivation. He understands aggression as best encompassed by two distinct motivational systems, basing this conceptualization on experimental work with infants and toddlers. The assertive aspect of the classically conceived aggressive drive is encompassed in the exploratory-assertive motivational system, wherein the focus is on the innate and forceful urge for competence and effectance pleasure present in the infant from birth. The rageful and destructive aspect of the aggressive drive is subsumed under the aversive motivational system, in which aversion is understood to encompass flight as well as fight and the fight response is demonstrated to be reactive to frustration or fear, rather than some innately pleasurable and inevitable murderous push from within. It is into the motivational system of aversion that the psychoanalytic concept of defense is incorporated. Lichtenberg's decision to separate aggression in this way is not arbitrary or based solely on reconstructions from the clinical situation, as were Kohut's views, but is strongly supported by experimental evidence based on clusters of behavior and affect that parse themselves out in this way. I am convinced that both time and reason is on the side of Lichtenberg's conceptual decision, and that psychoanalysis will have to yield to this vision of aggressive motivation.

In terms of the other classically recognized instinctual drive, libido, Lichtenberg conceptualizes a sensual-sexual motivational system. Like the other four systems, this system is seen as present at birth; it is a psychological entity with neurophysiological correlates, an entity beginning in the neonatal period and built around functional needs. As is true for the other systems also, the sensual-sexual system encompasses a line of development going from need to wish. The system includes the separate but related affect states of sensual enjoyment and sexual excitement, the former being derived from caregiver activities that sooth and express affection, activities that may lead either to relaxation or to a sexual excitement that, when age appropriate, leads to orgasm. This is obviously different from the classical view of sexuality, wherein all of sensuality is viewed as a variety of and precursor to the same sexual state. Lichtenberg argues that by distinguishing the two, their manifestations in every stage of development may be more accurately perceived. Thus, Lichtenberg views sensual-sexual pleasure as theoretically coequal with the other systems, including the attachment system so paramount in self psychology. He contends that self psychology has erred in relegating sexuality to a secondary position in motivation; he contends also that classical analysis has erred in misperceiving sensuality as being in all cases manifestations of sexuality, as well as in elevating sexuality to a cardinal position shared only by aggression in the motivational hierarchy. Moreover, both classical analysis and self psychology underestimate the motivational role of the enjoyment of nonsexual sensuality per se. Classical analysis conflates it with sexuality and self psychology limits it to its cohesion-promoting potential. Lichtenberg concludes that only by examining each situation to determine whether the sensual-sexual system is dominant can we assess whether sex is a motivator and trigger for disturbed cohesion, as is conceptualized in much of self psychology, or is the initiator of a symptomatic compromise formation, as is conceptualized in much of classical analysis.

My question for Lichtenberg is, Where is there room in your conceptualization of the self for anything other than your motivational systems? It seems to me that Lichtenberg's systems include id (motivation), ego (means for its fulfillment), and superego (its regulation), but I am questioning whether there is anything other than motivational-functional systems in his framework.

## REFERENCES

Kohut, H. & Wolf, E. (1978), The disorders of the self and their treatment: An outline. *Internat. J. Psycho-Anal.*, 59:413–25.

# Chapter 13

# The Selfobject Concept: A Further Discussion of Three Authors

### *James L. Fosshage*

Each of the authors of the three major new books on self psychology, as Estelle Shane so comprehensively and clearly delineated, is expanding and refining the theory' and clinical practice of self psychology (or, perhaps more accurately, the theories and clinical practices of self psychology). In his disarmingly straightforward and elegant writing about the treatment of the self, Wolf (1988) creates an empathic *ambience* for the reader, illustrative of the type of ambience that is an important ingredient of the self-psychological psychoanalytic endeavor. Bacal and Newman (1990), in their "mutually regulating" interweaving of self psychology and object relations theory, expand self-psychological theory and, buttressing their argument with a tightly reasoned and clinically based perspective, firmly anchor self psychology as a two-person psychology. And in his synthesis of infant research, psychoanalytic theories, and clinical evidence, Lichtenberg (1989) provides us with a comprehensive and detailed motivational model, undoubtedly the most conceptually parsimonious, explanatory, and elegant motivational model in psychoanalysis today, that serves as a basis for understanding self-experience and the genesis of self-structure. Clearly, self psychology is alive and well as the differences abound and the theory evolves. In this chapter I wish to consider briefly some of the complex issues related to bridging self psychology and object relations theory and to focus particularly on the selfobject concept as viewed by these different authors.

Although Kohut legitimized self concerns by extricating them from

229

Freud's concepts of primary and secondary narcissism, his original postulation of two independent lines of development, namely, the narcissistic and object relational lines, inadvertently repeated the error in classical theory of dichotomizing self and object relational concerns. Even when Kohut developed his theory into a supraordinate theory of self psychology, he never fully resolved this theoretical division between self development and object relational conflict. An example of this dualism in his last book, *How Does Analysis Cure?* (1984), is his contrast between the narcissistic rage emanating from self-injury and the anger emerging out of object relational conflict. Kohut considered the process of self-consolidation to be the primary developmental task and derailments of this process to be central in the formation of psychopathology, whereas he viewed object relational conflicts as ultimately manageable by a person with a firmly consolidated sense of self.

Questions emerge: Are self and object relational concerns divisible, and, if so, how can we differentiate between them? Is the selfobject dimension of object relations the only relevant dimension for understanding psychopathology? What are the other dimensions of object relations? If "selfobjects" refer to a dimension of object relations, is this not a relational model? And fundamental to all of these questions is, What do we mean by "selfobject"? These questions emerge out of our increasingly complex picture of the development of a sense of self within a self–selfobject matrix and of the multifaceted object relations *as a part of self-experience.* Lichtenberg's motivational systems theory provides five different motivational bases for the development of self-structure and interaction with others. Bacal and Newman's study is aimed at furthering this needed integration of self and object relational concerns.

Related to this issue of integration is whether self psychology is a one-person or a two-person psychology. Shane (this volume) reads Kohut as insisting that "the self, and not the self and its object, is at the center of self psychology." Wolf (1988) notes that Kohut insisted that self psychology is "an intrapsychic dynamic and not an interpersonal or object-relations theory" (p. 47). Bacal and Newman disagree and suggest that Kohut placed the self within a selfobject surround at center stage. All of these authors, I believe, agree that self psychology is an individual psychology in that we focus analytically on the individual patient and his or her experience and that the theories of psychological development and pathogenesis are firmly anchored in the self–selfobject experience. Where they appear to disagree is in the conceptualization of a selfobject (does it refer to an object or not?) and the nature of object relations theory (is it interpersonal or not?). Bacal and Newman believe that object relations theory is not an interpersonal theory, that is, a theory that focuses on interpersonal interactions instead of the patient's subjective experience of those interactions. (Incidentally, many interpersonalists also feel that they, too, focus on the individual's experience of the interpersonal interactions). In their argument Bacal and Newman quote Charles Rycroft (1968) who defines *object relationship* as the "relation of the subject to his object, *not* the relation between the subject and the object which is an *interpersonal* relationship . . . because psychoanalysis is a psychology of the individual and therefore discusses objects and relationships only from the point of view of a single subject" (p. 227). The focus on the subject's experience of the other offers one bridge, which Bacal and Newman delineate, between self psychology and object relations theory. Thus, the disagreement between Wolf and Shane, on one hand, and Bacal and Newman, on the other, involves the conceptualization of the selfobject, the central issue relating to how object relations, as a major aspect of self-experience, fits into self psychology.

In addressing the different meanings that theoreticians give to the term *selfobject*, let us begin by turning to Kohut in his last work, *How Does Analysis Cure?* Kohut (1984) defines "the *general* meaning of the term *selfobject* as that dimension of our experience of another person that relates to this person's functions in shoring up our self" (p. 49). He fills out this meaning of the term in an often-quoted passage:

> Throughout his life a person will experience himself as a cohesive harmonious firm unit in time and space, connected with his past and pointing meaningfully into a creative-productive future, [but] only as long as, at each stage in his life, he experiences certain representatives of his human surroundings as joyfully responding to him, as available to him as sources of idealized strength and calmness, as being silently present but in essence like him, and, at any rate, able to grasp his inner life more or less accurately so that their responses are attuned to his needs and allow him to grasp their inner life when his is in need of sustenance [p. 52].

Because selfobjects, as Kohut viewed it, are a dimension of our experience of others and the self–selfobject matrix is central in our theories of development and pathogenesis, self psychology is—and this is Bacal and Newman's thesis, with which I am in full agreement—fundamentally a two-person psychology or relational field (or intersubjective) model. The selfobject experience refers to self experience that can only be captured through the empathic mode of perception but is relational in that the experience, either through a symbolic or interpersonal interaction, involves the other. The selfobject dimension of experiencing others is ever present and shifts to the foreground or background as the needs of the self require (see Stolorow, 1986). Some self psychologists have been reluctant to view self psychology as a relational model (as Bacal and Newman note) for fear—unfounded, I believe—that it would steal away from the singular focus on the analysand's self-experience and become more interpersonal in focus. We can remain focused on the analysand's experience analytically and still maintain a two-person psychology model with regard to development, pathogenesis, and therapeutic action.

Let us turn to the authors' conceptualizations of the selfobject and selfobject experience. In *Treating the Self*, Wolf uses the concept of selfobject as follows:

> Precisely defined, a selfobject is neither self nor object, but the subjective aspect of a self-sustaining function performed by a relationship of self to objects who by their presence or activity evoke and maintain the self and the experience of selfhood. As such, the selfobject relationship refers to an intrapsychic experience and does not describe the interpersonal relationship between the self and other objects [p. 184].

The selfobject relationship is a subjective experience that is relational in that it involves the use of the other. However, I sense that Wolf extended the term *selfobject experience* when he said, "Any experience of the individual that evokes in that individual an organization of experiences into patterns that create order and a sense of being a person, of 'I am I', is a selfobject experience" (p. 6). He broadens the range of selfobject experience and through the omission of reference to objects deemphasizes the relational component. (Additionally, he omits including positive affective coloration as part of the selfobject experience. Does he mean to include self-organizing experiences with a negative affective tone as part of a selfobject experience, a radical departure from the usual meaning of the term?) Do we wish to call a self experience that is principally internally generated and occurs at a moment when the caretaker surround is, comparatively speaking, in the background (e.g., a baby's experience of competence pleasure in discovering that he can turn the lights on [see Papousek and Papousek, 1975]) a selfobject experience (according to Wolf's last meaning of the term)? Does calling this a selfobject experience blur the distinction with experiences in which the self-sustaining function of the other is in the foreground? Why not call the baby's pleasure simply a self-enhancing efficacy experience? To do so enables differentiation between a person's principally self-generated efficacy experience and the selfobject experience that Wolf designates as an efficacy [selfobject] experience. In describing this latter designation Wolf writes, "The essence of these phenomena is the self's experience of being an effective agent in influencing the object" (p. 60). In this instance Wolf's "object" refers either actually or symbolically to another person whereas the baby in our example is not primarily relationally engaged. However, I may now be differentiating too sharply between primarily self-generated experiences and those experiences that more directly involve others. Within a more consistent field model self-generated and other-generated should be viewed as two poles on a continuum of selfobject experiences. (An additional note: As Wolf describes the efficacy selfobject experience, he makes the important point that in the efficacy experience the self is experienced as the actor rather than as being acted upon, a distinction that, to me, could be viewed as two poles of another continuum for understanding the diversity of selfobject experiences.)

In viewing self psychology as a two-person psychology, Bacal and Newman emphasize the relational matrix and place the accent on the "object" in their definition of selfobject: "An object is a selfobject when it is experienced intrapsychically as providing functions in a relationship that evoke, maintain, or positively affect the sense of self" (p. 229). Although self psychologists are particularly attuned to the analyst's contribution to the patient's selfobject experience and ruptures, Bacal and Newman contend that self psychology's focus on the intrapsychic functions inadvertently has theoretically, but not clinically, minimized the specificity of the object and the actions of the object (I believe there's some truth to that). They write, "We want to balance Stolorow's caveat that the selfobject should be conceived of as a dimension of experiencing an object (Stolorow 1986:274) by emphasizing that this experience is also embodied in a significant object" (p. 231). They include more forcefully the object's availability for and participation in a selfobject experience, which within the analytic arena led Bacal to his conceptualization and technical emphasis on "optimal responsiveness."

Bacal and Newman, thus, view the selfobject relationship as a type of relationship. Moreover, a selfobject relationship is a type of relationship with a specific object. This leads them into equating a failed selfobject with a "bad object," an equation that Shane questions as undermining the distinction between selfobject and object, the central contribution and fundamental organizing principle of self psychology. Bacal and Newman offer a reformulation:

> When the self is fragmented, or seriously disunited . . . the significant other may, indeed, not be experienced as a selfobject at all. In other words, it may be experienced as simply a bad object—in that case, as a rejecting object. However, in most instances, the selfobject is not experienced as totally good or bad. We would use the term "selfobject" to denote, for short, a relatively good selfobject, and we would like to suggest that the term "bad selfobject" (that is, a relatively bad selfobject) may be meaningful in self psychology as a term that is analogous to, but more useful than, the term "hostile introject" in object relations theory—a term that has always referred to the internalized "bad object" [p. 4].

At this point it appears that their self psychology is accommodating to, not assimilating, object relations theory.

To repeat, I concur with Bacal and Newman's view of self psychology as fundamentally a two-person psychology or what I prefer to call a relational or intersubjective field model. However, to view a selfobject as a "dimension of our experience of another person"—to use Kohut's (1984, p. 49) words—rather than as a type of relationship enables recognition of the shifting multidimensions of one's object relations (which Bacal and Newman are attempting to address as well). To speak of a "bad selfobject" is a contradiction in terms if selfobject refers to the use of the object for *self-enhancing* purposes. (Incidentally, Kohut, 1984, also wrote, although I believe only once, of a "pathogenic selfobject" [p. 6].) These denotations tend to categorize and portray objects and relationships as unidimensional, as well as lend themselves to reifications, rather than reflect the complexity of feelings and attitudes toward and functions of an object. However, Bacal and Newman are attempting, as Kohut did, to capture important clinical phenomena, for example, the experience with an object who serves important selfobject functions but requires self-constricting accommodations. But to specify selfobject functions without personifying the term *selfobject* enables us to more accurately and comprehensively describe this dynamic scenario. For example, a person may maintain a masochistic tie because of its self-organizing function despite the fact that it also results in a negative self-image. To call this a bad selfobject tie does not provide a sufficiently detailed and experience-near understanding of this complex phenomenon. Bacal and Newman provide another example: a person about to embark on a new endeavor feels in need of another's support but recalls past disappointments that serve as an impediment. Rather than refer to a "memory of a bad selfobject," would it not be more parsimonious and less confusing to simply refer to the thematic memory or schema of the disappointing other (which includes traumatic selfobject ruptures)?

Bacal and Newman note that other experiences with objects are not adequately addressed in either the traditional psychoanalytic definition of object or in definitions of selfobject: "We have *contacts* of one sort or another with these objects, they may fulfill certain needs, but these needs may be neither sexual nor self-affirming" (p. 235). And that leads us to Lichtenberg, who has conceptualized five basic needs that serve as a motivational basis for self-experience.

Lichtenberg also views self psychology as fundamentally a two-person psychology. He writes:

> In agreement with much infant research, Kohut conceptualizes a constant interrelationship between *motive*, to achieve and restore self cohesion, and *environment*, the empathic responsiveness. . . . [and] the overarching concept that conveys the mutual relationship of self-regulation and regulation between self and environment is that of a selfobject experience [pp. 4–5, 12].

In an attempt to avoid reification of terminology and to consistently place the focus on the subjective experience of the individual, Lichtenberg shifts the focus from selfobject to the *selfobject experience* (I am drawing not only on his book but also on his recent paper entitled "What Is a Selfobject?"). Lichtenberg (1990) writes, "Selfobject experience designates an affective state of vitality and invigoration, of needs being met and of intactness of self" (p. 42). For him, the selfobject experience is defined as a specific affective state of intactness and vitality, with no mention, thus far, of the object. This affective state is presumably triggered variably, ranging from principally self-generated acts to object-related acts. The term *selfobject* refers to the *trigger* of the selfobject experience. For the infant, Lichtenberg (1990) refers to a "combination of having needs met and being vitalized by attunement responses" (p. 23), a combination that triggers selfobject experiences, strengthening the core self. In the clinical setting Lichtenberg places his emphasis on the analyst's affect attunement and empathic responsiveness or understanding as the trigger of selfobject experiences. His consistent emphasis is on the patient's use of the analyst and the analyst's listening and understanding stance to create needed selfobject experiences:

Thus in the clinical situation, by doing the ordinary work that promotes restoration of self (self-righting), and the reorganization of symbolic representations, the optimally responsive (Bacal, 1985) therapist triggers pari passu selfobject experiences [p. 29].

Although I agree with this characterization in the main, I would want to include under the rubric of "ordinary work" the wide range of analytic interventions that are necessary and occur in response to the needs of the patient. For example, I would want to include interventions like the one portrayed in Kohut's famous anecdote (infamous to some) wherein he offered his two fingers in responding to and conveying understanding of the patient's momentarily heightened need to feel the physical presence of the analyst.

On the basis of this review let me make several suggestions concerning the selfobject experience. To conceptualize selfobject experience as referring to any experience that is vitalizing and self-organizing (as Lichtenberg and Wolf propose) enables us to encompass a broad range of experience. Selfobject experience would include relatively solitary activities generated principally from within, which always occur within a relational matrix no matter how recessed in the background (e.g., a solitary work activity). It would also include those more relationally dominated experiences (e.g., an interaction with a friend who comforts us). Selfobject triggers vary from a walk in the forest to an intimate relational involvement. To describe *dimensions of selfobject experience* (e.g., internal to external triggers, of active agent to receptivity, of degrees of vitality) that quantitatively differ argues against the dichotomization of experiences. Thus, we can retain Kohut's invaluable emphasis on the development, maintenance, and restoration of a vital self anchored within a relational field. His emphasis that a consolidated, vital experience of self can fully occur only when there is an intrapsychic sense of empathic resonance with an actual or symbolic other provides one necessary and ubiquitous linkage between ourselves and others. Even when the activity is solitary and is not relationally dominated, an empathic resonance undoubtedly serves as a necessary ingredient and backdrop for a fully vitalized sense of self.

However, to refer to selfobject experience implicitly dichotomizes experiences into selfobject experiences and other experiences. Just as the erroneous division between selfobject and object can be resolved by referring to the selfobject dimension of relationships (Stolorow, 1986), so can the dichotomization of experience be resolved by referring to the selfobject dimension of experience. The *selfobject dimension of experience is always present* as our sense of self and vitality varies from ever so incrementally to considerably, over short or long periods of time.

In an attempt to differentiate between ordinary object relations and selfobject experiences, Wolf provides us with a story about purchasing gas for his car. When he was feeling "together," an experience of encountering an attractive woman, which activated the sensual-sexual motivational system, did not involve any change in self-state and, therefore, was not a selfobject experience but an object relational experience. In contrast, when he was feeling depleted, the same experience was vitalizing and was a selfobject experience. As with any story presented for illustrative purposes, the divisions are too sharply portrayed, although the division accurately reflects Wolf's position. I wish to close by retelling the story, from my perspective, using Lichtenberg's motivational systems theory in attempting to illustrate the complexity of our self experience of ourselves and others.

As I am driving along I may notice that my car is low on gas. I may then feel some additional alertness—to keep a sharp lookout for the nearest gas station. Because I am feeling relatively solid this particular morning, with a supportive sense of an empathic resonance of others in the background, I go into action—my exploratory-assertive motivational system comes to the fore and I feel confident that I will be able to solve the problem. The status of my self affects the functioning of my exploratory-assertive system, and a successful experience in mastering this problem reinforces my confidence and, therefore, affects my self-state. Having remembered where there is a gas station, I pick up a little speed with a sense of direction. As I do so, it crosses my mind how well my car handles, a type of sensual experience in combination with a bit of a mastery experience. That sensual experience, although minimally intense, adds to my good feeling, even though I was not in need of a sensual experience to bolster a vulnerable self at that moment. (Of course, I could always be unconscious of such a need, but, based on my experience, it's the best call I can make.) All of a sudden another car comes barreling around the corner cutting into my lane and threatening to sideswipe me; I swerve out of the way, yelling and swearing as he passes by me. In my actions my aversive motivational system had come to the fore in both a flight and fight fashion. Once out of danger, my heart begins to slow down. Because I was internally in a good place, I am able to calm down fairly quickly. My aversive system drops gradually into the background, although I may remain somewhat more vigilant for the duration of the ride. As I reflect on the incident in an attempt to further master it, I realize that my aversive reaction was quick and decisive. This is reassuring, even a bit invigorating, and these feelings accrue to the positive feeling about myself, which enabled me to organize the experience in this way in the first place.

Now, while at the gas station I encounter another customer, a woman whom I previously knew and found quite attractive and appealing. As I speak with her, both my sensual-sexual and attachment-affiliation motivational systems come to the fore and even though I am not in a vulnerable state, my sense of self is a bit vitalized by the experience.

Now, in contrast, let me describe the scenario if I had been a little out of sorts and unsure of myself that day: I note that I am low on gas, which irritates me and adds to the burdens of the day. My exploratory-assertive system goes into effect as I attempt to deal with the situation, and although I think of a nearby gas station, I do so without zest. This is more evidence of a slightly depleted self-state, which encumbers the exploratory-assertive system. I pick up speed, but my negative affect–toned self-organization prevents me from turning this into a sensual experience. After the near accident with the other car, my anger or aversiveness lingers longer in a general grumpiness. (An alternative response to my somewhat depleted state might be to drive excessively fast to feel vigorous again. If I consistently handled depletion in this manner, it would border on becoming what Lichtenberg calls a pathological selfobject experience: although it momentarily bolsters my sense of self, it does not enable me to resolve the issue of my depleted state in a self-vitalizing way.) To return to our story, I pull into the gas station and encounter the same woman. As I talk to her I am intent on getting a positive response from her. She smiles warmly, and I begin to feel uplifted.

Now, was a selfobject dimension operative in this second encounter with the woman? As Wolf pointed out in his story, this encounter is a type of selfobject experience used to restore a more positive sense of self. In addition, although in this second example my exploratory-assertive and aversive motivational systems were working, contributing to restoring a more positive sense of self, clearly they were encumbered by my particular self-state.

Was a selfobject dimension operative in the first story? My answer is yes. The range of experiences in the first story helped to maintain a consolidated sense of self, if ever so slightly. My point is this: the selfobject dimension of our experience, namely, that dimension of our experience that refers to our vitality and cohesiveness of a sense of self, is ever present, more or less. All experiences consciously and unconsciously variably affect our sense of self and, in turn, our sense of self affects all of our experiences. This is one conceptual route wherein object relations experience can be integrated as part of a broad range of self-experience.

## REFERENCES

Bacal, H. & Newman, K. (1990), *Theories of Object Relations*. New York: Columbia University Press.

Kohut, H. (1984), *How Does Analysis Cure?* ed. A. Goldberg & P. Stepansky. Chicago: University of Chicago Press.

Lichtenberg, J. (1989), *Psychoanalysis and Motivation*. Hillsdale, NJ: The Analytic Press.

———— (1990), What is a selfobject? *Psychoanal. Dial.*, 1:455–479.

Papousek, H. & Papousek, M. (1975), Cognitive aspects of preverbal social interaction between human infant and adults. In: *Parent-Infant Interaction* (Ciba Foundation Symposium). New York: Associated Scientific Publishers.

Rycroft, C. (1968), *A Critical Dictionary of Psychoanalysis*. Totowa, NJ: Littlefield, Adams.

Stolorow, R. (1986), On experiencing an object: A multidimensional perspective. In: *Progress in Self Psychology, Vol. 2*, ed. A. Goldberg. New York: Guilford Press, pp. 273–279.

Wolf, E. (1988), *Treating the Self*. New York: Guilford Press.

# Chapter 14

# Subjectivity and Self Psychology: A Personal Odyssey

## Robert D. Stolorow

The writing of this "odyssey" was stimulated by informal discussions that occurred during the Twelfth Annual Conference on the Psychology of the Self in San Francisco (1989), which raised questions about the relationship between self psychology and the theory of intersubjectivity. By tracing the origins of the concepts of the subjective world and intersubjectivity in my own intellectual development, I hope in this essay to clarify the nature of the relationship between these ideas and the framework of self psychology.

The formal roots of my interest in subjectivity go back to the period of my doctoral studies in clinical psychology at Harvard, from 1965 to 1970. During that period Harvard was a wonderful place for a clinical psychologist to grow up in intellectually. The clinical psychology program was actually not part of a psychology department; it was set in the Department of Social Relations, which had been formed by leading scholars from four disciplines—sociology, cultural anthropology, social psychology, and personality psychology—all of whom shared a common interest and background in psychoanalysis. Thus, instead of studying the experimental psychology of rats, I had the privilege of learning about social systems theory from Talcott Par-

I wish to thank Drs. James Fosshage, Frank Lachmann, Joseph Lichtenberg, Estelle Shane, and Morton Shane for their valuable criticisms and suggestions. The chapter is dedicated in loving memory to Dr. Daphne S. Stolorow, my treasured companion during the best years of my journey.

sons, culture and personality from John Whiting, and epigenesis and identity formation from Erik Erikson.

The clinical psychology program at Harvard was the first and last stronghold of a tradition in academic personality psychology known as *personology*. This tradition, founded by Henry Murray at the Harvard Psychological Clinic in the 1930s, held as its basic premise the claim that knowledge of human personality can be advanced only by the systematic, in-depth study of the individual person. This emphasis on "idiographic," rather than "nomothetic," research was a radical departure from the philosophy of science that then dominated, and has continued to dominate, academic psychology in this country. Murray's personology attracted a group of exceptionally creative students, many of whom contributed to his (1938) magnum opus, *Explorations in Personality*, a classic in the field of personality psychology. Two of Murray's most influential followers were Robert White and Silvan Tomkins.[1]

My two principal mentors during my doctoral studies were White and Irving Alexander, a visiting professor and protégé of Tomkins. From White I took seminars on analytic theory and the study of lives and acquired an abiding interest in understanding the uniqueness of each individual's world of experience. Alexander taught us psychological assessment the way he had learned it from Tomkins. Instead of preparing us to do psychological testing in hospitals, his course consisted in studying one person for the entire year by means of a variety of methods (analyzing autobiographical material, in-depth interviews, projective tests, etc.). Again, the emphasis was on systematically investigating the unique inner experience of the individual.

Unfortunately, White's retirement in 1968 was a virtual death blow for personology at Harvard, but attempts were made to revive the tradition in other settings. One such attempt began in 1972, when I was a candidate in psychoanalytic training in New York City. I became interested in pursuing an academic career in psychology and learned of a position opening at Rutgers, where Tomkins and George Atwood, who had been deeply influenced by Tomkins, were on the psychology faculty. I recall a phone conversation in which Tomkins

---

[1]To psychoanalysts, White is best known for his theory of effectance motivation, and Tomkins for his contributions to affect theory. Less well known is the fact that they were both major contributors to the personological movement in academic personality psychology. I suspect that few analysts are aware, for example, of White's (1952) *Lives in Progress*, a classic in the in-depth study of individuals. The history of the personological movement at Harvard, including White's participation in it, is chronicled in his privately published *Memoir* (1987).

urged me to come to Rutgers because, as he put it, with me on the faculty there would be a "critical mass" for the creation of a program in personology. I did join the faculty at Rutgers, and although there were several meetings devoted to planning a new personologically oriented doctoral program in personality psychology, it never got off the ground. The one concrete result of these efforts, a highly significant one for me, was a series of collaborative studies, first by Atwood and Tomkins and then by Atwood and me.

Atwood and Tomkins (1976) wrote a pivotal article, "On the Subjectivity of Personality Theory," which was published in a rather obscure periodical, *The Journal of the History of the Behavioral Sciences.* The basic premise of this article, which the authors viewed as a contribution to the psychology of knowledge, was that every psychological theory has roots in the psychological life of the theorist; the authors further claimed that the science of personality psychology "can achieve a greater degree of consensus and generality only if it begins to turn back on itself and question its own psychological foundations" (p. 166). Following this lead, Atwood and I (1979) embarked on a series of psychobiographical studies of the personal, subjective origins of the theoretical systems of Freud, Jung, Reich, and Rank, studies that formed the basis of our first book, *Faces in a Cloud,* which was completed in 1976. From these studies we concluded that since psychological theories derive to a significant degree from the subjective concerns of their creators, what psychoanalysis and personality psychology need is *a theory of subjectivity itself*—a unifying framework that can account not only for the psychological phenomena that other theories address but also for the theories themselves.

In the last chapter of *Faces in a Cloud* we outlined a set of proposals for the creation of such a framework, which we referred to as "psychoanalytic phenomenology," a term that has never caught on. Influenced by the writings of Schafer (1976) and G. Klein (1976), we envisioned this framework as a depth psychology of human experience, purified of the mechanistic reifications of classical metapsychology. Our framework took the subjective "representational world"[2] (Sandler and Rosenblatt, 1962) of the individual as its central theoretical construct. We assumed no impersonal psychical agencies or

---

[2]Later, we (Atwood and Stolorow, 1984) dropped the term "representational world" because we became aware that it was being used to refer both to the imagistic *contents* of experience and to the *thematic structuring* of experience. Hence, we decided to use "subjective world" when describing the contents of experience and "structures of subjectivity" to designate the invariant principles unconsciously organizing those contents along specific thematic lines.

motivational prime movers in order to explain the representational world. Instead, we assumed that this world evolves organically from the person's encounter with the critical formative experiences that constitute his unique life history. Once established, it becomes discernible in the distinctive, recurrent themes and invariant meanings that unconsciously organize the person's experience. Psychoanalytic phenomenology, in its essence, entailed a set of interpretive principles for investigating the nature, origins, functions, and transformation of the configurations of self and other pervading a person's subjective universe.

Although the concept of *inter*subjectivity was not introduced in *Faces in a Cloud*, it was clearly implicit in the demonstrations of how the personal, subjective world of a personality theorist influences his understanding of other persons' experiences; one of the sections of the introductory chapter is subtitled "The Observer Is the Observed" (p. 17). The first explicit use of the term *intersubjective* in our work appeared in an article (Stolorow, Atwood, and Ross, 1978) entitled "The Representational World in Psychoanalytic Therapy," also completed in 1976. In a section with the subtitle "Transference and Countertransference: An Intersubjective Perspective" (p. 249), we conceptualized the interplay between transference and countertransference in psychoanalytic treatment as an intersubjective process reflecting the interaction between the differently organized subjective worlds of patient and analyst.[3] Foreshadowing much work to come, we considered the impact on the therapeutic process of unrecognized correspondences and disparities between the patient's and analyst's respective worlds of experience.

It should be clear from the foregoing account that characterizing the theories of the subjective world and intersubjectivity as "growing out of" self psychology would be quite inaccurate. With roots extending back to the intellectual ambience of my graduate studies at Harvard, this framework was already outlined, in skeletal form, one year before the formal christening of self psychology in 1977. Self psychology, to be sure, would contribute to this skeletal framework

---

[3]Our use of the term *intersubjective* has never presupposed the attainment of symbolic thought, of a concept of oneself as subject, or of intersubjective relatedness in Stern's (1985) sense. Although the word *intersubjective* had been used before by developmental psychologists, we were unfamiliar with this prior usage when we coined the term independently in 1976 and assigned it a particular meaning within our evolving framework. Unlike the developmentalists, we use *intersubjective* to refer to *any* psychological field formed by interacting worlds of experience, at whatever developmental level these worlds may be organized.

much of its flesh and blood.[4] By 1976 I had written a number of clinical papers, some alone and some with Frank Lachmann,[5] that made extensive use of Kohut's (1971) new insights into the psychology of narcissism, but at that time I did not yet see a way of integrating these new clinical understandings into the more general theoretical program that Atwood and I were developing. The bridge between the two was eventually supplied by Kohut's (1977) *The Restoration of the Self*.

A nodal point in my own intellectual and professional development occurred in 1977 when the book review journal *Contemporary Psychology* invited me to review *The Restoration of the Self*, an invitation that I gladly accepted. It is difficult for me to convey the depth of satisfaction and intensity of excitement that I felt as I read this book. I was not primarily responding to the particulars of Kohut's formulations, as elegantly framed and profoundly true as I believed many of these to be. Instead, I was responding more to the revolutionary scope of his general theoretical proposals, in which he was throwing off the shackles of classical metapsychology and recasting psychoanalysis as "a developmental phenomenology of the self," as I called it in my review (Stolorow, 1978b, p. 229). This stunning new theoretical paradigm, involving a shift from the motivational primacy of drive to the motivational primacy of self-experience, seemed to me to fit like a glove with the suggestions for a psychoanalytic phenomenology that Atwood and I had set forth in *Faces in a Cloud*. Kohut was attempting, as we were, to reframe psychoanalysis as *pure psychology*.

Kohut's discussion of the empathic-introspective mode of observation in the last chapter of *The Restoration of the Self* led me to his original article on that subject, which I had not read before (Kohut, 1959). Reading this article, which demonstrates that the empirical *and theoretical* domains of psychoanalysis are defined and delimited by its empathic-introspective mode of investigation, was an even more exhilarating experience for me than reading the book, and the article continues to be my favorite of Kohut's works. What was so exciting and intensely verifying for me was that Kohut, by studying the

---

[4]As has been delineated elsewhere (Stolorow, Brandchaft, and Atwood, 1987), I regard self psychology's essential contributions to psychoanalysis to be threefold: (1) the unwavering application of the empathic-introspective mode of investigation as defining and delimiting the domain of psychoanalytic inquiry, (2) the central emphasis on the primacy of self-experience, and (3) the concepts of selfobject function and selfobject transference.

[5]These were later incorporated into our book (Stolorow and Lachmann, 1980), *Psychoanalysis of Developmental Arrests*.

relationship between mode of observation and theory in psychoanalysis, had come to exactly the same conclusion that Atwood and I had arrived at by studying the subjective origins of psychological theories, namely, that psychoanalysis, at all levels of abstraction and generality, should be *a depth psychology of human experience*. Kohut, I now believed, was truly a kindred spirit.

My first personal contact with Kohut came about as a direct result of my reading *The Restoration of the Self*. Citing two articles (Stolorow, 1976; Stolorow and Atwood, 1976) in which I had shown how his conceptualizations of narcissism and narcissistic transferences shed new light on the works of Rogers and Rank, Kohut implicitly included me, in the preface of the book, among a group of authors who had criticized him for failing to acknowledge sufficiently the contributions of others. I wrote him a note expressing my surprise at this and affirming that I was an enthusiastic admirer of his work, not a critic. With little delay he sent me a characteristically gracious reply, apologizing for his mistake. Shortly thereafter I sent him a draft of my review of *The Restoration of the Self*, which, it goes without saying, was unambivalently positive. Kohut, in turn, sent me a letter expressing both his gratitude for the favorable review and his sense of satisfaction in discovering that someone whom he had never directly taught could grasp the essence of his ideas. I suspect that it was my review, and Kohut's reaction to it, that led to my being invited to participate in the first national self psychology conference in Chicago in 1978 and also to join the Self Psychology Publications Committee, which Kohut formed for the purpose of furthering and disseminating self-psychological thought.

At this point I became firmly implanted within the self psychology movement, where I remain, but I did not stop working on the theoretical program, now greatly enriched by articulations with self psychology, that Atwood and I had envisioned. There were a number of articles (e.g., Stolorow, 1978a, 1979, 1985; Atwood and Stolorow, 1980, 1981; Stolorow and Atwood, 1982, 1983) in which we continued our efforts to free psychoanalytic theory from its metapsychological encumbrances and to recast its basic principles in terms of a pure psychology of the subjective world.

Another nodal point in this development occurred in 1979 when, at the second national self psychology conference in Los Angeles, I heard Bernard Brandchaft deliver a paper on negative therapeutic reactions that attributed these to patients' experiences of selfobject failure in the transference, to which the analyst's faulty interpretive stance had contributed (see Brandchaft, 1983). I happened to have with me the page proofs of a section of the book I had written with

Lachmann (1980) subtitled "The Therapeutic and Untherapeutic Action of Psychoanalysis" (p. 187), which made a very similar point, and I eagerly showed these to Brandchaft. I think we both felt an almost immediate intellectual kinship. Shortly thereafter, he invited me to present a paper at a conference on the borderline personality at UCLA the following year, and I accepted, suggesting that we write the paper together. In that paper we (Brandchaft and Stolorow, 1984) proposed that the psychological essence of what is called "borderline" is not a pathological condition located solely in the patient but phenomena arising in an *intersubjective field*, "a field consisting of a precarious, vulnerable self and a failing, archaic selfobject" (p. 342).

Thus began a series of collaborative studies (Atwood and Stolorow, 1984; Stolorow, Brandchaft, and Atwood, 1983, 1987) in which Atwood, Brandchaft, and I extended what we came to call "the intersubjective perspective" to a wide array of clinical phenomena, including development and pathogenesis, transference and resistance, conflict formation, dreams, enactments, and even psychotic states. In each instance, phenomena that had traditionally been the focus of psychoanalytic investigation were understood not as products of isolated intrapsychic mechanisms but as forming at the interface of interacting subjectivities. The intersubjective context, we contended, plays a constitutive role in all forms of psychopathology and clinical phenomena can no longer be comprehended psychoanalytically apart from the intersubjective field in which they crystallize. In psychoanalytic treatment, as Kohut (1982, 1984) also emphasized, the impact of the observer was grasped as intrinsic to the observed.

How does our concept of an intersubjective field differ from Kohut's concept of a self–selfobject relationship? One difference is a relatively minor one. An intersubjective field is a system of *reciprocal mutual influence* (Beebe and Lachmann, 1988). With regard to the selfobject dimension of experience, not only does the patient turn to the analyst for selfobject functions but the analyst also turns to the patient for such functions (see Wolf, 1979), although hopefully in a less archaic way. A parallel statement can be made about the child–caregiver system as well. Thus, to capture this reciprocity of mutual influence, one would have to speak of a self-selfobject–selfobject-self relationship.

A second difference is a more important one. *Subjective world* is a construct that covers more experiential territory than *self*. Thus *intersubjective field*—the field constituted by the reciprocal interplay between two (or more) subjective worlds—is broader and more inclusive than the self–selfobject relationship; it exists at a higher level of generality. To put it another way, intersubjective field includes dimensions of experience other than the selfobject dimension. It is broad enough, for example, to encompass the patient's (and analyst's) experience when the patient is *not* experiencing the analyst as a source of selfobject functions but as a source of painful and conflictual affect states. It is not sufficient, from our perspective, to identify and analyze a patient's experience of a rupture in a selfobject transference bond. It is crucial, in addition, to investigate the invariant principles unconsciously organizing the patient's experience during the disruption, when no selfobject transference tie is in evidence, and to identify the qualities or activities of the analyst that are lending themselves to being perceived as confirmations of those principles.

I wish to emphasize that, in our framework, the concept of an intersubjective field is not meant to replace the concept of transference in general or selfobject transference in particular. We define transference as referring to the ways in which the patient organizes his experience of the analytic relationship (Stolorow and Lachmann, 1984/1985; Stolorow, Brandchaft, and Atwood, 1987). So defined, transference is always multidimensional. A crucial dimension of the transference, delineated by Kohut, is the selfobject dimension. We refer to a second dimension as the repetitive and conflictual dimension. These and perhaps other dimensions continually move between the foreground and background of the patient's experience in concert with specific perceptions of the analyst and the analyst's activities. A parallel description applies to the analyst's transference, which analysts call countertransference. The larger system created by the reciprocal mutual interaction between the patient's transference and the analyst's transference is an example of what we call an intersubjective field or intersubjective context.

For me, the concept of an intersubjective field is a theoretical construct precisely matched to the methodology of empathic-introspective inquiry. What we investigate through empathy and introspection are the principles organizing the patient's experience (empathy), the principles organizing our own experience (introspection), and the psychological field formed by the interplay between the two.

I hope I have been able to make clear that the theory of intersubjectivity is not an outgrowth of self psychology and is certainly not intended to supersede it. Rather, the germinal concept of intersubjectivity developed in parallel with and became greatly enriched by the framework of self psychology. It is my view that the theory of intersubjectivity provides a broad methodological and epistemological net within which self psychology can creatively expand.

## REFERENCES

Atwood, G. & Stolorow, R. (1980), Psychoanalytic concepts and the representational world. *Psychoanal. & Contemp. Thought*, 3:267–290.

_____ (1981), Experience and conduct. *Contemp. Psychoanal.*, 17:197–208.

_____ (1984), *Structures of Subjectivity*. Hillsdale, NJ: The Analytic Press.

Atwood, G. & Tomkins, S. (1976), On the subjectivity of personality theory. *J. Hist. Behav. Sci.*, 12:166–177.

Beebe, B. & Lachmann, F. (1988), Mother–infant mutual influence and precursors of psychic structure. In: *Frontiers in Self Psychology: Progress in Self Psychology, Vol. 3*, ed. A. Goldberg. Hillsdale, NJ: The Analytic Press, pp. 3–25.

Brandchaft, B. (1983), The negativism of the negative therapeutic reaction and the psychology of the self. In: *The Future of Psychoanalysis*, ed. A. Goldberg. Madison, CT: International Universities Press, pp. 327–359.

_____ & Stolorow, R. (1984), The borderline concept: Pathological character or iatrogenic myth? In: *Empathy II*, ed. J. Lichtenberg, M. Bornstein, & D. Silver. Hillsdale, NJ: The Analytic Press, pp. 333–357.

Klein, G. (1976), *Psychoanalytic Theory*. Madison, CT: International Universities Press.

Kohut, H. (1959), Introspection, empathy, and psychoanalysis. *J. Amer. Psychoanal. Assn.*, 7:459–483.

_____ (1971), *The Analysis of the Self*. Madison, CT: International Universities Press.

_____ (1977), *The Restoration of the Self*. Madison, CT: International Universities Press.

_____ (1982), Introspection, empathy, and the semicircle of mental health. *Internat. J. Psycho-Anal.*, 63:395–407.

_____ (1984), *How Does Analysis Cure?* ed. A. Goldberg & P. Stepansky. Chicago: University of Chicago Press.

Murray, H. (1938), *Explorations in Personality*. New York: Science Editions, 1962.

Sandler, J. & Rosenblatt, B. (1962), The concept of the representational world. *The Psychoanalytic Study of the Child*, 17:128–145. New York: International Universities Press.

Schafer, R. (1976), *A New Language for Psychoanalysis*. New Haven, CT: Yale University Press.

Stern, D. (1985), *The Interpersonal World of the Infant*. New York: Basic Books.

Stolorow, R. (1976), Psychoanalytic reflections on client-centered therapy in the light of modern conceptions of narcissism. *Psychother.: Theory, Prac., Res.*, 13:26–29.

_____ (1978a), The concept of psychic structure: Its metapsychological and clinical psychoanalytic meanings. *Internat. Rev. Psycho-Anal.*, 5:313–320.

_____ (1978b), The restoration of psychoanalysis (book review of *The Restoration of the Self*, by H. Kohut). *Contemp. Psychol.*, 23:229–230.

_____ (1979), Psychosexuality and the representational world. *Internat. J. Psycho-Anal.*, 60:39–45.

_____ (1985), Toward a pure psychology of inner conflict. In: *Progress in Self Psychology, Vol. 1*, ed. A. Goldberg. New York: Guilford Press, pp. 194–201.

_____ & Atwood, G. (1976), An ego-psychological analysis of the work and life of Otto Rank in the light of modern conceptions of narcissism. *Internat. Rev. Psycho-Anal.*, 3:441–459.

_____ (1979), *Faces in a Cloud*. New York: Jason Aronson.

_____ (1982), Psychoanalytic phenomenology of the dream. *The Annual of Psychoanalysis*, 10:205–220. New York: International Universities Press.

_____ (1983), Psychoanalytic phenomenology: Progress toward a theory of personality. In: *The Future of Psychoanalysis*, ed. A. Goldberg. Madison, CT: International Universities Press, pp. 97–110.

———— & Ross, J. (1978), The representational world in psychoanalytic therapy. *Internat. Rev. Psycho-Anal.*, 5:247–256.

Stolorow, R., Brandchaft, B. & Atwood, G. (1983), Intersubjectivity in psychoanalytic treatment: With special reference to archaic states. *Bull. Menninger Clin.*, 47:117–128.

———— ———— ———— (1987), *Psychoanalytic Treatment: An Intersubjective Approach.* Hillsdale, NJ: The Analytic Press.

———— & Lachmann, F. (1980), *Psychoanalysis of Developmental Arrests: Theory and Treatment.* Madison, CT: International Universities Press.

———— (1984/85), Transference: The future of an illusion. *The Annual of Psychoanalysis,* 12/13:19–37. New York: International Universities Press.

White, R. (1952), *Lives in Progress.* New York: Holt, Rinehart & Winston.

———— (1987), *A Memoir.* Marlborough, NH: Homestead Press.

Wolf, E. (1979), Transference and countertransference in the analysis of the disorders of the self. *Contemp. Psychoanal.*, 15:577–594.

# Author Index

# Subject Index

## A

Abandonment, fear of, 8, 106
Abstinence
  in codependency, 152, 153
  relentless, 41
  traditional analytic attitude of, 40
Abstract art revolution, 182, 184
Accountability, in codependency, 151–152
Activity
  self and, 118–119, 120
  transitional selfobject relationship to,
    121, 135
Adaptation, 39, 174
Addictive personality disorder, 109–110
  analytic therapy for, intersubjective
    approach to, 121–124, 135–137
  case histories, 124–135
  etiology of, 136
  self psychology theory of, 110–121
Addictive trigger mechanisms (ATMs),
    110, 119, 120, 136
  ersatz selfobject relationships and, 118
  function of, 110–112
  self-anesthetization induced by, 111
  selfobject and, 112, 118–119
  things or activities functioning as, 121
  transference relationship and, 136

Admiration, spontaneous expression of,
  25
Adolescent girl, delusions and hallucina-
    tions in, 57–73
Adult children of alcoholics (ACA), 145
  case material, 156–161
Aesthetic of maternal handling, 176
Affect
  articulation, 107
  attunement
  in desomatizing selfobject transfer-
    ence, 104
  establishment of, 105
  Basch's view, 46
  containment, 107
  defense against, 47–48
  development, 105
  differentiation, 107
  experiencing of, 34
  regulation, 23
Affect spread, 34
Affect states
  child's caregiver's response to, 39–40
  self-dysphoric, 110
Affective bonding, 38
Affective constellations, 46
Affective development, Basch's view,
  48–49